More Praise for *Raising*

"I used to say there weren't any manuals for how to parent—until now. **An entertaining and evidence-based guide** to parenting in today's fast-paced, increasingly tech-saturated, mind-bogglingly complex, and busy wilderness."

—Lisa Coyne, PhD, assistant professor of psychology, Harvard Medical School, and CEO, New England Center for OCD and Anxiety

"Conveys the critical topics of struggle and resilience in a genuinely accessible language. This book is a **true golden nugget**, and I wish every parent could read it."

—Maria Svernell, clinical psychologist, Anna Freud National Centre for Children and Families

"Everything about this book speaks to any parent looking for **sound, easy-to-read, science-based advice** for raising emotionally healthy and resilient children."

—Michael Houston, MD, clinical professor of psychiatry and pediatrics, Department of Psychiatry and Behavioral Science, George Washington University Medical Center

"This book is **an excellent resource that will empower parents** to talk their kids through challenging situations while giving them the autonomy they need to find solutions that work for them."

—Angela Fletcher, PsyD, pediatric psychologist, Children's National Hospital, Washington, DC

"**Empathic, encouraging, and accessible** ... [this book] provides a broader framework for equipping our children with the tools they need to thrive."

—Matthew Biel, MD, MSc, professor and chief of child and adolescent psychiatry, Georgetown University Medical Center

Raising a Kid Who Can

Simple Strategies to Build a Lifetime of Adaptability and Emotional Strength

CATHERINE McCARTHY, MD
HEATHER TEDESCO, PhD
JENNIFER WEAVER, LCSW

WORKMAN PUBLISHING · NEW YORK

Library of Congress Cataloging-in-Publication Data is available.

ISBN 978-1-5235-1859-3

Design by Rae Ann Spitzenberger
Illustrations by Sarah Letteney

Images repeated throughout:
Creativika Graphics/Shutterstock; Net Vector (Shutterstock); olnik_y/Shutterstock; Tartila/Shutterstock.

Workman books are available at special discounts when purchased in bulk for premiums and sales promotions as well as for fundraising or educational use. Special editions or book excerpts can also be created to specification. For details, please contact special.markets@hbgusa.com.

Workman Publishing Co., Inc., a subsidiary of Hachette Book Group, Inc.
1290 Avenue of the Americas
New York, NY 10104

workman.com

Printed in the United States on responsibly sourced paper.

First printing August 2023

10 9 8 7 6 5 4 3 2 1

Contents

Welcome

The world of today can feel complicated, overloaded, moving at warp speed. Modern kids need to be ready to roll! The pace of daily life can leave them with little time to catch their breath before the next hurdle. We want today's kids, no matter what their age and stage, to be strong enough to gracefully navigate the inevitable ups and downs of everyday life. To be able to learn, grow, adjust, and bend—not break.

And what of our kids tomorrow? Are you having a little trouble even imagining the future world they will be living in? You aren't alone. We are in what many scientists believe is the most rapid period of change in all human history. And this pace of change will likely continue to accelerate even further for our kids: in technology, global connectivity, jobs, and ways of living.

Modern life can be exciting, scary, fun, unpredictable, and sometimes overwhelming. Parents have an obligation and an opportunity to take special care and equip our kids for our modern world. The good news is that we can protect and prepare them for both the ordinary challenges of today as well as for an uncertain future. And the opportunity is here for them to shift and evolve beyond us— to move us from an Age of Anxiety into a new Age of Adaptability.

We can't know what exactly might be coming down the road for our children. But we believe in putting our energy into focusing on things where we may have the most impact. Rather than trying to raise our children for a world that exists now, we believe modern parents should raise children for the world that will be, whatever that will be: the best possible, the problematic, and anything in between. Raising kids who are prepared for everything, derailed by nothing, and adaptable for whatever may come along.

In short, we believe in raising kids who CAN.

And the good news is that it's not as hard as it sounds.

A SIMPLE PARENTING PLAYBOOK
FOR THE AGE OF ADAPTABILITY

For years we've seen loving parents drowning in information and advice on how to raise their kids, which can frankly be exhausting. We've shared their frustrations. Not only is the pace of change accelerating, we are also in an age of information overload. So we set out to write just a single, simple playbook for parents, one that would offer the best professional parenting knowledge and advice out there, all condensed into one small, fun package, organized and skimmable, easy on the eyes and soothing to the brain.

Our inspiration was a Rick Steves travel guide—friendly, accessible, packed with information, but set up to make it easy to find what you need. We made sure we were as scientifically accurate as the *New England Journal of Medicine*. And then we added the best of everything we know based on our collective professional wisdom and boiled it down into the essential things every child needs in order to thrive in this modern age.

The result is the book you hold in your hands, a playbook for parents. Being an effective parent—in bad times and good times— is simpler than you think: You just need to know what to prioritize and how to put those priorities into practice. Our goal is to share the very best tools for healthy development and emotional strength in a easy format so that you can parent smarter, not harder.

So, who are we? We are three mental health professionals— a psychiatrist, a parent psychologist, and a child psychotherapist— whose work focuses on children, parents, and families. Together we have a combined seventy-plus years of experience and have worked with tens of thousands of families in our individual private practices. All three of us are professional child whisperers, coming to the job from three different but complementary lenses.

We are also parents ourselves, with grown or nearly grown kids. We know firsthand how relentless, stressful, confusing, and lonely this parenting job can be. We, too, have faced challenges within our own families. We have struggled with the same uncertainties and have made plenty of mistakes. Like you, we try to practice what we preach and to forgive ourselves when we fall short.

Anyone can google "separation anxiety" or "How can I get my kid to listen?" And there are a million magazine articles and blogs, usually with contradictory advice, on every parenting question out there. So why do you need another voice (or three) in your ear telling you how to do it? Because our office shelves are lined with research books and journals, which we refer to routinely in our clinical work. We attend major conferences featuring leading researchers in the field of child and adolescent mental health. We are up to date on the latest and best research. In other words, our work—and this book— is grounded in evidence-based, peer-reviewed research, combined with our own decades of experience in clinical work.

We have tried to make this book ridiculously simple. It is designed to be visual, efficient, useful, and fun.

This book is for you if:

→ **You want just one simple parenting book that tells you the most important things to know.** You are a dedicated parent, but you don't always want to own or read all those books lined up in the parenting section of the library.

→ **You want trustworthy, high-quality information and advice that is evidence-based and current.** You prefer streamlined, straight talk from professionals over sifting through conflicting and sometimes dubious Google advice. You appreciate the *Consumer Reports* or *Wirecutter* approaches to curating the best information. Just as *Consumer Reports* tests forty washing machines to recommend the top three, our essential principles are based on countless numbers of studies of kids and families. We have culled the best.

➜ **You want balance in your parenting life.** You don't want to become a professional parent; you want to be a person who (mostly!) loves to parent. You don't want to feel so worried about being a good parent, and you don't want to constantly second-guess yourself.

➜ **You want to parent your own way.** You'd like to know some basic principles but apply them in a way that aligns with your individual style, values, and circumstances, as well as with your individual kid's needs, style, values, and circumstances.

Parents, Kids, and the COVID–19 Pandemic

Though we had long considered writing this book, we finally put pen to paper in the summer of 2020—frankly, as our own way to cope with the COVID-19 pandemic. To put it mildly, it was a difficult time to be in the field of child mental health. Evidence quickly mounted that kids and their parents were struggling in new and, at times, devastating ways. While we were inspired by the many families who found ways to manage the fear and uncertainty that were swallowing up daily life, we could also see more serious cracks begin to form. Small challenges became major impairments. We watched our young patients shift from presenting a bit of anxiety to refusing to go to school. We saw the occasional tantrum become protracted daily meltdowns. We saw sadness turn to full-blown depression.

The good news? We also saw the opportunities in the adversity. Kids learned to be newly flexible. We all remembered our collective human need for meaningful connection. As a society, we practiced tolerating uncertainty. And seeing all this, we came to believe that parents can nurture a next "greatest generation" of mentally strong kids, helping them develop, out of the ashes of the pandemic, a new superpower: adaptability.

➜ **You want a book that's fun to read and easy on the eyes.** Doodles and infographics keep your brain amused—and might even help you remember a parenting tip or two. You don't have to sweat every decision or agonize over every mistake. It's okay to not take this parenting thing too seriously.

As professionals and as veteran parents, we know full well that there is no such thing as a perfect parent or a perfect child. Parenting is the ultimate long game, and everyone gets unlimited opportunities to get it "right." You could have weeks, months, or even years of parental inertia, inattentiveness, or missed signals, but nothing with your kids is irrevocable. Indeed, missed moments are to be expected, and each one is a chance for growth. Children—in fact, all humans— do not ever "finish" learning and growing, they just continue evolving. Our brains are adaptable by design, and they are especially moldable until we are in our mid-20s. So it really *is* about the journey. There is no finish line, judge, or final score.

THE TEN ESSENTIALS

We believe that, in order to thrive, every child needs:

1 Rest, recreation, and routine

2 Attention skills and self-control

3 Tolerance for difficult feelings

4 Tools to accept and manage anxiety

5 Psychological flexibility

6 Independence

7 Self-motivation

8 Compassion and gratitude

9 Resilience

10 Parents and caregivers who strive to embody these essentials, too—and who embrace that they themselves, just like their children, are works in progress

These ten principles did not magically appear to us. We talked and brainstormed and whiteboard-ed and sticky-noted for countless hours as we wrestled to distill what we knew, trying to crack the code of the essential properties of healthy humans. Our different professional lenses allowed us to find the common threads and the underlying truths in psychological development. What emerged were our ten top priorities for raising kids.

These Essentials, as we call them, fall in order in this book and are designed to build upon one another. They are the essential qualities of well-being that parents can nurture in their kids, with a little guidance. They are *not* a linear checklist of skills and characteristics to acquire—human development doesn't work like that. Instead, they are qualities that evolve and become more deeply wired over time. These Essentials form a set of priorities that we can return to again and again over the course of our kids' childhoods.

Our Essentials are innately human, with no expiration date. And kids' brains are wonderfully plastic and do not fully form for decades, so parents have a million unique opportunities to help wire their kids, no matter their age, for psychological strength.

Using these Essentials as a road map of sorts, parents can help kids develop the neurobiological capacity to evolve into happier, healthier humans. You might get lost; you might take a wrong turn. Don't panic! Just refer back to your map and remind yourself of your priorities. And don't kick yourself for any detours along the way.

We believe in putting our energy into controlling the things we can. What follows next are our top ten Essentials, whether for an age of anxiety, our post-pandemic decades of recalibration, or for an increasingly complex modern world. Difficult things happen. We sometimes have the opportunity to wrestle something good out of them. The human brain is not fully developed into our mid 20s, so we have a massive window of neuroplastic opportunity. We have the chance to help mold and shape our children's actively developing brains into learning crucial coping skills that will set them up to thrive in adulthood. Our Essentials are specifically designed to help raise kids who can evolve beyond our generation into members of a new Age of Adaptability.

HOW TO USE THIS BOOK

We hope your copy of this book will be well-worn, dog-eared, highlighted, and constantly moving from the bedroom to the kitchen to the bathroom. It is designed for you to drop in, drop out, read in multiple sittings, in multiple years, throughout your parenting journey. Each chapter covers one of the Essentials and is organized to allow easy skimming. These ten principles build upon one another, yet every chapter can be read as a stand-alone topic, so feel free to jump around.

Each chapter is built upon the same structure:

➡ **The Takeaway:** A quick glance at the key points in the chapter. Sometimes that's all you need!

➡ **The Setup**: A brief story from one of our patients or clients that illustrates the Essential in action.

➡ **Why Is This Essential?** Why did this topic make our top ten?

➡ **Curious About the Science?** Here we offer a few highlights from the relevant psychological and neuroscience research, boiling down the greatest, latest, and/or most interesting findings.

➡ **What Does It Look Like in Your Family?** One of the biggest challenges with parenting books is that they are written without knowing each reader's individual family. In our professional capacity, the first thing we do when we meet a family as new clients is to "take a snapshot"— that is, we assess where they are and what help they need. We have created some simple assessment tools so you can determine for yourself whether you might need a little help with any of the Essentials in this moment. They will help you customize the approaches laid out in this book and make them your own.

➡ **Take a Look at Your Child:** Questions here will help you consider how your child is doing with family relationships, friendships, learning, and sense of self. Looking at these categories and how they apply to the essential principle under discussion, how curious versus concerned for your child are you? Using markers, colored pencils, or a stray crayon or two, mark up the Concern-O-Meter with arrows to indicate where you think your child lands in this moment in time.

CONCERN-O-METER

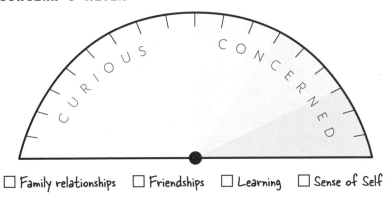

☐ Family relationships ☐ Friendships ☐ Learning ☐ Sense of Self

→ **Take a Look at Yourself:** This section asks bigger-picture questions to help you clarify your own parenting values and goals, and identify your natural parenting style as it relates to the essential principle at hand.

HOW DO YOU THINK YOU TREND?

(target zone)

→ **Plays for Your Playbook:** This section is the heart of the book, offering a variety of concrete tips and tools that we provide to our patients. Browse and experiment. Play around to find the ones that fit your family best. Maybe even pick some plays that are uncomfortable or wildly different from what you usually do. At different ages and stages some will be more applicable than others, so there is value in rereading this book for the same kid as that kid grows older. Certain tips will also be more useful for some kids than others. Ultimately, you decide what to try.

→ **Wrapping Up:** The bottom line.

→ **Deeper Dive:** This book is designed to be ten parenting books condensed into one. If you want to delve deeper into a particular topic, here you'll find the books and other resources we love best and most recommend to the parents we work with.

PLAYBOOK PEARLS

In each chapter, observant readers may find some universal themes in our parenting tips, tools, and tricks. Here are a few general best practices to consider.

Hold Up the Mirror

We want our kids to learn how to see themselves, both on the inside (their feelings, thoughts, and motivations) and on the outside (their behavior and interactions with others). We can do this by holding up a mirror; share with them our observations about how they are acting or feeling, and help them make connections between their emotions and their behavior. It's important to share your observations neutrally, like a reporter, rather than judgmentally, like a pundit. Say what you see, not what you think or feel. ("I see that you're really mad at your sister for knocking over your LEGO tower. Your hands are all balled up and you look like you want to kick something.")

Encourage Your Kids to "Take a Selfie"

Self-understanding leads to self-regulation. We want kids to gain enough self-awareness to be able to evaluate themselves—to be able to take their own selfie rather than rely only on us taking a snapshot of them.

Copycat

A parenting truth is that our kids learn more from watching what we do than from listening to what we say. Modeling what to do through our own actions is a highly effective way to parent.

Narrate Your Thought Process

A specific form of modeling is narrating out loud what kids often can't see: your interior thoughts, feelings, and decision-making. Narrating is a thinking-out-loud technique in which you describe what you are doing as you are doing it. Often it works best when you include the why: "I'm feeling really grouchy, so I'm going to go take a short walk because I know it will help me feel better."

Unmask Yourself

We encourage parents to share their own struggles, both past and present, with their children. Rather than alarming them, we find it to have the opposite effect; kids are relieved and encouraged to know that their parents are humans who also make mistakes and sometimes feel uncertain, sad, or overwhelmed. By "unmasking" ourselves, we help our kids see difficulties as part of the normal human condition. It can also allow children to develop their intuition. If a kid senses that their parent is hurt or upset, we generally recommend that the parent share or confirm that feeling (within reason, without overloading). This way, children can learn to trust that their inner sense about others is often correct.

Give a Feelings Shower

One of the biggest mistakes we see parents make is trying to talk to a part of a child's brain that is currently offline. When a kid becomes emotional, the rational, organized part of their brain often shuts down, and logic and problem-solving become impossible for a time. In these moments, we encourage you to talk only to the part of your child's brain that is still active—that is, the emotional center. The best way to connect with this part of the brain is to give a "feelings shower" with your words: Recognize, validate, and empathize with your child's strong emotions to help them regulate and bring that executive brain back online.

Do Nothing

Sometimes the absolute hardest—and most effective—thing to do as a parent is not to do anything at all. To say nothing, to do nothing, to zip our mouths, to stifle the urge to act, to just wait and see what

 happens. When we give our kids space to feel, suffer, or figure things out for themselves, we give them the ability to stretch and grow by their own effort.

WHAT'S GOING ON IN YOUR KID'S BRAIN

efore you dive into the heart of this book, we want to provide some context about what exactly is going on in your kid's brain. It's not essential that you understand the nitty-gritty of neuroscience, brain development, and neuroplasticity, but a brief overview of these things will give you the "why" that will guide you toward implementing the "how" of the Essentials.

The human brain hasn't changed much in the past 30,000 years. This means that the brain helping your kid survive a busy twenty-first-century day is unfortunately hardwired to survive a different kind of day from our prehistoric hunter-gatherer ancestors. The brain is ready to help your kid stay alert and on the move. In the face of stress, the brain is wired to be fearful, reactive, and anxious—useful emotions when you're trying to avoid a tiger attack, but less useful when you're trying to prepare for a chemistry test.

The human brain's survival response is not always well-suited for modern life, including the experience of uncertainty, which is a hallmark of the world we live in today. We need to adapt our stone-age brain to function in a modern world. The good news is we can help our kids overcome their currently less useful, primitive instincts and instead leverage the immense power of the newer, more adaptable parts of their minds. We have the opportunity to help our kids develop increasingly rich and efficient connections to the most highly evolved parts of their brains.

PREFRONTAL CORTEX (PFC) HIPPOCAMPUS

BED NUCLEUS OF THE STRIA TERMINALIS (BNST) AMYGDALA

EMOTIONS, MEMORY, AND THE BOSS OF THE BRAIN

The amygdala and hippocampus are some of the more ancient parts of the human brain. They are close to the very oldest parts of the brain—the brain stem and cerebellum—which control the most vital life functions, such as heart rate, breathing, body temperature, and balance.

The amygdala is part of the limbic system, which codes and processes emotion: fear, sadness, anger, happiness, and pleasure, to name a few. The amygdala is our threat detection center. It is always scanning for potential danger—even as we relax and binge-watch

Netflix—and stands ready to sound the alarm so that, should a crisis occur, we can react immediately, before thinking a single conscious thought. (Consider how your body might react to touching a hot stove—your hand snaps back before you can consciously think "hot!" or even react with an "ouch!".)

AMYGDALA

A perceived threat sets off the amygdala's alarm bells and triggers our "fight-or-flight" response, which unleashes into our bloodstream a mighty bundle of stress chemicals, including adrenaline, norepinephrine, and cortisol. The term *fight-or-flight* was coined more than a hundred years ago. Today, this emergency survival reaction is now more accurately referred to as "freeze, fight, or flight." Freezing is a powerful defense—not moving can help prevent detection by a predator. However, in this book, we stick to the more common term *fight or flight*.

With this chemical blast, we feel our amygdala's alarm in a very physical and sudden way. The amygdala directs blood and strength to the most essential body parts needed to survive the perceived crisis: Our heart rate increases to quicken our blood flow. Blood is redirected from nonessential places, such as our skin, fingers, toes, and gastrointestinal tract, to the more essential larger muscle groups, like our thighs and biceps. We breathe faster to take in more oxygen and sweat to cool ourselves down. In an instant, we are physically prepared to react as fast as possible to save our life.

But for all of its powers, the amygdala is not discriminating. It often can't tell the difference between a tiger and a test—and most inconveniently, the amygdala can perceive our *thoughts* as threats. For example, for those of us who are afraid of snakes, simply picturing a snake in our mind could trigger our amygdala's danger response. Neuroscientist Joseph LeDoux, one of the early researchers of anxiety, was able to map out, within the brain itself, how our unconscious

threat detector, the amygdala, synaptically interacted with our conscious thoughts. Ta-da! We now could see how these survival circuits create the human experience of anxiety.

The hippocampus is the part of our brain that is responsible for processing memory. It forms and organizes memories of our experiences so we can remember them for later use. It also records the emotions connected to these experiences. The amygdala and hippocampus are next-door neighbors. This friendly neighbor status allows them to permanently connect our feelings with our memories of a situation without needing to tap into the more thinking parts of our brain. Situations that make us emotional, especially the scary ones, are immediately recorded in our memory. This evolutionary adaptation allows us to remember to avoid those situations that make us feel fearful or anxious in the future. Again, that's great for avoiding the tiger den you noticed on your afternoon walk through the savanna. It's not so great for tackling that chemistry test.

The good news is that the sometimes-unruly amygdala and related structures are overseen by the newest and most intrinsically human part of the brain, the cortex, a six-layered masterpiece that has evolved over millennia. The cortex is composed of intricately interconnected brain cell matter, a remarkable system overlaying the primitive brain. The very front part of the cortex, the prefrontal cortex (PFC), was especially enlarged and sculpted in humans.

The PFC is the wise, rational, reasoning part of the brain. It is often referred to as the "executive" of the brain, like the CEO of an organization. We like to call the PFC the "boss of the brain." The PFC houses some of our language processing centers, and helps us focus, sustain attention, and not get distracted. It helps us slow down and make good choices—to think clearly, control our

FEAR of FEAR

FEAR

more primitive impulses, and analyze information to make the best decisions. The PFC allows us to see the middle ground—the gray between black and white. It helps us avoid thinking in extremes or engaging in "all or none" thinking. As the locus of our self-control, the PFC also applies the brakes on our amygdala to regulate anxiety and emotions—the wise Yoda to our feisty young Skywalker. Simply put, the PFC sets humans apart from other animals. Thanks to our PFC, we can plan ahead, strategize, manage our time, create contingency plans, and think bigger-picture thoughts that transcend time and space.

As mental health professionals, we often help care for a primitive brain attempting to respond to a modern world—a world that has less physical danger (most of the time) but constant other experiences that our ancient brains code as being equally dangerous, like forgetting your homework, dropping your tray in the school cafeteria, missing the school bus, or having to interact with a stranger at the coffee shop. We help our patients tap into the strengths of their PFC while regulating the not-always-helpful emotional responses from their amygdala and related brain pathways. And the good news is that our brains are open to this sort of help, thanks to neuroplasticity.

NURTURING NEUROPLASTICITY

Neuroplasticity is the ability of neurons to continually network in the brain, forming, organizing, and reorganizing connections. These connections are called synapses. Neuroplasticity allows the brain to change and grow more complex by molding and shaping different synaptic networks.

Dr. Jay Giedd and his colleagues at the National Institute of Mental Health revolutionized the way we look at child brain development. Their research showed that the PFC is the last part of the brain to develop and remains a neuroplastic "work in progress" through young adulthood. Giedd's study looked at MRIs of young people's brains every two years from the ages of 3 through 25. The MRIs showed dramatic changes in the thickening, thinning, molding, and shaping of the PFC during the child and teen years.

The brain develops in a wave of neuroplasticity from back to front. Development starts in the primitive areas at the back of the brain after birth. It then progresses forward to the front of the brain, finally reaching completion of the brain's advanced frontal regions when we reach the age of approximately 25. This explains why young adults, despite their adult-like physical bodies, can still make impulsive, reckless decisions; the boss of the brain, the PFC, has not fully formed, connected, and taken charge.

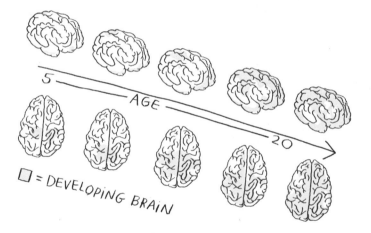

In babies and young children, brain neurons grow like bushes. As kids enter their teen years, their brains begin to prune the smaller, lesser-used branches and twigs to allow the more-used branches to grow stronger and faster. The brain hardwires whatever we practice: riding a bicycle, learning an instrument, shooting a basketball, staying calm when feeling angry. Children don't come into the world being able to do these things automatically; they need to practice so that the neuroplastic brain hardwires these skills.

In terms of brain development, the child and teen years are both windows of opportunity and periods of vulnerability. Everything that kids practice, learn, and hardwire in these years holds major consequences for the development of emotional regulation, attention, and self-control. Practicing multiplication tables hardwires in that skill, while avoiding multiplication tables may hardwire a child's thought that they are not as competent as their peers. Practicing staying calm when angry also can be hardwired into a kid's brain, making it easier for them to stay cool under pressure as they get older. On the flip side, exploding every time they feel angry can also become hardwired, making that behavior more difficult (though not impossible) to change or improve.

Dr. Giedd's study, along with other research, points to the teen years as a particularly critical period for brain growth and development. Dr. Giedd coined the phrase "use it or lose it" to

CLIENT FILE
Fish Have Amygdalas, Too

Catherine had a sweet, anxious 7-year-old patient* who had a passion for fishing. She taught him how some of the "lower" parts of the brain that carry emotions and memories are actually ancient vestiges from our evolutionary past, and can be found in different forms in all the animals that descended from the same common ancestors. Catherine talked about how even modern-day reptiles and fish have a rudimentary amygdala and hippocampus. They can "feel" fear and connect it with memory, which allows them to avoid future dangerous situations (such as a certain boy's favorite fishing hole). Her little patient responded with shock, saying, "Wait a minute, FISH have amygdalas, TOO?" His dad later reported that the boy was very gentle with any fish he caught after that: soothingly assuring them as he released them that it was okay, he was just fishing to visit them, and they were safe in the fishing hole.

* Our client stories throughout this book are based on real-life examples from our practices, but we have changed key details and created composites from multiple client experiences.

describe this period of neuroplasticity, meaning that frequently used neural pathways are strengthened, while seldom-used pathways are eliminated. By the time we reach adulthood, our brain is using the synaptic networks it built through habit when we were younger to guide our thoughts, feelings, and behaviors.

"YIKES" vs. "MEH": THE BRAIN UNDER STRESS

That PFC boss of the brain is miraculous, but it's not impervious to strain. Two constants of modern life—stress and uncertainty—are PFC kryptonite, and they can make it hard for the boss of the brain to do its job as the calm, rational locus of control. And when our PFC is impaired, we have less ability to think rationally and feel calm.

Yale neuroscientist Dr. Amy Arnsten has spent more than two decades researching the effects of stress on the PFC connectivity network, all the way down to the molecular and chemical level. Her research shows that chemical messengers in the brain, including norepinephrine (related to adrenaline) and dopamine, can both positively and negatively affect the strength and power of the PFC. When we are under stress but feel alert and in control (such as when we're facing the pressure of a big deadline or a choir solo performance), the release of norepinephrine and dopamine helps optimize PFC brain control. This "top-down control," as it's called, can help us successfully manage intense, often unpleasant feelings of stress. Conversely, high levels of *uncontrollable* stress (such as when we are living through a global pandemic) activate the amygdala response, which impairs the PFC. This isn't always a bad thing! When we are in immediate danger, we want to act quickly, from instinct rather than trying to work through our decision-making process (and possibly getting hit by a bus while doing so). But long-term exposure to high levels of chronic stress has been shown to lead to additional changes in the PFC that can be further detrimental to its functioning.

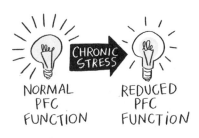

NORMAL PFC FUNCTION — CHRONIC STRESS — REDUCED PFC FUNCTION

Acute stress activates the PFC to provide the motivation to get up and go in the face of a challenge (*Yikes! I better start studying for that math test!*). Chronic stress lowers our PFC function, dimming our drive and our energy levels (*Meh. What's the point?* *continues to scroll TikTok*). The result is a loss of focus, often experienced as a kind of brain fog, less awareness of time and space, and difficulty with higher-level decision-making and abstract reasoning.

As noted by Dr. Giedd and his colleagues, neuroplasticity is paradoxical. The brain's plasticity—its ability to grow, strengthen, and prune neural connections in response to the environment—can have negative effects as well as positive ones, leaving kids' brains more vulnerable to the effects of chronic high stress. Research shows that stress can cause neurons to die and neural networks to shrink or retract. Stanford researchers led the first study comparing MRI brain scans of teenagers taken before the pandemic to MRIs taken a year after the pandemic started. The teens assessed after the pandemic shutdowns had brain MRIs that had prematurely aged and thinned, with more advanced brain age and neuro-anatomical features typical of individuals with a history of significant childhood adversity and trauma. As our favorite neuropsychologist, Dr. William Stixrud, often says, "The more anxious and stressed you are, the more anxious you become."

There are so many things that can knock our PFC off track—economic uncertainty, toxic family dynamics, poorly performing schools, and even more systemic issues such as the long-term effects from the stress of poverty, violence, and racism. And many of these stressors are out of parents' control. It's deeply challenging to help your kid keep a routine if you never know when your next work shift is going to be; motivation can be hard to cultivate if your neurodivergent kid needs more support and the school isn't helping. And for many of us, the pandemic created new vulnerabilities in our family and social structures, opening us up to the damaging effects of chronic stress on our children's still-developing brains. This neurological reality has potential implications for some individuals' long-term mental health and well-being.

Highly stressful events often come with an ever-present cloud of uncertainty. Like most vertebrates, we humans find uncertainty to be stressful; our brains associate survival with predictability. We are wired to constantly work to reduce and resolve uncertainty.

However, during the pandemic we encountered radical changes; the "corona coaster" went up and down on a week-by-week and sometimes day-by-day basis. We often felt like we could not depend on anything to remain constant or consistent. Our inability to resolve the chronic daily uncertainty of the pandemic placed a level of chronic stress on us that was exhausting to sustain.

Recent research has shown that the feeling of "anticipatory anxiety" comes from a part of the brain near the amygdala called the bed nucleus of the stria terminalis (BNST), sometimes also known as the "extended amygdala." Recall that the amygdala is tied to our feeling of fear and immediate response to threat. The BNST is involved in sustained fear reactions, and in the long-lasting icky unease that is typical of anxiety and switched on by apprehension. Our collective BNSTs certainly had a lot of wear and tear over those pandemic years.

BED NUCLEUS OF THE STRIA TERMINALIS (BNST)

Chronic uncertainty can cause us to lose our sense of control and develop feelings of powerlessness. With powerlessness comes the risk of losing hope. Dr. Martin Seligman described the concept of "learned helplessness": the idea that when people experience a stressful situation repeatedly and feel like they cannot see a way out, they may eventually give up trying to change or solve the situation, even when paths to the solution present themselves. Learned helplessness at any age can lead to anxiety and depression; in childhood, it can have lifelong consequences.

The good news: Studies reveal that PFC connections can regrow during sustained periods without stress, allowing a worn-out PFC to heal. After all, the boss needs a vacation, too.

MODERN PARENTING IN AN AGE OF ADAPTABILITY

Humans are remarkably adaptable. In evolutionary time, we have taken over the entire planet in the blink of an eye. Our physical adaptability has allowed us to thrive over time, evolving to survive wars, famine, predators, and (yes) plagues. We adapted within groups driven by social connections, communication, and relationships with other humans. We adapted to develop communities that depend on individual specialists, freeing up energy that was previously devoted to survival. With our evolutionary gifts of intelligence, the ability to use language, and our crème de la crème PFCs, we became able to plan, strategize, explore, invent, specialize, and work together in complex systems on a global scale.

However, the overwhelming speed and complexity of modern life is outpacing our psychological adaptability. Society is changing *fast*, and our ancient survival-based wiring is not equipped to handle our psychological needs when managing our modern world. In what scientists call an "evolutionary mismatch," our brains were wired for specific settings and stressors, but our current environment no longer matches those conditions. Our prehistoric brains, wired for survival, are in constant fight-or-flight mode, understandably overstressed, and overflowing with adrenaline, all of which builds our anxiety levels to an all-time high.

We think it is high time to capitalize on the most evolutionarily advanced boss of the brain, that logical, wise, calm, and Yoda-like prefrontal cortex to build a true superpower: psychological adaptability. It begins with teaching kids to see their brains in action and to optimize their PFC superpower while their brains are still taking shape, thanks to the long window of neuroplasticity. We can help kids identify their emotions, which allows them to create some separation between feelings, thoughts, and reactions. This process can help kids maximize their focus, attention, emotion regulation, and locus of control.

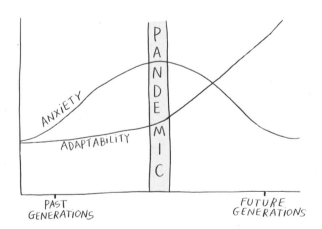

PANDEMIC

ANXIETY

ADAPTABILITY

PAST
GENERATIONS

FUTURE
GENERATIONS

We believe in putting our energy into controlling the things we can. What follows next are our ten top Essentials, whether for an age of anxiety, our post-pandemic decades of recalibration, or for an increasingly complex modern world. Difficult things happen. We sometimes have the opportunity to wrestle something good out of them. If the human brain is not fully developed until the late 20s, we have a massive window of amazing neuroplastic opportunity. Our Essentials are specifically designed to help raise kids who can evolve beyond our generation into members of a new age of Age of Adaptability.

DEEPER DIVE

The Whole-Brain Child: 12 Revolutionary Strategies to Nurture Your Child's Developing Mind by Daniel Siegel and Tina Payne Bryson

> Dan Siegel (a psychiatrist) and Tina Payne Bryson (a psychotherapist) are two of the most important voices in the field of brain health and emotions. This easily accessible book includes illustrations of the metaphors they use for how a child's brain develops and grows over time, with specific strategies you can use to build healthy synaptic connections.

The Teenage Brain: A Neuroscientist's Survival Guide to Raising Adolescents and Young Adults by Frances E. Jensen with Amy Ellis Nutt

> Dr. Jensen, a neuroscientist and mother, provides the latest understanding of brain development while using her own real-world examples parents can resonate with. We often share sections of this book with teenagers, too, so they can better understand their own behavior in light of their neurobiology.

Getting Your Three Rs

REST, RECREATION, AND ROUTINE

THE TAKEAWAY

✔ The roots of good mental health are rest, recreation, and routine.

✔ Sleep has a massive impact on cognitive function and mental well-being. Unstructured play provides critical thinking skills, movement activates brain connections, and routine relaxes the brain and sets it up for success.

✔ If your kid has hit a rough patch, it's likely that at least one of these elements is out of whack.

THE SETUP

Catherine was recently asked to assess a young boy for ADHD based on concerns expressed by his teacher. During her initial evaluation, the boy confessed that he was secretly reading late into the night with his flashlight under the covers. She "prescribed" a no-flashlight rule for a week. Soon after, unbidden, the teacher wrote a note to the parents about what a difference the "doctor's visit" had made in their son's ability to pay attention at school.

WHY IS THIS ESSENTIAL?

As parents, one of our most important jobs is to help our kids build a strong foundation for psychological health so they can function well both in crisis and in calm. The roots for good mental health (at any age) are rest, recreation, and routine. We call these the Three Rs.

Inevitably, there will be times when one or two or all three of the Three Rs will be out of whack. We have all experienced the frequent tension between the demands of modern life and the Three Rs. Rushed meals, fewer opportunities for movement and exercise, wacky sleep cycles— if too frequent, these daily disruptions raise concern about long-term consequences for mental health and brain development in our children.

The Three Rs are intrinsically connected; imbalance in one affects the others. For instance, the bulk of the sleep disturbances we saw in children during the pandemic were likely exacerbated by a lack of movement and dysregulated routines. Kids (and their parents) lost the boundaries of their daily schedules. Bedrooms morphed into classrooms. With limited playground time and reduced sports schedules, the structure for movement, exercise, and outdoor time largely disappeared. Results? Reduced quality of sleep.

We want you to find balance. If your child seems a little unmoored, is struggling in some way, or is just having a bad week, take stock of the Three Rs. Remember, your child's brain never takes a break. It works equally hard, day and night. Whether managing all your child's vital life systems or their motor, sensory, and cognitive processes, the brain continues to take care of your child's body all the time, even when they are asleep. Even a small adjustment in just one of the Three Rs can make a big positive difference for your kid.

CURIOUS ABOUT THE SCIENCE?

What Science Says About REST

The old adage "sleep is the best medicine" applies to more than just physical illnesses. Sleep is one of the most critical components for body and brain health, impacting everything from cognitive function and mental well-being to growth, height, and immunity. Reduced or disrupted sleep can completely unravel frontal lobe attention and self-control, both in children and in adults. Sleep problems are correlated with multiple psychiatric disorders, including anxiety, depression, and ADHD. Sleep deprivation has been shown to quadruple the risk of teenage depression and significantly increase the risk for teen suicidality.

A recent study from the University of California at Berkeley concluded that deep sleep seems to be a natural inhibitor of anxiety. The study showed that a night of good sleep reduces activity in the amygdala, whereas a sleepless night can trigger amygdala activity and cause up to a 30 percent increase in anxiety levels. When we are sleep deprived, our body and brain benefit from adrenaline to keep us awake and alert.

But adrenaline is also designed for moments of potential danger, which means that we become more reactive, more anxious, and more likely to lose control of our emotions.

Another fascinating function of sleep is related to the flow of cerebrospinal fluid (CSF), the lubricating fluid that bathes our brain and keeps it cushioned inside our hard skull casing. New research has shown that the channels in the brain expand while we sleep, allowing large waves of CSF to flow through and flush out toxins and debris. We can think of this sleep-time CSF flush as a nightly "power-wash" of the brain, preventing the buildup of adrenaline and toxic waste by-products.

Research has also shown that sleep plays a critical role in learning and memory. For example, in one research study, people who studied information in the evening, had a good night's rest, and then were tested in the morning performed better than those who studied in the morning and were tested that same evening.

We see lots of sleep struggles in our young patients. One reason is stress, which affects sleep on multiple levels—when we sleep, how long we sleep, how easily we fall asleep, and how soundly we sleep. Another is excessive screen time and/or screen use too close to bedtime. Our brains require rest and rejuvenation from screens and devices. As early as 2010, researchers showed that when students unplugged and significantly reduced their screen use, they reported a dramatic improvement in their quality of life.

Other studies have found that adults unplugging completely after the workday resulted in feeling recharged for the next day. As we discussed earlier, modern life's constant connectivity and disruptions—the incessant pings from emails, texts, tweets, and digital notifications—exhausts our brains. Unplugging our devices may refresh the prefrontal cortex (PFC), creating motivation, energy, and engagement with the world.

With our busy lives, we know it can feel impossible to prioritize a healthy night's sleep over our kids' grades, sports, family time, and chores. This is an area where we ourselves find it especially hard to practice what we preach. But we promise: *Everything* you and your child struggle with will get better if you first have the foundation of a healthy night's sleep. There is never a time when consistent, right-sized sleep won't help. There are no magic pills to raising a healthy, well-adjusted kid, but sleep may come closest to the promise of immediate improvement in at least some aspect of your child's life—and your own.

What Science Says About RECREATION

Humans are built to play. Experts in human evolution have shown that fun and recreation—exercise, movement, laughter, time spent outside, time to be social, unstructured playtime—are essential for the growth and development of children's brains and even the survival of our species.

CLIENT FILE
Exercise for Worriers

Jennifer was working with a parent of a worried 8-year-old named Sadie. Sadie had a lot of anticipatory worries that kept her from being able to go to recess or hang out with friends. Some worries were related to outdoor sensory experiences, such as thunderstorms or being stung by a bee; others were more home- or school-related, like fear of a home robbery or someone throwing up on the bus.

Poor Sadie's fight-or-flight system was turned on for much of her day. She needed a way to methodically release the anxiety-triggering chemicals that her nervous system, feeling constantly under threat, was producing. Jennifer decided to put her on an "Exercise Program for Worriers." They enlisted her older brother to skip, walk, and/or jog with her to school each morning. Her school counselor had her join a speed walkers group—meeting up with other like-minded kids to walk for the last ten minutes of lunchtime. Her grandmother officially timed her while she ran around her apartment building two times right when she got off the school bus. Every time she had a worry at home, she was encouraged to jump twenty times on the tiny indoor trampoline her family had in the TV room. Even without any formal talk or play therapy, within two weeks Sadie and her family reported her anxiety levels at less than half what they had initially been.

To begin, the experience of unstructured play is crucial for nerve cell connections being made in kids' growing PFCs. (Emphasis on *unstructured*, meaning free play without rules or directions from parents, teachers, coaches, or other adults.) Unstructured play is also a critical ingredient for teaching the brain two important life skills: the ability to predict what will happen, both with people and the world, and the ability to manage uncertainty and surprise. Studies have shown that older kids who are highly playful report less stress and better coping skills than their less-playful peers.

Play also brings movement, an essential component for a healthy life. When we stay in the same position for long periods of time, the body circulates less oxygen. When less oxygen circulates in the bloodstream, the feeling of fatigue increases and results in lower energy efficiency and motivation levels.

Spending time outdoors is essential, too. Studies show that simply spending ninety minutes outside, in a natural setting, stimulates beneficial changes in the PFC. Daily contact with nature lowers stress, improves mood, and reduces anxiety. Time spent in green spaces and outdoors can improve cognition in children with attention deficit disorders.

One exciting recent discovery is a little-known metabolic factor called brain-derived neurotrophic growth factor (BDNF). BDNF is naturally created in the body, especially during exercise. In the lab, when scientists put BDNF on nerve cells it caused neurogenesis (the creation of new nerve cells) and supported the survival of existing nerve cell pathways. Harvard professor and BDNF guru Dr. John Ratey calls BDNF "Miracle-Gro" for the brain.

BDNF boosts memory and IQ, increases the thickness of the cortex and hippocampus, and helps protect neurons. There is evidence that BDNF stimulates neurogenesis in older adults, including people with Alzheimer's. Conversely, lower levels of BDNF have been associated with depression, cognitive decline, and even a shorter life span.

As far as we know, there is no way to manufacture BDNF. We can't take a BDNF pill to support brain health. However, there are ways to encourage the brain to make more of it—one of which is regular exercise. According to Dr. Ratey, this means getting to at least 70 percent of your maximum heart rate for thirty minutes, four or five times a week. Exercising once or twice a week may feel good and can relieve stress, but to receive the deluxe brain benefit, our kids need to be running, jumping, chasing, and playing cardio-intense sports more regularly. And we want them hot with exertion, short of breath, covered in sweat. This type of physical effort uses more brain cells and using more brain cells activates the genes that make BDNF.

Last but not least, as Stanford neuroscience researcher Dr. Allan Reiss has shown, humor is also important for cognitive and emotional development. Both child and adult brain networks are activated in positive ways by humor and play, delivering enormous servings of dopamine, along with some mood-enhancing serotonin.

More than ever, we need to step up and incorporate movement, daily play, and humor into our everyday life. The good news is that evolution has designed kids for exactly this purpose. All you have to do is make sure your kids have ample opportunities to laugh, move, and play.

What Science Says About ROUTINE

One of humanity's most amazing neurological gifts is our ability to anticipate the future by learning from past and current events. With this power, we can work to prevent bad things from reoccurring. But this also means that our human brains fear uncertainty. Uncertainty diminishes our sense of control, which can cause anxiety (both immediate and anticipatory). It can make us feel overwhelmed and trigger a sensation of "brain fog." Uncertainty causes our obsessive anticipatory circuits to come up with endless "what if" scenarios, conjuring up worst-case scenarios and catastrophe.

Routine is an antidote to uncertainty. Routine relaxes the brain and sets it up for success. As parents, we can help our kids feel more organized and focused by maintaining structure and routine. Having a routine reduces the need for on-the-spot decision-making and supports self-regulation by taking the guesswork out of daily life. It gives kids a boost of empowerment by supporting a sense of self-control.

Even the illusion of structure can convince that boss of our brain, the PFC, to think, "I've got this." Picture the sense of calm you might feel upon entering your child's classroom on back-to-school night and seeing a daily activity schedule neatly written on the whiteboard. Or the relief and satisfaction you might see on your kid's face when they cross off a homework assignment on their to-do list. Whether we are young or full-grown, our sense of control is optimized when we can rely on a general framework of what will happen each day. Having a routine engages our PFC and regulates those pesky anxiety loops—and it's a more constructive way to hack into our dopamine circuits than playing video games for two hours.

Structure is a kind of mental health. Several studies have found that having active daytime routines promotes healthier sleep cycles. Another study showed that family routines help reduce oppositional and negative behaviors in children. Solidifying the morning routine reduces stress not only in the morning but also later in the day. Knowing what we can expect, and having rituals and plans we can count on, whether fun or monotonous, gives both parents and children daily anchors in a sea of uncertainty. Do not underestimate the power of a solid routine!

Routines and "Real Life"

While we tout the importance of routine, we also need to be gentle and flexible. Routine is not rigidity. Sometimes our work or home lives are necessarily unpredictable—for example, when parents travel for work or have changing shifts, when someone in the family is going through a serious illness, or when childcare is unreliable. Even if some parts of family life are chaotic, parents can still work to stabilize what they can. Look for opportunities to build ritual and routine (for example, a military parent might pre-record bedtime stories before a lengthy deployment). And in times of change or transition (a big move, a divorce, a pandemic), implementing new routines and rituals might be the first priority. Even in families with great predictability to their days, some routines will go lopsided. Some days may become unexpected pajama days. But other days might be planned pajama days that can go on the family calendar.

WHAT DO THE THREE Rs LOOK LIKE IN YOUR FAMILY?

Take a Look at Your Child

* *Family relationships:* Does your family structure provide support for the Three Rs (Rest, Recreation, Routine)? Do you prioritize them for your child? Is one R particularly challenging for your family?

* *Friendships:* Does your kid engage in both structured and unstructured time with friends? Do they have opportunity for sleepovers and playdates, but not to the point of exhaustion? When they are with their friends, do they spend any time outside? Do they run, move, jump, and chase?

* *Learning:* Do teachers, coaches, or other adults involved in your child's life express any concern about your child being sleepy, lacking attention or focus, or lacking interest in movement?

* *Sense of self:* Can your child notice what they need for themselves in all Three Rs? Do they connect their mood to the quality of their sleep the night before? Do they notice if they can concentrate better after walking the dog? Can they speak up or adjust when they feel they are getting out of balance?

CONCERN-O-METER

Pick a color for each category. Draw a colored arrow for each to give yourself a visual picture of your child in this moment.

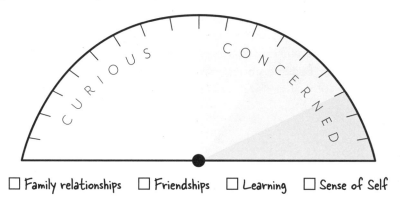

CURIOUS · CONCERNED

☐ Family relationships   ☐ Friendships   ☐ Learning   ☐ Sense of Self

Take a Look at Yourself

✳ *Are your values aligned with your parenting choices?*

Simple as the Three Rs might be, this Essential may require you to do some soul searching to honestly identify your priorities for your child. (Travel sports or downtime? More sleep or better grades?) Every family has constraints and competing needs that may impact their ability to make the Three Rs a priority. What elements of your daily/weekly/monthly/yearly life are fixed (work hours, childcare needs, financial limitations) and what are flexible? Accepting that you may not be able to change everything, what can you adjust to better serve your long-term goals for your kid?

✳ *If your kids are young, are you taking advantage of your ability to have a direct effect on the Three Rs?*

The age of a child matters greatly in how we can effectively address the Three Rs. With very young children, it is much easier for parents to create a routine and ensure it is followed, as well as to control the amount of sleep kids get, the food they eat, and the recreation in their days. Are you paying attention and following through?

Be Honest with Yourself

If you're a hypocrite, own it! If you're ambivalent, admit it! Who isn't? Perhaps you don't garage your cell phone, but you can get a good night's sleep anyway. Perhaps you really value good grades and think your child can get by with less sleep for a year or two in order to make that happen. Before you determine where you want to be with your child's Three Rs, determine where you are with yourself and your priorities. We aren't recommending that you be perfect, or even perfectly consistent—only that you be honest, with yourself and your kids.

If your kids are older, are you using your parental influence to encourage them to observe the Three Rs, and are you consistent in your messaging and actions?

As kids get older, parents' control shifts to influence, and adolescents' barometer for hypocrisy is huge. At this stage, leading by example and having thoughtful conversations is more effective than issuing mandates. It may become more difficult to enforce the Three Rs, but it's still extremely important to give them your attention: practice them in your own life and prioritize them in your parenting and messaging to your children.

What are your favorite things to do with your kids?

Does time spent with your kid also contribute to the Three Rs? Relaxing with your kids provides important connection time that can help kids cope with stress. Have you found unplugged activities that you and your kids enjoy doing together? What about family inside jokes, laughs, and all-around silliness?

HOW DO YOU THINK YOU TREND?

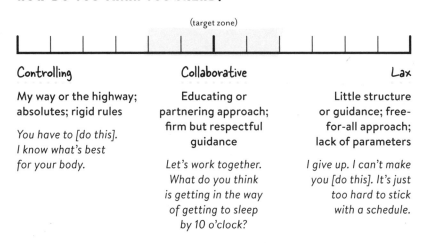

(target zone)

Controlling
My way or the highway; absolutes; rigid rules
You have to [do this]. I know what's best for your body.

Collaborative
Educating or partnering approach; firm but respectful guidance
Let's work together. What do you think is getting in the way of getting to sleep by 10 o'clock?

Lax
Little structure or guidance; free-for-all approach; lack of parameters
I give up. I can't make you [do this]. It's just too hard to stick with a schedule.

PLAYS FOR YOUR PLAYBOOK: REST
Supporting Good Sleep

There are a thousand ways, and reasons why, kids might have a tough time with sleep. If they have trouble falling asleep, are they struggling to turn off their thoughts, do they have worries about monsters, or are they still physically amped up? If they fall asleep but then wake up a lot, are they seeking your reassurance, craving your warm body, or still learning how to put themselves back to sleep? If they wake up before dawn, are they feeling anxious about the day, or are they hardwired early risers?

If you want to help your child improve the quality of their sleep, try some of the tips below. See if you notice any shifts in your child's functioning (or your own). And as always, remember that sometimes the techniques that don't appeal to you are exactly the ones that you might end up finding the most helpful.

➡ **Notice whether your child's brain is able to go "Off Duty."**
The brain has a daytime setting, when it is "On Alert," and a nighttime setting, when it is "Off Duty." On Alert always overrides Off Duty, so if a child feels On Alert, they won't be able to access their sleep system. As an example, studies show that people don't get good-quality sleep the first night they are in a hotel—even if their mind is calm, the body is still set to On Alert, not yet used to the surroundings. Ask yourself, does my child feel chill enough to go Off Duty, or is their On Alert system still engaged? Many of the following Plays can help your child get to their Off Duty state.

➡ **Set a sleepy mood.** Melatonin, a brain chemical that promotes sleep, develops in the body during times of low light. Create an atmosphere of low light in the house, especially in your child's bedroom at least an hour before bedtime, so your child's brain can release a melatonin boost for a naturally sleepy body. Reduce the use of electronics—cell phones, tablets, computers, and other screens put out a blue light that signals the brain to stop producing melatonin. (Remove devices from kids' rooms at night when they are young so they don't get in the habit of sleeping with them. Model good sleep hygiene by having a family "phone bedroom" where phones can "sleep"—and get charged—outside of the bedrooms.) Small doses of a melatonin supplement have shown benefits in resetting the sleep cycle, so if your child still struggles with sleep after trying other methods, consider discussing a melatonin supplement with your pediatrician.

➜ **"Pretend" to sleep.** Lots of kids assume they should be able to go right to sleep once they lie down, but for many people, getting to sleep takes up to twenty minutes. Some children may feel like they are doing it wrong, somehow, if they are just lying there waiting for sleep. Let them know we all "pretend" to sleep for a while before we actually fall asleep—knowing that this is how everyone does it may bring them some comfort and confidence.

➜ **Sleep is best, but rest is a close second.** If a kid can't seem to fall asleep or can't get back to sleep after waking in the night, assure them that lying quietly is also rejuvenating. It is also a practice they can control, unlike sleep. So make high-quality rest the goal (and sleep will often follow).

➜ **Go for boring.** Help your child find the sweet spot of bedtime activities that are interesting enough to keep their mind from going to those late-night worried places, but boring enough to help their bodies wind down and bring on sleepiness. Familiar music and books (whether audio or print) are especially soothing. For younger children, read them a book they know by heart. For older kids, recommend familiar books from their childhood, especially comforting or lighthearted novels and comic books that are easy, quick reads and don't tax reading comprehension at that late hour.

➜ **Use sensory activities.** Bring your child's body into the present, away from the past (which may be a source of sadness and regret) and away from the future (a possible source of anxiety). Try working into the bedtime routine items that engage the physical senses: a soft and fluffy blanket, a hot-water bottle, lavender aromatics, mint tea, low-fi music, or even a lava lamp whose light your child can watch shift and change.

➜ **Go for repetition and ritual.** Do bedtime activities in the same order. Repetition trains your child's brain to recognize certain lower kinds of light, clothes, beverages, and hygiene routines as signals to slow down and turn on that Off Duty setting.

➡ **Practice progressive muscle relaxation activities.** You can find audio recordings of these progressions online or on various apps. They are usually just five to ten minutes long and give the brain a "job" of concentrating on each individual part of the body, in turn. The practice encourages the brain to quiet while simultaneously relaxing muscles and releasing stress.

➡ **Try slow exercise in the evening.** Exercising the muscles in the evening with slow movements, like stretching or resistance training, has been shown to bring on quicker and deeper sleep. For example, a slow uphill walk an hour before bedtime can be a helpful sleep-inducing activity. High-intensity aerobic activity, on the other hand, can raise body temperature and create too many endorphins to allow sleep.

➡ **Use slow breathing to turn on the "Off Duty" sleep setting.** Use slow, measured breathing to reset the body for sleep. Slower, deeper breathing is a way for the body to communicate to the brain that the

Recommended Sleep Guidelines

Here are the recommended minimum and maximum hours each age group should regularly sleep during a twenty-four-hour period for optimal health:

Ages 4–12 months	12–16 hours (including naps)
Ages 1–2 years	11–14 hours (including naps)
Ages 3–5 years	10–13 hours (including naps)
Ages 6–12 years	9–12 hours
Ages 13–18 years	8–10 hours

Source: American Academy of Sleep Medicine, endorsed by the American Academy of Pediatrics

If you're concerned your child may not be getting enough sleep, track their sleep for a week, jotting down their sleep and awake times and any other information that might help you get to the bottom of their sleep issues.

environment is safe enough for sleeping. Try teaching your child a technique like four-square breathing. Or try one of the many apps and devices that guide users through slow-breathing practices, such as the Dodow—a device whose soft light slowly "breathes," expanding and contracting, on the ceiling, allowing you to synchronize your own breath with it.

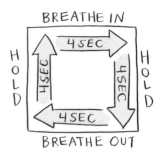

➜ **Capture nighttime worries on paper.** If your child has trouble sleeping because they are worried about practical matters, like drafting an outline for an upcoming paper, their brain is having trouble discriminating between what needs to be done now versus later. It is On Alert and continuing to send signals to itself that, for example, that outline should be done *right now*. Research shows that writing down these worries and noting when we plan to address them ("I will draft that outline tomorrow at 4:30") soothes the brain and tricks it into feeling that the task is being handled. If your child is worried about safety-related things, then their list could be combined with a reality check on how likely it is that these dangers will occur (even in less-safe neighborhoods, the likelihood of an intruder on any given night is statistically close to zero).

➜ **Consistency is key.** A recent study looked at the sleep habits of more than two thousand first-year medical residents. The researchers found that variability in sleep habits significantly affected their mood and depression—no matter how many total hours they slept. In an interview with the *Washington Post*, the lead study author, Yu Fang, said, "Keeping a regular sleep schedule is as important as, if not more important than, having enough sleep time for one's mental health."

➜ **Factor in your child's age and biology.** Adolescent bodies can struggle to sleep before 11 p.m. Do not fight their biology or shame them for it. Focus on consistency over number of hours slept.

➜ **Get outside in the morning.** Research shows that getting five to ten minutes of morning sun or daylight promotes sleep by supporting the circadian rhythms that control our natural sleep-wake cycle.

BED TIME!

➡ **Set an alarm for going to bed.** Bookend the day by setting an alarm to signal the start of your child's nighttime routine. You can even let them plan to hit the snooze button so they can give themselves a ten-minute warning.

➡ **Track your child's sleep patterns.** One of Heather's parents thought her kid was sleeping relatively well, but when she actually started tracking it, she found that every Wednesday her son struggled to fall sleep. After checking with his teacher, she realized that he was quietly anxious about his weekly spelling test that happened every Thursday. Sometimes a little curiosity can go a long way.

➡ **Teach your child about the science of sleep and the body.** The more they know, the better the decisions they can make down the road.

➡ **Lower the temperature.** Studies show lowering the temperature to around 65°F in the room before bedtime and during sleep reduces the amount of time it takes to go to sleep and improves sleep quality throughout the night.

PLAYS FOR YOUR PLAYBOOK: RECREATION
Supporting Healthy Movement

In today's modern world, so much of a kid's day can be taken up with sedentary activities. Some are necessary, such as long commutes to daycare or school. Some are required, such as staying on your carpet square in preschool or sitting still during during a religious service. Some are by choice, such as crafting, playing video games, or reading. Staying in balance sometimes requires us to look for intentional opportunities for our kids to move their bodies.

If you want to help your child increase physical and playful movement, try out some of the tips below. See if you notice any shifts in your child's functioning (or your own). And as always, remember that sometimes the techniques that don't appeal to you are exactly the ones that you might end up finding the most helpful.

➡ **Play physical games with your kids.** Throw a baseball, shoot hoops, sling a Frisbee, kick a soccer ball. Or take it down a notch and play hopscotch, hide-and-seek, or Simon Says. Create "Family Olympics" hour where everyone in the family makes up an event or two—make

Screen Time and Our Dopamine Dial

Technology use is so pervasive and thorny that we have written an entire digital playbook section (see page 220) to help address these challenges. However, one popular form of recreation for many kids is screen time, so we address it here as well. We encourage parents to maintain some balance in their child's use of technology and offer the wisdom of Dr. Clifford Sussman, a leading expert on screen addiction.

Dr. Sussman labels activities such as video games, streaming media, and social media, which produce instant and continuous stimulation, "high-dopamine activities" (HDAs). Activities that yield more delayed gratification are termed "low-dopamine activities" (LDAs). There are plenty of fun LDAs: sports, crafts, music, hobbies. Some LDAs are less welcome: homework, exercise, chores.

Dopamine is the feel-good and reward chemical messenger in our brain, and we get a blast of it any time we get what we want right away. All addictive things—drugs, drinking, gambling, et cetera—have one quality in common: immediate gratification. And that includes digital addictions.

With frequent HDA screen time, the brain gets flooded with dopamine. This digital bingeing produces so much dopamine that our usual daily dose of dopamine loses its potency and effect. Over time, our kids start to develop an increased tolerance to dopamine, making their brain desire more stimulation. Previously enjoyable LDAs will become boring, paling in comparison to the dopamine hits from the thrill of HDA excitement. The end result is what's called "reward deficiency syndrome." This dopamine-depleted state is marked by even more loss of interest in LDAs, and irritability and boredom during most off-screen activities.

Dr. Sussman illustrates this in a pattern familiar to many of us: "A weekend of heavy gaming leads to Monday-morning classes seeming even more boring, which drives kids to seek extra stimulation through more gaming."

It's time to focus on dopamine detoxing, so that children can turn their attention to, and remember how to find joy in, the lovely LDAs of real life.

it silly, let them roll their eyes, but watch and see as they come back next week to ask to do it again.

➡️ **Bring back neighborhood play.** Look for opportunities to be outdoors and informally gather with others. If possible, make sure your kid has plenty of time to play tag with neighborhood kids or shoot hoops with friends at the local park or in the driveway (not just hustle off to basketball practice). If you are a working parent who relies on structured activities for childcare, look for after school/day care programs that value and allow a lot of time for unstructured play. Or, instead of a more traditional after-school program, go in with a group of local families to hire a babysitter to take the kids to the park for a couple of hours and keep out of their way!

➡️ **Assign a few chores throughout the day that involve micromovement.** This could be walking the dog, getting the mail, or even emptying the dishwasher. Make a habit of "all hands on deck" to carry groceries into the house or to load the car for a trip.

➡️ **Dance!** Bring your kid to your Zumba class, play a dance video game on the Xbox, or ask your kid to teach you a popular TikTok or *Fortnite* dance. Crank up the music while you're doing the dishes and dance in the kitchen. Forget about how you look and lean into laughing at yourself with your kids.

➡️ **Turn down the HDAs and turn up the LDAs.** Kids are naturally drawn to activities that give them immediate gratification in the form of feedback or rewards, such as video games and social media. Yet having too many things "on demand" changes their brains, making them less responsive to the dopamine reward stimulation, and so they feel less pleasure over time from the same activity (much like a drug user). Be careful not to let your child spend too much time on instant-gratification activities. (For more on HDAs and LDAs, see page 41.)

LDA
DIYS
READING
BIKE RIDING
EMBROIDERING
PLAYING WITH THE DOG

HDA
VIDEO GAMES
YOUTUBE
SOCIAL MEDIA
BINGE-WATCHING
TV SHOWS

→ **Take a walk.** Research demonstrates many benefits to walking. One recent study showed that walking on a treadmill for twenty minutes increased kids' control of their attention and improved their performance on academic achievement tests. You'll get an even-greater benefit if you get outdoors into fresh air and use the walking time to connect with your child.

→ **Let them catch you exercising regularly.** Talk about which activities you enjoy, how they make you feel, and how you motivate yourself to do them.

→ **Don't let organized sports crowd out free play.** Organized sports bring many benefits to families, but kids also need time and space to play freely, on their own and with peers, to benefit from the powerful combination of both movement and creativity.

One of Jennifer's young clients, April, loved her Tuesday softball team, but it was also hard work—she had to wait her turn, follow directions, and be a good listener. She told Jennifer her favorite game was "Puma Lands," which she played with three friends at recess. They ran "free, across the savanna," collaborating on story lines and using their wild imaginations.

→ **Give your kid a movement tracker.** Research supports the idea that tracking a behavior helps change the behavior. A movement tracker like a Fitbit, a running watch, or a simple pedometer can be worth the investment. Make it more appealing to your child by rewarding certain movement goals or creating challenges as a family.

→ **Create balance with low-tech delayed-gratification options.** Activities that don't have built-in feedback and rewards (such as reading, playing card or board games, doing puzzles, exercising, or playing outside) are crucial counterbalances to all the instant gratification available to kids today. Steer your kids toward these activities and make sure they have a healthy balance between instant- and delayed-gratification options.

PLAYS FOR YOUR PLAYBOOK: ROUTINE
Supporting Healthy Structure

If you want to focus on increasing or improving your child's routines, try out some of the tips below. See if you notice any shifts in your child's functioning (or your own). And as always, remember that sometimes the techniques that don't appeal to you are exactly the ones that you might end up finding the most helpful.

➡ **Make a Ta-Da! list.** Checking things off a daily to-do list that includes even the littlest tasks can give your child a nice blast of dopamine, that feel-good reward neurotransmitter. If your child is having trouble getting started, they can begin with a list of things they have already accomplished, even if it's as small as "brushed teeth." Ta-Da!

➡ **Give them the gift of preplanned limits.** Structure reduces the need for willpower. We all struggle to make decisions in the moment, and kids are far more likely to select the "junk food" of instant-gratification activities over other activities. Discuss with your kids what a healthy balance looks like, and plan with them ahead of time how to parcel out their time each day.

➡ **Tie activities to the time of day, not the amount of time.** It's a lot easier to make screen time from 4:00 to 5:00 p.m. than it is to limit it to 60 minutes. You can eliminate at least some arguments and power struggles—and foster an important life skill—by keeping it simple and giving your child the responsibility to adhere to the pre-decided schedule. The goal should be to transition from you, as the parent, overseeing technology usage (by setting and following through on limits) to your kids slowly developing their own ability to self-regulate.

➡ **Show increments of time graphically.** Research shows that kids of all ages better understand time when it's visual. Use a calendar system that allows you to block off chunks of time (such as fifteen-minute increments), rather than just creating a list of what happens when. Fill in (and potentially color-code) the scheduled activities, from

TUESDAY

3:00
3:30
— VOLLEYBALL
4:00
4:30
5:00
5:30
6:00 — HOMEWORK
6:30
7:00 — DINNER
7:30

getting ready for school to travel/transition time, school day, and any after-school practices, activities, or commitments. Also fill in high-dopamine activities (screen time) and low-dopamine activities (downtime). All this will help your child see the balance between the types of activities and identify where they have free time. Use the calendar to talk with your child about how they are spending their time and to get their input on the amount of scheduled versus unscheduled time, and HDAs versus LDAs.

➜ **Stack the deck with environmental cues.** Make it easy for your child to choose low-dopamine activities. You know how to help your kids eat a higher-quality diet by putting the fruits and veggies at the front of the refrigerator. You can fill your home with "grab and go" low-tech activities. Keep a puzzle in progress on a table; have a basketball toss or dartboard on the back of a door; have a whiteboard for drawing on or magnetic poetry tiles on the refrigerator; post a running list of family board-game champions in the living room; keep comics, crosswords, Sudoku, and engaging magazines scattered around your house.

➜ **Show your kids how you unplug and engage in low-tech activities.** Let them catch you reading a book or doing a crossword puzzle. Lead the way to having device-free dinners by putting out a "phone bin" when you sit down at the table. Use conversation starters to draw your kids into engaging discussions. (You might ask, for example, "If you could have one superpower, what would it be and why?") Play old-fashioned car games like I Spy or the Alphabet Game.

➜ **Be sure your kids have time to be bored.** Boredom is a desirable and essential ingredient in kids' lives. It forces them to practice emotional regulation, and it fosters creativity. A tremendous amount of learning happens in these moments: self-awareness and insight about what they enjoy, as well as resourcefulness, independence, and efficacy when they figure out ways to occupy their time and attention. Yet no one chooses to be bored, so parents must create these opportunities for their kids.

➡ **Emulate preschool structure.** Remember the preschool routine of morning greeting, free time, circle time, putting away the carpet squares, recess, and the goodbye song? All of these offer young kids with short attention spans a helpful structure for their day. But structure can be helpful for kids of all ages. You can encourage older kids to alternate more rigid routines, chores, and check-ins with free time to do what they want throughout the day.

➡ **Routines don't have to take a lot of time to be meaningful.** Consider having a quick, regular check-in time before school and again at bedtime. You may not always have time for family dinner, but even just a two-minute check-in with your child where you ask them to tell you a "high" and a "low" from their day creates ritual, connection, and a more organized, relaxed brain.

➡ **Take a broader view.** If your older child appears overwhelmed with their routine, take some time together to step back and look at how they spend their days. It can be helpful for them to actually sketch out a chart or graph to see how they are spending their time—and where they might find more balance.

➡ **Build in autopilot responsibilities one at a time.** Habits are soothing and grounding for the brain, and once they're "wired in," they take little to no mental effort to complete. Give your kids responsibilities one at a time, diligently focusing on each one until your kid can complete it on autopilot. Tell them what you are doing and why. Soon, a "painful" chore becomes an easy one.

> *"Sally, from now on, when you get home from school, before you do anything else, before you even go to the bathroom, your job is to empty and wipe out your lunch box. At first it will be annoying and hard to remember, but I'm going to help you—and annoy you!—to practice every day. By next month, you will have built a little 'lunch box robot' in your brain that just does it for you, every day, and you won't even have to think about it."*

> *"David, I can't ever find the car keys these days! I need you to practice putting the car keys on the hook by the door every single day when you come home until it becomes habit, and then you won't have to think about it. I know this may sound weird, but can you humor me right now and go back out to the car with the keys, pretend to turn it off, and then walk in and put them on the hook? Please do that every single time you forget, not to punish yourself, but to help you wire the action into your brain."*

➡ **Create slow family routines at night.** These might include lower lights, soft music, a favorite easy TV show, or reading in the same place at the same time. Rely more on routine as the day gets closer to night, when both you and your kid have less bandwidth and emotional flexibility. Sameness is grounding. Sameness feels safe. Kids revel and thrive in predictability.

➡ **Routines don't have to be daily—they can be weekly, monthly, or yearly.** Find days of the week to have family rituals: Sunday game night, or Saturday brunch with heart-shaped waffles. Even yearly rituals are special: an act of service on Martin Luther King Day, or a family hike on the first Saturday in October. Your kids may roll their eyes at the time, but we know from talking to kids that these ritualized activities, and memories, are meaningful to them.

➜ **Show your child what a clean room and organized belongings look like.** Kids don't naturally know how to keep their rooms and belongings organized so they can access and find things. Instead of just ordering your kid to clean their room or organize their closet, help them do it. While you're helping them, provide some perspective. Let them know that while cleaning and organizing are often dreaded activities, once started, they can be pleasant. Take a picture of the room, closet, or shelf in its clean, organized state so your kid can refer back to it the next time they tackle the chore.

➜ **Bring joy and fun into routines when you can.** Model how to enjoy the work of caring for your home, and reframe the idea of chores as opportunities for grounding. Try dancing to music while cleaning up the living areas, using dishwashing to have a moment of mindfulness, or listening to your favorite podcast while folding laundry. When you're doing housework with your kids, let them make a cleanup playlist of their favorite songs. If they are young, a "cleanup song" can lighten the task.

WRAPPING UP

Strong brains start with healthy habits. Taking care of the basics always pays the biggest dividends, even under stressful conditions. Every other Essential that follows this chapter will become easier with sufficient rest, recreation, and routine as your child's foundation.

DEEPER DIVE

Spark: The Revolutionary New Science of Exercise and the Brain by John J. Ratey with Eric Hagerman

> This book will change the way you think about exercise, not just because it is good for you, but because it can remodel the brain for peak performance. Simple and straightforward, it is a motivator you will not be able to get out of your head.

Child of Mine: Feeding with Love and Good Sense, revised and updated edition, by Ellyn Satter

> This book is a classic, valuable guide for parents of picky eaters. While some of the nutrition information isn't especially current, the warm, calming advice on how to parent picky eaters is well researched, and can help parents (especially of young children) feel confident in how they approach mealtimes and nutrition.

CliffordSussmanMD.com

> Our colleague Dr. Clifford Sussman, a child and adolescent psychiatrist, is an expert on internet and video game addiction. His website has many excellent resources for concerned parents, including articles and videos that explain the issues and offer solutions.

Diet and Feelings Are Connected

More and more studies are showing that the food we eat affects brain development and composition, brain function, and mood. Fats, or lipids, account for nearly 60 percent of our brain composition, and come in the form of fatty acids. The "good" fatty acids—the building blocks for the very best cell membranes—are omega-3 and omega-6. These healthy fatty acids also build myelin, the insulation that wraps around our nerve cells and allows them to transmit electrical signals super-fast, like a superconductor.

We cannot make our own fatty acids; we must eat them. Eating omega-rich foods like nuts, seeds, and fatty fish is crucial for creating the most primo and fast-acting brain.

In contrast, "bad" fats, like processed trans and saturated fats, may compromise brain health. Consuming processed fats and refined sugars results in poor insulation around our nerve cells and lousy structure for 60 percent of our brain.

Certain compounds in some foods can stimulate brain cells to release mood-altering neurotransmitters such as serotonin, dopamine, and norepinephrine. A diverse and healthy diet and consistent pattern of eating help maintain a good balance of your neurotransmitters and can help keep your mood more stable.

The antioxidants found in fruits and vegetables are powerful micronutrients that rid the body of free radicals (molecules that destroy the body's cells) and keep our brains alert and working longer and more optimally. Itsy-bitsy amounts of iron, copper, and zinc are also important to early cognitive development and continued good brain function.

Even though the brain accounts for only about 2 percent of our body weight, it uses up to 20 percent of our energy fuel. Fuel for all body cells comes in the currency of glucose. Our PFCs are particularly sensitive to drops in glucose. Glucose fuel comes from the digestion of carbohydrates, in the forms of sugar, starch, and fiber. Glucose from carbohydrates that break down slowly (that is, low-glycemic-index carbs) will last longer and be used more evenly, sparing us the ups and downs of the high-glycemic roller coaster.

A decline in mental function is one of the first signs of a nutrition deficit. Moving away from simple sugars to more complex carbs improves sustained attention and can help stabilize mood. A Mediterranean diet, consisting of mostly unprocessed grains, fermented foods (which are full of natural probiotics), fish, fruits, and vegetables, not only has benefit for multiple organ systems but repeatedly shows benefit in optimizing brain health.

Another psychiatric hot topic is the gut biome, comprising the trillions of bacteria living in the gut. This gut brain research is only in the earliest stages, but it's fascinating. The gut is sometimes referred to as a second brain because it has its own nervous system, called the enteric nervous system. This "gut brain" is a network of millions of neurons that signal to each other in the same manner as the neurons in our cerebral brain, using the same electrochemical neurotransmitters. An astonishing 95 percent of our serotonin, that special neurotransmitter related to our mood and anxiety, is produced in the gastrointestinal tract, all linked to those good bacteria in the gut biome. Some research indicates that we can reduce anxiety and improve our mood when we make dietary changes to enhance the good bacteria in our gut. Our gut biome is in many ways more complicated than our genome; it is "more unique than our fingerprint," according to biome-brain expert Dr. Laura Steenberger.

There is a lot of emerging evidence that the gut biome can affect the brain. As an example, when mice are raised without good gut bacteria and compared to genetically equivalent mice with normal gut bacteria biomes, they exhibit lots of major behavioral changes, including anxiety, reduction of motor function, and social effects. Other studies show that stress causes changes in the bacterial composition of the gut biome.

What if you have a picky eater? Never fear—research shows that as long as parents are offering a wide variety of foods throughout the week, most picky eaters end up naturally choosing balanced nutrition. If you have a picky eater, focus more on offering a wide variety of foods over time than on what, and how much, they are consuming at any given meal.

For a deeper dive on nutrition, we suggest reading Columbia University psychiatrist Dr. Drew Ramsey, who is creating a goldmine of useful and fascinating research on food and the mind. He will give you real *food for thought*.

Learning to Focus

ATTENTION AND SELF-CONTROL

THE TAKEAWAY

✔ Our child's young brain is still taking shape, so there is a limit to how much self-control we can expect from them.

✔ The first step is helping our child build self-awareness and self-acceptance of their current capacity, without being too critical.

✔ Then comes the second step: building their capacity for increased self-control and attention.

THE SETUP

Jennifer worked with a second grader who struggled at school: talking too much to her neighbors, humming loudly, and wandering all over the classroom. Other kids often found her distracting and annoying, and sometimes teased her. Each time her teacher, Mrs. Lee, would talk with her about her behavior, Carmen would cry, saying she didn't think she was bothering anyone!

Jennifer suggested to Mrs. Lee that instead of reminding Carmen to stay in her seat, she try to help her better see herself as others saw her. To that end, they played "The Carmen Movie Game." Every hour Mrs. Lee would ask Carmen to guess how Mrs. Lee would rate Carmen's behavior as if she was watching Carmen in a movie: specifically, staying in her seat, sitting quietly without humming, and not talking to her neighbors. If Carmen could correctly guess Mrs. Lee's rating, she was awarded a point. At first Carmen couldn't guess correctly. But soon, she naturally began correcting her disruptive behavior. After all, she wanted to be a good friend and classmate—she just needed help noticing herself and seeing how her behavior impacted others.

WHY IS THIS ESSENTIAL?

The ability to maintain attention, focus, and self-discipline, even during times of crisis, is one of the most important skills to hardwire.

But it takes time to cultivate these neurobiological fruits. We have to be patient with our kids' daily (sometimes even hourly) ups and downs with attention and self-control. And our kids need to be patient with and kind to themselves as they work—and sometimes struggle—to develop their skills.

Research on attention, willpower, and self-control is sometimes contradictory. Some research shows that attention and self-control are limited resources that become depleted, like a muscle that has to recover after exercise. Other research shows that attention and self-control can be strengthened and grown. We suspect both are true, and we believe this mixed research has something important to teach us. Our kids need us to help them with two seemingly contradictory things: building more self-acceptance of their current capacity, and building additional capacity so their attention spans and self-control can continue to grow. Paradoxically, growth happens only once we first develop awareness and acceptance of our current capacity and its limitations.

CURIOUS ABOUT THE SCIENCE?

Self-control is the ability to regulate thoughts, emotions, and behavior in the face of temptations and impulses. Most experts in the field believe that self-control is an indispensable ingredient in the ability to function well in the world.

The boss of the brain, the prefrontal cortex (PFC), is responsible for our self-control, the granddaddy of all the executive functions. The PFC neural pathways are still taking shape through our late 20s, so there is a limit to self-control in children and young adults. However, research shows there are ways to increase the strength and number of synaptic pathways in a developing brain, no matter what age, and the more complicated connections a brain makes, the better control we have over thoughts and actions.

Multiple (and beautiful) imaging studies have provided a map of how attention and self-control develop over the course of childhood and adolescence. Functional MRI (fMRI) studies have looked at the adult brain and the adolescent brain while they were performing a simple self-control task. Although both groups had similar abilities at the self-control task, the brain activity greatly differed between the two groups.

The fMRI showed the adult brain had smooth, simple synaptic routes that clearly lit up when completing the task—think interstate highways between two cities. In contrast, the adolescent brain had clunky, twisted synaptic routes that meandered in various directions, like a tangle of country roads between towns. The adolescent brain worked much harder and more creatively to stay in control whereas the adult brain was able to rely on autopilot. From the outside, it may look like your adolescent is easily and competently practicing self-control. But on the inside, their brain is rushing around in circles, trying to make its way through an unmapped, energy-sucking maze of synaptic pathways in order to maintain self-control within their underdeveloped PFC.

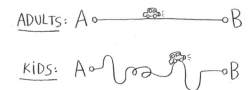

This contrast is even more pronounced in younger children's brains. Studies show children can sometimes exhibit even better self-control than adults, at least for brief periods. But kids can sustain this self-control only for short bursts, and only under optimal conditions. Even under normal stress, their ability to control themselves can quickly drop dramatically. They get hungry and misread cues. They get exhausted and start to slow down. They get frustrated and begin to make serious mistakes.

When the Three Rs (rest, recreation, and routine) are firmly in place, kids are better able to complete tasks, stay focused, and have self-control. The development of self-control advantageously wires a child's brain, helping to reduce the risk of mental disorders in adulthood.

Attention Deficit/Hyperactivity Disorder (ADHD)

Optimizing attention is always going to be harder for children (and adults) who have ADHD. This playbook is just as applicable to a child with ADHD. However, when a kid has ADHD it is important to keep in mind that some of these plays should be scaled down and practiced more often for a brain that can't help being a bit delayed.

ADHD can be a confusing and still sometimes controversial diagnosis. However, in 2021 the World Federation of ADHD (eighty foremost experts in ADHD from twenty-seven countries across six continents) published an international consensus statement evaluating the decades-long science of ADHD. It addresses many misconceptions about ADHD and states unequivocally that ADHD is a real medical disorder with potentially devastating consequences when not properly identified, diagnosed, and treated. It also summarizes the best, most rigorously researched treatments that are available.

A few highlights of its 208 evidence-based conclusions:

* Imaging research continues to show the small differences in the brain between people with and without ADHD. Dr. Philip Shaw at the National Institutes of Health (NIH) was one of the first experts to show through MRI studies that, on average, the brains of ADHD children mature about three years later than those of their peers.

* ADHD is highly treatable. Several medications have been demonstrated to be safe and effective for reducing the symptoms of ADHD. Non-medication treatments for ADHD are less effective than medication treatments for symptoms but are frequently useful to help manage problems that remain after medication has been optimized.

* Untreated ADHD can lead to many adverse outcomes, including the development of clinical depression.

The bottom line: If you suspect that your child potentially has ADHD, we encourage you to get an initial screening through your pediatrician. Early identification and treatment can have a significant positive impact on your child and their future.

WHAT DO ATTENTION AND SELF-CONTROL LOOK LIKE IN YOUR FAMILY?

Take a Look at Your Child

Family relationships: Do you find yourself repeating your child's name or instructions for them over and over? Is your child able to engage in an age-appropriate way at the dinner table? Do you dread lengthy unstructured time such as vacations?

Friendships: Can your child mostly wait for their turn? Do other kids appear annoyed with or avoid your child? Is your kid able to sometimes let other kids lead and to follow along?

Learning: Can your child manage basic structure and rules at school most of the time? Do you find yourself tracking, organizing, or even producing their homework or projects? Can they mostly manage their school belongings and homework? What kind of feedback are you getting from their teacher about how your kid compares to their peers?

Sense of self: Is your child able to entertain themself for at least short periods of time? Do you see them growing in their ability to manage their impulses? Do they need to have what they want right away, or can they sometimes wait?

CONCERN-O-METER

Pick a color for each category. Draw a colored arrow for each to give yourself a visual picture of your child in this moment.

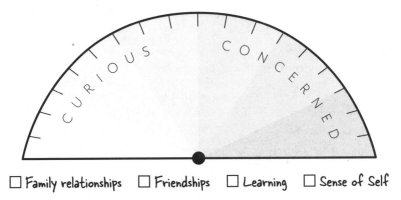

☐ Family relationships ☐ Friendships ☐ Learning ☐ Sense of Self

Take a Look at Yourself

Are attention and self-control challenging for you?

A child's struggles with attention and self-control can be particularly challenging for parents who share this struggle with them. In these cases, parents sometimes become frustrated with, rather than empathetic to, their child's difficulties. It's natural to want your kids to succeed in areas that have caused you distress, but it's impossible to "teach" kids how to develop more quickly. It's more effective to lay the foundation for them to grow when they're ready. Ask yourself: How have your own attention and self-control issues affected your expectations for your child? How does it feel to see them struggle with issues that may have been or continue to be difficult for you?

Do attention and self-control come easily to you?

For people who don't struggle with attention and self-control, kids' waxing and waning focus can feel like a lack of effort, not a lack of ability. If this applies to you, how can you better understand and support your child's developmental state so that they can be encouraged, not discouraged?

Pay attention to your self-talk.

Are you kind or critical to yourself? Chances are this voice gets communicated to your kids, whether or not you speak it out loud. Can you start being more encouraging of yourself?

HOW DO YOU THINK YOU TREND?

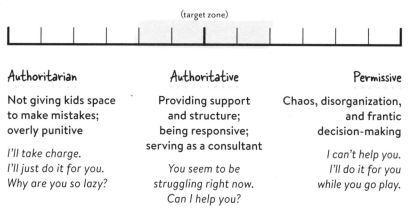

(target zone)

Authoritarian

Not giving kids space to make mistakes; overly punitive

I'll take charge.
I'll just do it for you.
Why are you so lazy?

Authoritative

Providing support and structure; being responsive; serving as a consultant

You seem to be struggling right now. Can I help you?

Permissive

Chaos, disorganization, and frantic decision-making

I can't help you.
I'll do it for you while you go play.

PLAYS FOR YOUR PLAYBOOK

If you want to help your child develop increased attentional capacity and improved self-control, try out some of the tips below. The first step focuses on plays that help your child build their self-awareness and self-acceptance. The second step focuses on plays that can help your child build their capacity for increased self-control and attention. See if you notice any shifts in your child's functioning (or your own). And as always, remember that sometimes the techniques that don't appeal to you are exactly the ones that you might end up finding the most helpful.

Step One
Build Self-Awareness and Self-Acceptance

Before you can help your child build their attention and self-control, you both must first be able to accurately evaluate their current capacity, and accept that current capacity without judgment. Self-awareness is a crucial first step. It is difficult, if not impossible, for a kid to make a change or improve self-control without first seeing their current capacity clearly. Many mental health professionals call this sense of self "mindsight." The term was coined by the neuroscientist Dr. Dan Siegel, who, along with authoring many amazing books for both parents and professionals, also founded the Mindsight Institute. Mindsight is the ability to see yourself, both from the inside and as others see you from the outside, clearly in the moment.

But self-awareness and mindsight alone are not sufficient for a kid to grow skills or make a change. Often when kids are self-aware, they are unfortunately also highly self-critical of themselves. Kids want to do well and be in control. Self-judgment about any of their own struggles with self-control or willpower can create a great deal of embarrassment (in older kids especially), even if they seem on the outside like they don't care. And counterintuitively, any judgment they feel toward themselves actually makes them less likely to be successful. Acceptance paradoxically breeds the ability to change,

while judgment breeds discouragement. Self-awareness plus self-acceptance keeps the PFC on, giving kids the room and capacity to change.

→ **Teach kids that their willpower and self-control can change from day to day and hour to hour, just like the weather.** Lack of willpower is temporary (like a rainy day, we often can't control when and how it happens), but feeling guilt and shame over a temporary lack of willpower can decrease kids' future willpower. Kids begin to see their temporary lack of self-control as a trait rather than a state. Over time, this idea that they can't pay attention or control their impulses can become a part of their identity, a self-fulfilling prophecy.

→ **Notice and work to reduce your own judgment.** Pay attention to the phrases you normally use to remind your child to do something. Try not to say things like:

> *"Why don't you ever get ready for bed on time? Why don't you ever listen to me at bedtime? I have asked you three times already!"*

Not All Procrastination Is a Problem

For some humans (but not all), procrastination works as an activator to force attention and motivation—even if it also causes stress. When pressured, the brain interprets the task at hand as an emergency, and, for some, this increases alertness and enhances memory. The stress caused by waiting until the last minute even releases adrenaline chemicals, similar to common ADHD medications.

If your child is not getting their work done because they are worried, afraid, avoidant, or demoralized, we encourage you to address the issue. However, some kids use the moderate stress of the approaching deadline to motivate themselves into doing their work. If your child is energized by waiting until the deadline is near and is able to complete their work successfully and without beating themselves up, procrastination may be an appropriate strategy for them.

→ **Help your child develop awareness of their internal resources.**
Sometimes your child isn't even aware they are depleted—but
noticing how much fuel one has in their own tank is the first step
to self-control. You can help your child begin to quantify their
own ability to concentrate and stay in charge of their emotions
and behavior through simple rating scales. Or, for younger kids,
you can use a stoplight (red, yellow, green) to indicate readiness.

*"Sam, is your stoplight red, yellow, or green for learning to tie your shoes
this morning?"*

You can ask your kid to assess how much charge is left in their
"battery."

*"Ari, you seem a little drained. How much charge do you think is left in
your battery this evening?"*

Or try a visual tool, like a drawing of a "stress bucket"—your kid
can see how full their stress bucket is and what it is filled with at
this moment.

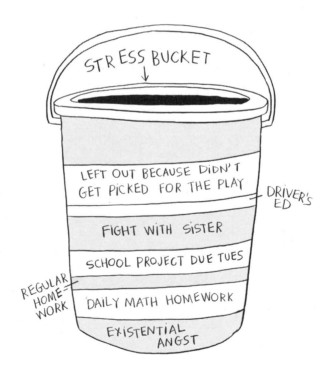

→ **Model your acceptance of your child's current state, framing it as understandable and temporary.** Validate their current difficulty while encouraging perseverance with a task or offering help if you see they are depleted.

> *"The later it gets, the harder it is for all of us to do boring tasks. But you still need to brush your teeth. I'm going to help you a bit here."*
>
> *"You did such a great job getting dressed this morning, but now it is the end of the day, and you are so tired. Would you like a little help from me?"*

→ **Help kids figure out what they need.** You may notice they are depleted well before they notice themselves. Help them think about how to renew their attention. What do they need? Sleep? A chance to run around the house a few times? A snack?

> *"You seem worn out to me. I think you are expecting too much of yourself right now. It's after 3:00—maybe feed your attention a sandwich and come back to it in twenty minutes?"*

→ **Say your thinking process out loud.** It may sound awkward and silly at first, but modeling self-talk can help kids develop their own internalized speech systems to self-regulate. Start with talking out loud as you go about finishing a daily routine or mundane task.

→ **Help your child develop their own internalized self-talk by asking detailed questions that break self-control into steps.**

> *"Billy, you look exhausted, but you just have one chore left, and it is emptying the dishwasher. [Here you open the dishwasher door for Billy, a nonverbal prompt.] I always do the bottom rack first. What order do you like to do it in? What's the easiest part? What's the worst part? When do you know you are almost done? For me, it's when I get to the silverware."*

→ **Provide useful information to kids before transitions occur.** Many kids are "time blind" when concentrating. Switching to a new task can feel intense or even shocking to those who didn't anticipate it coming, causing the fight-or-flight system to turn on and the PFC to turn off. Lots of advance notice, with verbal warnings and visual cues like calendars, timers, and clocks, can reduce this shock and help kids to stay in control of their brains.

Talk to Yourself

We humans are the only animal with true internal self-control. We are also the only animal with internalized language. This is not a coincidence. Internalized self-talk is highly correlated with the ability to delay urges. The more thoughtful the self-talk, the better. We recommend that parents model mature self-talk for their kids everywhere they go! Speak your thinking process out loud, whether you are trying to make yourself complete a dreaded task or finish a long-term project. We want kids to develop more and better internalized speech, and we can help support them by demonstrating our emotional and planning self-talk step-by-step, as if we were working on a math problem.

> *"Ugh. I'd love to binge-watch this show. But I will be happier if I'm well rested for work tomorrow. So here I go. Finding the remote. Clicking the power button. Standing up. Going to bed."*

Announce out loud how you notice your own limits and how you recharge.

> *"My self-control battery feels low. I am going to take a quick walk around the block to power back up before I make dinner."*

➜ **Don't be so sure that music or a video is distracting.** Many kids use music or even play videos in the background while they are reading or doing homework. A common worry is that this is distracting. But, in fact, the concentration of some kids (and even some adults) actually benefits from having something else in the background. These kids aren't actually multitasking; instead, the background noise appears to be almost "entertaining" a distractable part of their brain so that they can maintain attention better and longer. If your kid uses these aural and visual aids when studying, ask them more about their strategies and how and when they help (for example, when reading, many kids do better if the music they're listening to doesn't have words).

Step Two
Build Capacity for Increased Self-Control and Attention

Once you and your child are aware of and have accepted their current capacity for attention and self-control (and acknowledge that it can vary by the day or hour), you can then help your child strengthen and grow their capacity. As you recall, we call a kid's ability to see themselves clearly, both from the inside, and from the outside as others might see them, mindsight. Now we want to add two more skills to mindsight: helping kids also develop improved foresight and hindsight.

Foresight is the ability to see yourself in the future, while hindsight is the ability to recall yourself in the past. As Dr. Russell Barkley, one of the foremost researchers on children and attention, says, kids who struggle with self-control are "nearsighted to the future and forgetful of the past." Helping kids build their foresight and hindsight is crucial for developing skills in attention and self-control. After all, if your child forgets how hard a willpower task was yesterday but thinks it will be a breeze today, they will be constantly caught by surprise, and thus frustrated with themselves. And frustration erodes self-control.

➜ **Predict difficulties.** Help kids imagine potential struggles in their immediate future, allowing them to be prepared, minimize frustration, and perhaps make better choices. This has the added psychological benefit of putting kids in charge, sometimes even challenging them to prove you wrong. So, for example, suggesting to them it might be difficult to keep themselves from turning on Roblox when they are doing homework both helps kids predict and be prepared for the challenge. And it might also motivate them to do exactly the opposite. (But not always! Roblox is insanely fun.)

> *"It's so nice out; it's probably going to be really hard to come in from lunch today."*
>
> *"Your wiggles might get stronger just before your teacher starts reading to the class."*
>
> *"Don't be surprised if it's harder for you to concentrate in your last class, since it's late in the day."*

Don't Expect Consistency

Growth and change are not linear. Improvement and regression are inherent in child development. Once a child takes their first step, we don't expect them to start walking right away. Yet as our kids get older and their growth becomes more internal and subtle, we forget this truth. And when our child is struggling in some way, we are so happy and relieved when we see improvement that we tend to assume they can maintain that improvement. It can be disappointing when there is some inevitable backsliding.

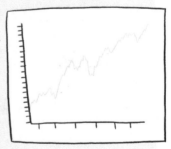

We suggest that parents think of their kid's development like the stock market: Expect many small fluctuations from day to day, and focus on the trend line over time.

➜ **Ask your child for predictions.** Wonder out loud how today will be. Ask kids to rate their readiness to learn or concentrate. Stay curious, not judging. How do they think a certain event planned for today will turn out? What three things could happen next? How will playing with the challenging neighbor down the street go? These kinds of questions allow kids to predict and plan ahead of time, when they are calm and available to think. Then they have a plan ready to go in the moment of difficulty.

➜ **Teach kids to engage with their Future Self.** Many kids with self-control or attention issues struggle to see themselves in the future. Their Present Self is happy playing a video game, so why would they switch over to studying? Help them remember that their Future Self is also them. If they can picture themselves more clearly in the future, having compassion and empathy for that Future Self, almost like they might with a friend, they are more likely to be able to manage their Present Self's attention and willpower. You can teach them to picture themselves tomorrow, next week, or next year. They can even compose notes from their Future Self to remind them how they'll feel when they finish; studies show this can actually increase willpower and perseverance with hard tasks.

> "Dear Evan, thanks for doing extra work on the group presentation last night, even though the hockey game was on. I really appreciated how prepared you made me this morning when I had to stand up in front of the class! Thanks a million! Sincerely, Future Evan."

➜ **Share your memories of their past struggles to help them develop hindsight.** It can be uncomfortable for parents, and may even seem cruel, unhelpful, or counterintuitive, to remind kids of their struggles. But nonjudgmentally reminding them that, for example, paying attention in math class this past week was really difficult and then asking them to predict how this coming week will go allows them to

IN THE TRENCHES

Catherine and the Exploded Death Star

When it came to reading and following instructions, my son Tommy consistently struggled to stay focused. I would say things like "Slow down; just take your time" and "Read the instructions first," all the while secretly knowing that I myself am cut from the same cloth.

One year I bought a LEGO Death Star, a long-coveted reward for Tommy for doing his dreaded nightly reading. When the payoff day arrived, he sat down and worked diligently at the Death Star for nearly eight hours straight, following the instructions meticulously. Unbelievable. The ability to hyper-focus is sometimes a by-product for kids who have attention difficulties, and that day was a hyper-focusing fiesta for Tommy. He came to a stopping point when it was nearly half done. He'd added an adorable Han Solo, who peeked out of the infamous trash compactor.

Then disaster struck. We had a number of younger kids over, and to this day, nobody will admit who did it, but by the end of the evening the entire Death Star was in a million pieces. My son stoically surveyed the scene and said nothing, but from the look on his face, I could tell that he was devastated. After the guests left, he cried, "Give it away! I'm not building that again!"

The exploded Death Star mess became an emblem of frustration and giving up. It sat on the floor in a pathetic pile for weeks. My son wasn't touching it; he also wasn't reading again.

I had tried to gloss over my own struggles with attention, but his despondency changed my mind and I outed myself. I admitted that I also can't stand following directions, get super-bored easily, and have difficulty paying attention to things that take a long time. After listening, Tommy decided he wanted to rebuild the Death Star, but on one condition: I had to assist him in the "boring part" of finding the shapes. I agreed to become his personal LEGO assistant, hour after hour finding the pieces he needed.

The rebuilding was slow and frustrating. We each struggled with our own attention and self-control challenges. In the end, we did not finish it perfectly. Yet I keep the mini Han Solo on my desk even today as a reminder of the bond my son and I built as we worked together to rebuild the Death Star—and to master our self-control.

use hindsight and forethought as tools to problem-solve, now, before they get to the place where they might become frustrated. This is when kids can often come up with great solutions on their own, before they are faced with the same dilemma down the road.

"You often have a harder time standing quietly when you are next to your sister."

"Last week it was super hard for you to end your screen time."

"Do you remember what happened yesterday just before lunch? Do you think it could happen again today? Do you remember the consequence?

It can be hard to remember in the moment."

CLIENT FILE
Validate (But the Answer Is Still No)

Heather was working with Julia, a single mother of three young children, two of whom had significant challenges in impulsivity and angry outbursts toward her when she set limits for them. Heather helped her practice embedding validation and curiosity into her limit-setting (not kind *or* firm, but kind *and* firm). Julia came back with this story:

"We were driving past McDonald's and the kids all started yelling at once, 'Mom, stop! We are starving! We want McDonald's drive-through! Mom, stop!' So I added some validation and curiosity to my saying no, to see what would happen. I told them, 'I smell it, too! It smells delicious! We are having leftover chili for dinner tonight, but man, I can sure see why you guys would rather have McDonald's! Darn! Too bad we can't have it, but if we could tonight, what would you guys order?' They all started shouting out their favorite foods and didn't even really attempt to convince me to stop anymore. I never expected that just seeing their point of view was actually half of what they wanted in the first place—when they saw I didn't fight them with my usual 'That food isn't good for you' speech, they seemed to be able to manage my 'no' much better!"

→ **Turn whining into whispers.** One of our favorite parenting authors, Dr. Tina Payne Bryson, has a tip to help kids who are whining feel connected and heard. She suggests bringing the child close and asking them to whisper what they are saying into your ear. As she says, whisper and whine are incompatible.

→ **Help kids prepare like a pessimist.** While we strongly encourage compassion and a lack of judgment over the changeable weather of self-control, we don't encourage lots of optimistic predictions. This is because numerous studies show that focusing on "wins" in self-control actually decreases our chances of maintaining that control later, while getting curious about and predicting our own failures is highly correlated with increased willpower. If your child is trying to develop a habit of doing their homework right after school and they succeed on Tuesday, rather than just celebrating, it's good to also ask them what might keep them from the same success on Wednesday. It's important to be fully nonjudgmental as you ask them to predict future failures. We should all expect failure. It's human.

WRAPPING UP

As we noted at the start of this chapter, research on attention, willpower, and self-control is often contradictory. We are suggesting a way to bridge the differences: First, help your child understand and accept the organic and fluctuating nature of attention and self-control including their own limitations, then challenge them to develop them anyway. Because once they understand and accept their current capacity, paradoxically, kids are better able to strengthen and grow their attention and self-control.

DEEPER DIVE

The Explosive Child: A New Approach for Understanding and Parenting Easily Frustrated, Chronically Inflexible Children, fifth edition, by Ross W. Greene, PhD

> In its fifth edition, *The Explosive Child* stands the test of time. Dr. Greene's collaborative problem-solving model provides a compassionate approach to understanding and parenting children who frequently exhibit emotion dysregulation and other challenging behaviors related to self-control.

Taking Charge of ADHD: The Complete, Authoritative Guide for Parents, fourth edition, by Russell A. Barkley, MD

> Dr. Barkley is considered one of the definitive masters of helping kids with attention issues. While designed for parents who have a child with ADHD, his approach is perfect for any parent who wants to help their child develop more attention and self-control.

The Willpower Instinct: How Self-Control Works, Why It Matters, and What You Can Do to Get More of It by Kelly McGonigal, PhD

> This book lets you feel like you are actually sitting in Stanford University psychologist Dr. McGonigal's wildly popular course "The Science of Willpower." She concisely explains the science of self-control, including (as the title says) how it works, why it matters, and how to get more of it.

For Kids

Puppy Mind by Andrew Jordan Nance

> A delightful picture book talking about how attention can wander (and be trained) much like a puppy.

Feeling Uncomfortable

TOLERATING DIFFICULT FEELINGS

THE TAKEAWAY

✔ Kids need to be able to do more than just name their feelings—
they need to learn to accept and tolerate their difficult feelings.

✔ A nonjudgmental stance and willingness to feel negative feelings
decrease their intensity and duration.

✔ We have an evolutionary instinct to relieve our kids' suffering in the
moment—but more valuable is sharing with them (and ourselves)
that they can function well even when they feel uncomfortable.

THE SETUP

Jennifer had just started working with Sam, age 7, when she got a call from the school nurse. Sam often had worries and came to the nurse's office frequently, asking for his mom to come pick him up. His school counselor had taught him some techniques for trying to calm down when he was worried, like counting to ten, taking slow breaths, and reminding himself his mom was safe. Jennifer worried that Sam misunderstood what these tools were really for: not to get rid of his worries, but to help his body and mind be patient and help him tolerate the times he was especially worried. The nurse asked for advice, saying Sam was freaking out. No kidding! Jennifer could hear Sam in the background, crying, "The tools in my toolkit aren't working! I'm still scared! I need more tools! *Give me more tools!*"

WHY IS THIS ESSENTIAL?

Unlike earlier generations, kids today often know a great deal about how they feel. Some can even openly share uncomfortable feelings, such as sadness, anger, or hurt. This is a credit to the psychological savvy of parents today. Being able to label our feelings—I feel scared, I feel frustrated, I feel worried—is a game-changing mental health skill. But it is not enough. Kids may be better able to label their feelings, but they are less skilled at accepting and tolerating difficult feelings. Many kids are under the impression that happy feelings are "normal" while uncomfortable feelings are "bad." They think that the "bad" uncomfortable feelings need to be fixed so they can return to the "normal" happy feelings. In our professional practices, we are less concerned about the intensity of feelings, which can widely vary among kids, and more concerned about duration of feelings.

But all feelings are fleeting. They are not meant to be felt for any length of time. Joy is transient, and not at all the normal state of a person's mind. Neither is sadness. This is a fundamental parenting challenge: to teach our kids to notice and name their uncomfortable feelings, but just as importantly to see them as moving states that ebb and flow—to accept and tolerate every feeling as a natural, normal part of the human experience. Uncomfortable feelings are not meant to be "solved" like a math problem. Emotions are chemical experiences in our bodies, and they come and go beyond our conscious control. Thus, there are no tools for changing the feelings themselves, nor should there be. But there are tools that can help us tolerate more difficult emotions. And tolerating negative feelings is an essential skill.

We encourage you to see difficult feelings like the weather: We don't get to control it; all we can do is prepare for it, enjoy it when it's good, and tolerate it when it's not. You can put your effort toward preparing your child for the natural ups and downs; help them pack their metaphorical suitcase for every kind of emotional weather. Teach them how to know what the weather is, accept it, and remember that it will change. As parents, we should prioritize helping our child label and accept their difficult feelings—not fix them. Experiencing discomfort is the price we pay for a rich and meaningful life.

CURIOUS ABOUT THE SCIENCE?

When a child is grumpy, telling them to cheer up usually makes them grumpier. And telling a child who is angry to calm down usually makes them even more angry. That approach doesn't work for adults either. There is clear evidence that suppressing emotions can lead to some serious problems down the line, including an increased risk of depression, anxiety, substance abuse, and eating disorders. Research has also linked emotional suppression to physical health issues, including chronic pain, heart disease, and lowered immune function. Emotional suppression can also affect our sense of empathy and our ability to connect with others.

Conversely, a nonjudgmental stance and true willingness to feel more negative feelings actually decreases a person's discomfort over time, both in duration and in intensity. Nonjudgmentally naming and accepting negative emotions, such as fear, annoyance, sadness, or anger, actually appears to decrease the intensity of that feeling, to reduce reactivity, and to elevate feelings of general well-being.

Stanford professor and stress expert Kelly McGonigal references a study that found participants' ability to hold their breath underwater (that is, people who were able to tolerate feeling uncomfortable) for longer periods of time correlated with their ability to function well under difficult circumstances.

Brett Ford and her colleagues at University of California at Berkeley devised a series of clever experiments to assess a nonjudgmental approach toward negative feeling states. Working with a group of more than 1,300 people, they found that some people are natural "habitual acceptors" of negative feelings. In some ways, these people were more pessimistic than their counterparts. They expected negative feelings to occur and

didn't judge themselves for feeling them. These more pessimistic but accepting people had less impulsive, reactive behaviors and more durable mental equanimity. They also had increased feelings of well-being even during difficult situations, whether in the lab or in their real lives.

In contrast, these studies found that optimism, while a lovely trait in many ways, can be a barrier to equanimity and acceptance. If someone always expects to feel mostly positive feelings, they may be regularly taken by surprise and even feel like a failure when negative emotions naturally bubble up. And this surprise can lead to fear of the feelings, or even guilt for having them—the opposite of acceptance.

A number of studies have shown the importance of children's ability to function well even when they are experiencing distressing feelings—and the dangers inherent when they are not able to. Evidence strongly suggests that low distress tolerance is a specific risk

Do Young Children Have Ihuma?

As part of the meticulous research for her book, *Hunt, Gather, Parent: What Ancient Cultures Can Teach Us about the Lost Art of Raising Happy, Helpful Little Humans*, NPR journalist Michaeleen Doucleff and her 3-year-old child, Rosy, lived with and investigated child-rearing practices in three of the oldest world cultures, including the Inuit of northern Canada.

Doucleff found that modern Inuit parents approach their fearful or raging children with calm acceptance. They see attempts to try to teach more adult behaviors to an irrational child as foolish and wasteful of their energy.

Doucleff quotes anthropologist Jean Briggs, who in the 1960s lived with and collected fascinating language from the Inuit that displays their cultural view of children's feelings: "The Utku (Inuit) expect little children to be easily angered (urulu, quiquq, ningaq) . . . and to cry easily when disturbed (huqu), because they have no ihuma: no mind, thought, reason, or understanding. Adults say they are not concerned (huqu, naklik) by a child's irrational fears and rages, because they know there is nothing really wrong. . . . Because children are unreasoning beings, unable to understand that their distresses are illusory."

PRO TIP

Look for Feelings Under Feelings

Many of us have a "default" feeling. When the chemical experience of emotion is turned on, we tend to quickly put that emotion in our most familiar bucket. But often there are more feelings underneath this default feeling—feelings that may be more useful (even if more painful) data points. The feelings underneath the default feeling are important to know because they are ultimately the feelings that need to be addressed. Recognizing and naming these "underneath" feelings will show you and your child the feelings that actually need to be seen and accepted. For example, your daughter comes home and slams her books on the table. She then marches into her room, clearly angry. Perhaps a friend was rude to her and called her names. But as she digs deeper beyond the anger, she finds embarrassment. Underneath embarrassment, there is hurt. And underneath that, there is sadness. These underneath feelings could be useful data points: she might want to speak with this friend, take a break from this friend, interact with a different friend as a way to shift her mood, or perhaps just feel the pain of the feeling and wait for it to fade.

ANGER

EMBARRASSMENT

HURT *Sadness*

LONELINESS

factor for the development of depression. The "window of tolerance" is a concept first created in 1999 by UCLA psychiatrist Dr. Daniel Siegel. Dr. Siegel defines this "window" metaphor as the healthy zone of our personal emotional responses and body reactions where we each function best to life's unexpected stressors and adversities. Children's windows may be smaller or larger depending on wiring and life experiences, and thus vary in the range and intensity in which they can comfortably experience, process, and integrate stress responses.

As parents, we must override the evolutionary instinct to relieve our kids' suffering in the moment. Science tells us that kids function best and recover more quickly when they can recognize, name, and, most importantly, accept their feelings. Tolerating feelings paradoxically allows them to move through the body and mind faster that fighting (or flighting) them.

To illustrate this point, we often use the analogy of a feelings cave verses a feelings tunnel. Instead of seeing uncomfortable feelings like a dead end, a scary cave you enter and may feel there is no way out, try to imagine uncomfortable feelings being more like a tunnel. Sure, it's just as dark and scary when you enter, but as you stop avoiding and instead move through these feelings, accepted feelings shift and change, and you will eventually come out to daylight.

WHAT DOES TOLERATING DIFFICULT FEELINGS LOOK LIKE IN YOUR FAMILY?

Take a Look at Your Child

Family relationships: Does your family have a large feelings vocabulary? Are family members comfortable talking about their feelings with one another? Are family members able to share more difficult feelings just as openly as more pleasant ones? Does your family try to "fix" each others' feelings, or end up walking on eggshells to avoid strong or out of control feelings?

Friendships: How well does your child manage their own feelings when they are engaging with their friends? Can they share their feelings with their friends in age-appropriate ways? Can they recover in a reasonable amount of time when challenged (for example, after losing a board game, not getting their favorite ice cream flavor, not being included at the playground)? Do they seem overly sensitive to rejection?

Learning: Can your child manage strong feelings within learning/ academic environments, or do feelings appear to overwhelm or distract them? Do they seem to give up or shut down quickly when faced with mild challenges (like homework, tests, having an opponent do better than them)?

Sense of self: Does your child appear to know how they feel most of the time? Do they tend to have just one default feeling (for example, when you ask how they feel, they always say they are annoyed), or can your child express a range of feelings? After about the age of 7 or 8, can they begin to acknowledge contradictory feelings ("I feel a little sad and also a little relieved")? In our professional practices, we see kids struggle with the intensity and duration of strong feelings. While we help kids manage their strong feelings, we don't focus on the *intensity*, which is often more of a fixed trait. Instead, we help them learn to shorten the *duration* of intense feelings, so they can recover more quickly and not let a strong feeling hijack their day. Duration can be shortened with acceptance of the intensity, but then shutting down the repetitive thinking that can accompany and reactivate the feeling. How long does it take for them to be able to shift, pivot, and recover? Do they seem to become helpless or stuck when faced with strong feelings?

CONCERN-O-METER

Pick a color for each category. Draw a colored arrow for each to give yourself a visual picture of your child in this moment.

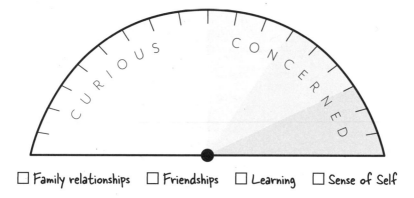

☐ Family relationships ☐ Friendships ☐ Learning ☐ Sense of Self

Take a Look at Yourself

How well do you tune in to your own emotions?

Are you aware of how you feel most of the time? Do you talk about your feelings with your kids? When you do talk to them, do you use a range of age-appropriate feeling words, from basic (angry) to nuanced (irritated, livid, sullen)?

How do you react to your child's uncomfortable or negative emotions?

How comfortable are you with difficult emotions in your child? Do you struggle with or give into the urge to fix the situation for them? Could you shift your responses to validate their emotions without taking any action?

How does your extended family handle emotion and stress?

Are there echoes of how you were raised in how you respond to your kids? If you are repeating patterns, is it by conscious choice?

What is your threshold for tolerating your child's distress?

Do you feel activated by your child's difficult feelings? Do you rush in to fix things or soothe them? Or do you find yourself judging them or getting irritated when they're overwhelmed by a big feeling?

HOW DO YOU THINK YOU TREND?

(target zone)

Get Over It	Bearing Witness	Early Rescuer
Lacking empathy; refusing discussion; avoiding, denying, or minimizing emotions	Being present; accepting feelings; being quiet; naming and describing	Swooping in; overfunctioning; quick fixing; Band-Aid-ing; solving; protecting
It's not that bad; don't be a drama queen; toughen up; you're fine; feelings are weaknesses.	*I'm with you; I see you; this is hard right now; feelings are painful but bearable.*	*I'll make it better; let me cheer you up; this feeling is bad, let's fix it! I can't stand to see you so upset.*

PLAYS FOR YOUR PLAYBOOK
Building Awareness and Accepting Feelings

If you want to help your child develop a greater vocabulary for their feelings and improve their ability to accept and tolerate uncomfortable emotions, try out some of the tips below. See if you notice any shifts in your child's functioning (or your own). And as always, remember that sometimes the techniques that don't appeal to you are exactly the ones that you might end up finding the most helpful.

➜ **Use lots of feeling language, with fine granularity.** Instead of the feelings basics of mad, sad, glad, and scared, use more specific and colorful language. You might, for example, tell your child that you feel despondent, low, hurt, felled with grief, bummed out, hopeless. Even though your average 6-year-old might not fully understand these words, parents who use such language offer texture and model subtle differences between similar feelings.

> *"I feel really embarrassed by what my boss said. But as I think about it more, I think I'm also a little hurt that she didn't like my presentation. And maybe also a little scared. I really want that promotion and maybe now she won't give it to me. Whew. These are hard feelings, but it feels good to at least say them out loud."*

➜ **Teach kids how to "bust a FAB."** Naming your feelings is the first step toward accepting them. Jennifer had a teen client who taught her how to do the FAB sentence completion:

I **F**EEL... hurt
ABOUT... not being included
BECAUSE... I worry you don't feel we're close friends anymore

➜ **Notice body language and label feeling states.** Feelings are chemical in nature and often reveal themselves as body sensations. You may see your child hold their stomach, tense their shoulders, or clench their fists. Describe what you see in their body (or yours) and label the feeling in front of your child.

> *"I see your hands are balled up so tightly. I wonder if you might be angry at your sister."*

> *"Whoa, my throat feels really tight after that phone call. I must be really hurt by what my brother said."*

➡️ **Notice and label feelings as a way to create a pause between your thoughts and actions.** Use feeling words as a wedge between emotion and response to create more time and space for a less impulsive reaction.

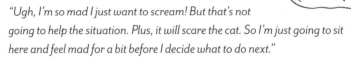

> *"Ugh, I'm so mad I just want to scream! But that's not going to help the situation. Plus, it will scare the cat. So I'm just going to sit here and feel mad for a bit before I decide what to do next."*

➡️ **Mix it up with words from different languages.** Other cultures have much to offer us in terms of deepening our understanding of human emotion. Emotions don't fully exist outside our chemical/physiological experience until we label and make meaning from them, and different cultures do that differently.

> *"You know how a lot of Scandinavian countries have months where it's dark all day long? Well, I just learned a new word, 'hygge.' It's Scandinavian for that cozy warm feeling you can have when you are home and it's cold and dark outside, and yet you are safe and loved and content. I think that's a good word for my feeling tonight as we make hot chocolate before we start our family movie on this rainy night."*

> *"What a day! I'm standing in front of the fridge with a bad case of 'kuchisabishii.' I just learned about it from a friend at work—she says the Japanese have a special word that literally translates to 'lonely mouth.' It means mindless eating when we are bored or feeling down. I bet you know that feeling, too."*

➡️ **Narrate accepting your own feelings.** Show your kid how to name, accept, and be nonreactive to feelings by narrating your own inner world in front of them as much as possible. And then, importantly, describe how you accept them and don't plan to *do* anything about them. Kids need to see that parents often have difficult emotions. They also need to see that we are not scared of them, we accept that these feelings happen, and we can cope without having to act on them.

> *"I can't believe I'm saying this, but I took one look at Aunt Janelle's new boots and I felt so jealous! Like I was back in middle school all over again. Oh well, I guess my jealousy chemicals took a little trip around my body today even though I'm pushing 40 and don't care much about footwear these days!"*

The Shrug

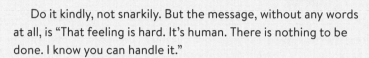

A useful (but difficult) parenting technique for modeling how to tolerate big feelings in our kids is The Shrug. The formula is simple:

1 Validate the feeling.

2 Shrug.

Do it kindly, not snarkily. But the message, without any words at all, is "That feeling is hard. It's human. There is nothing to be done. I know you can handle it."

➜ **Understand that feelings are like hiccups.** Don't try to fix or change your child's feelings, or your own. Feelings are like hiccups—you don't have control over the chemical nature of the experience, and there is no need to judge your experience of a feeling any more than you would judge yourself for having hiccups.

➜ **Use nonjudgmental language to describe difficult feelings.** Instead of talking about "bad" feelings, find other terms to describe them, like "uncomfortable." Feelings are neither good nor bad; they are simply human.

➜ **Know the difference between avoidance and distraction.** Avoidance is when you don't want to even acknowledge you feel uncomfortable, which can make that feeling more powerful. Distraction is naming and accepting your feelings, then deciding to take action to gently shift your attention to something new and interesting. Try to notice the difference between when your child is engaging in avoidance (a problematic strategy) versus distraction (a potentially useful strategy).

"That driver just cut me off—I'm so mad! What gives him the right?! Oh, I just hate bad drivers; what can I do? [Take a slow, audible breath.] Nothing, I guess. Shall we listen to the radio so I can think about something else?"

➜ Feelings are data points, so use them as clues.
Approach a feeling with curiosity. What might
it be telling you?

> *"Sounds like you are really mad that you were*
> *not invited to her party again. That really*
> *stinks. Do you think that anger is trying to*
> *give you clues on what you might do?"*

➜ Bear witness. We can support our kid by being present in the face
of their distress. Bearing witness communicates our confidence that
our kid can survive the heightened emotion. One of the phrases you
can channel is "I'm with you, buddy." Sometimes you might say it out
loud, and sometimes you might just silently "live" the phrase next to
your child without saying a word.

➜ Doing nothing is powerful parenting. Naming a feeling and then
doing nothing to fix it is the most difficult—and most effective—
kind of parenting we can do. Learning this technique may take effort
and practice on your part, but it is an important skill to master to
support your child's tolerance for difficult emotions.

**➜ Prepare your kids (and yourself) for difficult feelings ahead so they
aren't taken by surprise.** An early warning can help kids keep their
PFC turned on even once their emotional system is flooded with the
biochemicals of difficult feelings. For example, if your child tends to
be fearful at a birthday party, you can show acceptance by reminding
them of that on the way to the party and telling them not to be too
surprised if it happens again. You can also validate the experience by
adding that sometimes a noisy crowd can make lots of us feel stressed
out—and that's okay.

> *"I don't know what will happen today, but I know that in this past week*
> *you have gotten really upset at the dinner table when your brother starts*
> *to tease you. He can bring out some very frustrated feelings in you. It looks*
> *really hard. I can see why you feel that way. I wouldn't be surprised if that*
> *happens again for you this evening. (Shrug)."*

> *"I know you are so worried about not getting that internship. We don't*
> *know what the summer holds for you, and who knows, if you don't get it,*
> *it could feel kind of crushing for a while."*

You Are Not Your Thoughts

When we think thoughts, especially thoughts about ourselves, we can become attached and "hooked" to them. People can take a temporary aspect of themselves ("I didn't study enough for that test") and turn it into a more universal idea or fixed trait ("I'm a lazy bum"). However, believing and universalizing every random thought we think is not a recipe for good mental health.

One technique for seeing thoughts as separate from our true whole selves is to examine those thoughts from the outside, almost like watching a movie of your mind while calmly eating some popcorn. Thus:

"I am a lazy bum."

can turn into

"Look at that, I am having the thought that I'm a lazy bum."

which could be unhooked even further into

"Wow, now I'm noticing that I'm having the thought that I'm a lazy bum."

Paradoxically, once we unhook from a negative global idea about ourselves, we are actually more likely to not become that idea. After all, a lazy bum doesn't bother to study for the next test. But a person who sometimes makes a lazy choice can also be someone who buckles down next time.

➡ **Teach that any feeling is tolerable.** Feelings need to be validated so that they do not become amplified. Teach your kids the "validate and tolerate" technique: 1) Name and rate your feeling on a scale of 1 (hardly feeling it) to 10 (completely overwhelmed by this feeling). 2) Set a timer for 10 minutes. 3) Rate how you feel again 10 minutes later.

"You seem really despondent that your friend isn't texting you back. Scale of 1 to 10, how icky is it? Ugh, a 9? Ouch! Hang in there. I might set the timer and check in on you again in 10 minutes—is that okay?"

CLIENT FILE

Rating the Pain

A high school student who worked with Catherine was dreading going to the sports banquet at his school, feeling so anxious he couldn't really breathe every time he thought about it. He was going back and forth on whether he should skip it, even though he had run track that year. Just talking about it made his palms sweat. But Catherine persisted, wondering what he was afraid of, asking for details. At first he didn't want to think or talk about it—it was just too painful. But he stuck with it despite the discomfort and came to realize that his greatest fear was he might stand around awkwardly and not have anyone to talk with. He laughed, saying the discomfort of that happening at the banquet would only be a 4 in discomfort for 2 hours, instead of a 3 of discomfort, dread, and indecision for the next week. As soon as he decided he would attend, he noticed that he felt an initial panic, but then within minutes his body and mind started to relax.

→ **Be aware: Older kids see negativity everywhere.**
Teens tend to read even neutral faces and responses as angry or suspicious. This is evolution at work—caveman kids needed to be more careful, even a bit paranoid of others, to survive. Brain studies show adolescents read even neutral human expressions as a threat. This is why when you say something with only mild annoyance, your adolescents may tell you to stop yelling at them. They are not exaggerating; they truly do feel things more keenly.

> *"Oh gosh, you felt like I was furious when I asked you to pick up your socks. I'm actually not that mad; I just wanted to get your attention, so I didn't have to say it again later tonight. My bad for scaring you. And please pick them up."*

→ **Don't take it personally!** All parents can feel wounded by their kid's angry outburst or palpable disappointment, but kids' feelings are almost always due to a combination of factors, some of which we

Sh— Happens

To many people, the most uncomfortable of the *sh—* words has five letters, not four: *shame*.

Shame appears to be a useful universal emotion, grounded in evolution. We can even see the common origins of shame in mammal studies; for example, gorillas who are at risk for being ostracized will pose in a body position that most humans would easily identify as shame—a body protected and rounded in on itself, shoulders slumped, head down, eyes downcast. In early human societies, a feeling (and exhibition) of shame by someone who'd made a mistake might have elicited empathy from their community, allowing that person to maintain their membership. Even in modern times, shame is still a driver for retaining connection; for example, studies show that a previously unfaithful marital partner who openly described and demonstrated a deep feeling of shame to their partner in front of a therapist were more likely to still be married to the same partner two years later.

So shame has an important social function, just like many other emotions. And research has begun to show that avoiding feelings of shame, just like avoiding feelings of fear, can actually be more destructive to a person than simply noticing, naming, and accepting those feelings.

Unfortunately, one way humans try to avoid or "fix" their shame is by using the internal habit of regular self-criticism. We reflexively berate or belittle ourselves ("I'm the worst, I'm unlovable, I can't be depended on, I will screw this up, I am lazy, I always mess up"). Constant, automatic self-criticism is destructive to our sense of self, but it is effective in allowing us to avoid the feeling of shame.

Feeling shame is a natural evolutionary part of being human. And accepting that feeling as painful but normal, without having to twist and turn it inside out into something else (such as self-criticism or anger), ultimately leads to fewer long-term consequences and less suffering than trying to avoid it.

don't even know about and many of which are out of our control
(for example, who sat next to them at lunch or how thunder forced
their recess indoors). It helps our kids if we don't pile on
by taking their messy or undesirable responses personally.
Heather had clients who really struggled to find empathy
for their 5-year-old's frequent tantrums at home. They
lamented that she was an angel at school and everywhere
else, and the fact that she reserved her explosive behavior
for them felt very personal and hurtful. Heather reminded them that
kids melt down with people with whom they feel safe and loved, and
it took away some of the sting.

FURIOUS

➡ **Be authentic about your own difficult feelings.**

> *"It makes sense that you'd feel so angry with me after I yelled at you
> like that. I lost control over something awfully small, and I am so sorry.
> This is something I am working on."*

➡ **Don't offer a lecture to a person who needs a hug.** Assess whether
your child's emotional brain is activated, and if it is, respond to it
with comfort. Save the discussion for another time.

➡ **Develop a family mantra.** We know families who have used
lines from popular music, movies, and TV shows as reminders to
just tolerate and wait when things feel hard. For example, there is
"Let it be" from the Beatles, or "Be a goldfish" from the TV show
Ted Lasso (since goldfish theoretically don't have memories, they
aren't burdened by previous mistakes). Dory from *Finding Nemo*
says "Just keep swimming," and in *The Last Jedi* Luke Skywalker
reminded himself to "Breathe, just breathe." Or choose the classic

---

PRO TIP

The Ouch

A validating accompaniment to The Shrug. If your child can
name their feeling ("I'm so embarrassed Jackson
posted that ugly picture of me on Instagram")
you can respond with a very genuine but
accepting "Ouch." Finish with a shrug.

Jennifer Goes Back to Preschool

I was in counseling with a wise therapist years ago. I was in a not-fun place, struggling with some newly emerging anxiety. This therapist told me he believed that while I intellectually knew the names of all the feeling states, I didn't really ever allow myself to fully feel them. "Don't think of anxiety as a feeling. Think of anxiety as a physiological state that happens in your body *before* you know and feel what your true feeling really is," he explained.

He had me return to the basics. Every time I started to feel anxious, I stopped to just notice. First, my body: Tight throat? Gritted teeth? Stiff shoulders? Then, like taking clothes from a closet, I would try on some basic preschool feelings—mad, sad, glad, scared, surprised—to see what fit. What emotion seemed like the best fit for my physical state? Was I feeling resentful? Jealous? Feeling left out? Out of control?

At first the task felt impossible. On my first try of just noticing my body, I was surprised to find I honestly couldn't tell if I was feeling annoyed or just hungry. But the more I stuck to this practice, the easier it got. When I ran through the possible feelings, I would eventually hit upon the "right" word and then feel my entire body shift slightly. The word would be like an auger, drilling down inside of me, making me feel grounded. When I stopped ascribing everything to "anxiety" and instead just felt my body and searched through those preschool feelings, it seemed like I was less fighting against myself. The feeling could come, I could know it, and I could later feel it drift away. Even today (at least when I can remember to do so) I come back to this technique again and again. It is simple and powerful.

"Keep calm and carry on" or "This too shall pass." Adopting a few of these sayings can create some inside-joke reminders that everyone struggles at times, and that's okay.

→ **Check the oven temperature.** When your kid has a strong emotional reaction (such as yelling, stomping around, hitting, or kicking), it's a sign their emotional reptilian brain has turned on. Think of them like an oven that has just instantly preheated to 1,000 degrees. When the emotional outburst ends, their oven turns off, but it is still really, really hot! Kids need time to cool off before talking about their outburst. Wait to have any discussions until your kid's emotional oven is no longer too hot to touch.

WRAPPING UP

Many kids are under the impression that happy feelings are normal, while uncomfortable feelings are bad. Worse, they think uncomfortable feelings can and should be fixed. But feelings are not meant to be solved, just felt and tolerated, and sometimes used as data sources. Tolerating discomfort is an essential skill that allows us to be fully present with our feelings. And it's an achievable goal. Learning to tolerate uncomfortable feelings makes kids mentally stronger and helps parents avoid the trap of trying to make their children happy at the expense of preparing them for life's full range of emotions.

DEEPER DIVE

Emotional Agility: Get Unstuck, Embrace Change, and Thrive in Work and Life by Susan David, PhD

> With *Emotional Agility*, internationally recognized business consultant and psychologist Dr. Susan David created a game-changing mindset that is applicable to systems big and small. Dr. David explains how to embrace emotional agility and make feelings work for you instead of against you. You'll hear more about Dr. David's work in our discussion of Essential #5.

Hunt, Gather, Parent: What Ancient Cultures Can Teach Us About the Lost Art of Raising Happy, Helpful Little Humans by Michaeleen Doucleff

> NPR journalist Michaeleen Doucleff and her 3-year-old child, Rosy, lived with and investigated child-rearing practices in three of the oldest world cultures. An eye-opening book on how other cultures view childhood and parenting including practical tips on adapting these practices into our own families.

For Kids

Inside Out, directed by Pete Docter

> This Disney movie is a neurobiologically accurate depiction of a child's brain and the positive outcomes that can happen when a child begins to accept and listen to even difficult feelings, not just the pleasant ones.

Master of Mindfulness: How to Be Your Own Superhero in Times of Stress by Laurie Grossman, Angelina Alvarez, and Mr. Musumeci's 5th Grade Class

> A picture book developed for kids, by kids, with real-world examples of using simple mindfulness techniques.

Zach Gets Frustrated by William Mulcahy

> A picture book with specific frustration management techniques based on therapeutic strategies.

Alexander and the Terrible, Horrible, No Good, Very Bad Day by Judith Viorst

> A classic early reader. Most every kid can relate to Alexander and his feelings during his very bad day.

How to Become More Highly Evolved

Mindfulness and meditation fortify the brain so that both everyday and pandemic-sized stresses are easier to manage.

A meditation or mindfulness practice can literally grow physical connections in the brain so the different parts of the brain can "talk" to one another and have more healthy conversation. For example, while some parts of your child's brain might be telling them to slam the door on their pesky sister, other, more thoughtful parts of their brain might be reminding them that using their words may be more effective in getting her to stay out of their room—and keep them from getting in trouble! When these different parts of the brain can speak to each other, your child is more likely to be able to make the more productive choice, rather than being overwhelmed by the snap-decision urgency of their reptilian brain.

Enhanced connections between different parts of the brain allow us to use more of our whole brain power at once and can keep more of that healthy brain engaged, even during difficult times. This is how we as a species can become more highly evolved.

Brain images studies provide evidence for the role of meditation and mindfulness in enhancing these neural connections. Numerous studies have shown that even short periods of consistent meditation can physically change brain structure and increase synaptic connections. For example, in just eight weeks, participation in a mindfulness course that focused on meditation yielded measurable brain changes in a group of adults, including increases in gray matter density in multiple regions of the brain.

Mindfulness and meditation share many characteristics, including helping the brain shift out of autopilot and into being in the present moment. Both are essentially a form of paying attention, on purpose. Paying attention activates the frontal lobe, strengthening concentration, speech, problem-solving, and planning. But mindfulness and meditation are each practiced a bit differently.

Mindfulness can take place anytime, anywhere. It is simply the process of drawing yourself out of your past or future and into the present moment. Being right here, right now. You can be mindful while brushing your teeth, walking, or even driving a car. As a driver, you are not going to be distracted by practicing mindfulness. Quite the opposite: You will be safer. You are fully paying attention to the present moment.

You can feel your hands on the steering wheel. You can see the car in front of you drifting over the lane line. You can feel the engine and notice whether your acceleration or braking is smooth or raggedy. You can hear a car coming up quickly behind you.

Mindful awareness can be practiced solo or in a group. Often it can involve fun sensory activities. Building in time as a family for mindfulness and brain-building activities can provide all of you an opportunity to strengthen your brains and be ready for whatever future stressors may come your way.

Meditation is the gold standard of mindfulness activities. You can be mindful while doing pretty much anything, but meditation is a practice of focused mindfulness, often done at the same time of day, perhaps even in a quiet room, sitting in a certain position. If you want even more brain benefits from your mindfulness activities, meditation is the way to go. If mindfulness is to the mind what exercise is to the body, mindfulness can be as simple as taking the stairs instead of the elevator, while meditation is like working up a deep sweat at the gym.

Is mindfulness or meditation relaxing? Not always. Sometimes paying deep attention to the present can be painful or overwhelming. Often it can be boring. But that's okay. Like they say at the gym, no pain, no gain.

Avoiding Avoidance

ACCEPTING ANXIETY

THE TAKEAWAY

✔ Anxiety is harmless, but avoidance of the things that make our child anxious can be damaging.

✔ Your child's anxiety wants attention and protection, even if you know they are perfectly safe. Soothing and reassuring may inadvertently train our child to believe that the *only* way to feel better is through your attention or protection.

✔ Helping our kids manage anxiety is often as simple as listening to and understanding their fears, then lovingly shrugging our shoulders, signaling to them we know they can handle whatever worries come along.

✔ Anxiety is contagious. We parents need to be real with ourselves about how our own anxiety might be impacting our kids and takes steps to better manage our feelings.

THE SETUP

Heather was working with the aunt and guardian of twin middle school girls who were struggling at school with a number of "mean girls" and some challenging teachers. When the aunt walked the girls home from school at the end of the day, she heard about so many ways in which her girls were struggling, hurt, afraid, or being treated poorly, which made the aunt feel worried and sad. By the time they were home, often one or both girls would be in tears, and neither could settle down to do homework, leaving the late afternoon and evening stressful for all. Heather encouraged the aunt to reduce her own anxiety with some breathing techniques before the walk home, but the aunt was skeptical.

One day the aunt had some dental work done, and the dentist had given her antianxiety medication before the procedure. She was still feeling the effects when she went to pick up the girls later that afternoon, so she was a little more flat and less engaged when the girls began to download the pains of the day. The aunt told Heather how eye-opening that walk was. Her own lack of worry seemed to have a direct effect on the girls, who moved on from describing their difficulties and started chatting with each other about other more neutral parts of the day. When they got home, the girls made their own snacks and managed their own homework, leaving time to watch a favorite show that evening.

The aunt began trying the calming breathing techniques before pickup. She explained to Heather, "That dental work opened my eyes. It's as if my own sadness and worry and, frankly, love for them fed their afternoon struggles. While they still have difficulties at school, at least now their afternoons are a time for recovery and rest, not reliving their problems."

WHY IS THIS ESSENTIAL?

Our contemporary era has been called the Age of Anxiety for a reason. Even before the pandemic, we and our children were burdened with what we believe were unprecedented levels of anxiety. If there ever was a time in history to become a resident expert on how to teach our kids to better manage anxiety, that time is right now.

Anxiety itself, while often deeply uncomfortable, is in a technical sense harmless. The harm comes from our natural response to the anxiety: avoidance. Like all humans, kids naturally avoid situations that make them anxious, but avoidance only makes things worse. Avoidance trains our kids' brains to believe they cannot handle the situation. The remedy is counterintuitive: Avoiding anxiety makes anxiety grow. Approaching anxiety makes anxiety wither away.

Avoidance comes in many disguises, many of which can make avoidance hard to spot. It can be as simple as not going outside if you've been stung by a bee. It can be as protective as lashing out at the one person you are most afraid might leave you. And it can be as insidious and sneaky as continuing to think and think and think about a worrying situation, trying to plan for every possible

$$ANXIETY + AVOIDANCE = MORE\ ANXIETY$$

$$ANXIETY + APPROACH = LESS\ ANXIETY$$

contingency—giving yourself the illusion that you're making progress toward reducing the worry, when in fact all that planning is just another way to avoid taking action. Here is a good rule of thumb: You can't think your way out of a behavior you behaved your way into.

Through our own own actions and reactions, we can either foster or hinder our children's anxiety management. Anxious children understandably crave their parent's proximity as a way to reduce their feelings of fear. And as loving parents help their children manage their fears (by soothing, reassuring, and providing more proximity), the more anxiety is initially reduced for their children. It helps! But anxiety *over time* often becomes more intense as these children rely more and more on their parents to cope. Through experience, children start to believe that the only "solution" to feeling distress is proximity to and attention from their parents. We as parents need to be wary of unwittingly teaching or helping our kids to avoid anxious feelings. Instead, we need to create a space that allows them to feel accepted and understood, practice being uncomfortable, to sit with difficult emotions, and to show them they can manage.

CURIOUS ABOUT THE SCIENCE?

Compared to other animals, mammal babies are born particularly helpless. When threatened, a mammal baby's only real survival mechanism is to signal a caregiver for help. And mammal parents are hardwired to act to protect their child. However, a child's signals go off more often than necessary. A rustling of leaves could be a poisonous snake—or maybe just the wind. Our fear systems are designed to overrespond *just in case*. Evolution favors the anxious over the happy. Our DNA ancestor is the worried lizard, not the relaxed one—he got eaten.

Modern life continues to have life-threatening dangers. So many of our children experience major disruption, uncertainty, loss, or trauma in their lives. They may live on the edge of poverty, face discrimination, or experience marginalization. However, there is an evolutionary mismatch between what our children needed in the past and what our children need today. Statistically, we are significantly safer than our ancestors were in the prehistoric world for which our

Rethinking Stress: What Is it Good For?

"For there is nothing either good or bad, but thinking makes it so."
—*Hamlet*

Stanford psychologist Dr. Kelly McGonigal, first introduced as an expert in the science of willpower for Essential #2, has also helped transform how we look at stress. Stress is a kind of tension we feel under challenging circumstances. Specifically, Dr. McGonigal challenges us to consider that it is our "toxic relationship with stress"—not stress itself—that is problematic. Research studies support the idea that shifting our mindset about stress changes our stress response, and that a "stress-is-enhancing-not-harmful" mindset may have lasting positive effects.

Experiencing stress may actually have positive correlations with life span. Stress can prime the brain for action, attention, learning, or retrieval, and researchers at the University of California at Berkeley have shown that moderate stress levels can increase cell growth in the hippocampus.

We often remind our clients that there is an upside-down U-shaped relationship between stress and performance. Too little stress can lead to inaction or stagnation, while too much stress can create a host of negative psychological and physical effects. But the zone in the middle—the sweet spot—is where stress can spur growth.

We can think of stress like a vaccine. People often experience mild symptoms from receiving a vaccine (muscle soreness, fever, headache) and sometimes misinterpret these symptoms as evidence of illness. In reality, their symptoms are actually evidence that the vaccine is having the desired effect of provoking the immune system to mount an antibody response. We experience short-term pain for long-term gain. We can help inoculate our kids against the negative effects of too much stress by helping them see the benefits of moderate stress and welcoming it when it comes.

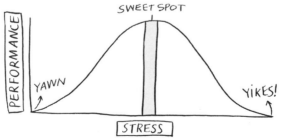

brain's threat detector is designed. And yet our children are more anxious than ever.

Pre-pandemic, the National Institutes of Health found that nearly one in three children ages 13 to 18 will develop an anxiety disorder, and depression will increase by 24 percent. Even before the pandemic's amplifying toll, there have been increasing concerns on the state of child mental health.

Across the scale of human physiology, the amygdala may be more or less sensitive to potential dangers. A crack of thunder that scares one child may be barely noticed by another. Children who are especially sensitive to fear stimuli send frequent cries for help to their parent, and MRI studies have shown a correlation between increased amygdala size in children with anxiety disorders.

Oxytocin is a stress-reducing, connection-enhancing chemical that is released during, among other things, parent-child contact such as eye contact, breastfeeding, touch, and loving interaction. New research suggests that especially sensitive and fearful children have less natural oxytocin available to them. That may be one reason why they often call on a parent to help manage their fears: The interaction with their parent produces oxytocin and yields the soothing, safe feelings they have trouble producing on their own.

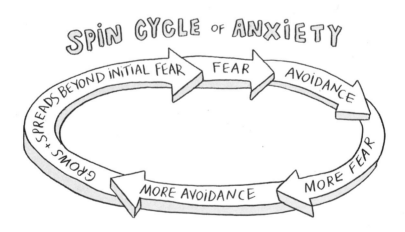

SPIN CYCLE OF ANXIETY

SPREADS BEYOND INITIAL FEAR · FEAR · AVOIDANCE · MORE FEAR · MORE AVOIDANCE · GROWS +

The Anxiety "Parent Traps"

Parenting an anxious child is difficult and often counterintuitive. Anxiety is an unpleasant state and thus hugely motivating to avoid. Children often call for their parents to "help them" in ways that cause the anxiety to accidentally grow. Parents need to learn to spot the ways in which children, consciously or not, can pull parents into contributing to their anxiety.

An anxious child typically seeks:

* **Reassurance** (*tell me it's going to be okay*)

* **Help with avoidance** (*help me change the situation*)

* **Rescue** (*save me from my panicky feelings*)

But if you respond to your child's desires in these ways, you may actually contribute to their overall anxiety. Instead of falling into these parent traps, use the Plays for Your Playbook (starting on page 109) to help your child improve their tolerance of anxiety's discomfort. You don't want your kid to never feel anxious; you want anxiety to lose its potency. Kids need to experience for themselves that while anxiety is temporarily uncomfortable, it doesn't last forever and is ultimately harmless.

Cortisol, a chemical the body releases during times of stress, is another biological measure that can show the contagious nature of anxiety. Recent science has shown that a parent's response to a child, and even the parent's own anxiety, can reduce or amplify the cortisol response of their child. And perhaps surprisingly, the kid may be affecting their parent right back—your child's cortisol secretions may influence and increase your own personal cortisol response. In other words, the chemical relationship between parent and child stress is complicated and goes both ways.

These new studies looking at oxytocin (connection) and cortisol (stress) during parent-child interactions scientifically support what parents may already have intuitively known and felt for themselves: Anxiety is a dance between parent and child. But there are many beneficial ways parents can lead.

Loving parents are naturally driven to soothe their child and relieve their distress. The old idea that children become anxious because their parent is coddling them or engaging in an early rescue has been challenged by new research. Eli Lebowitz, director of the Program for Anxiety Disorders at the Yale Child Study Center, and author of *Breaking Free of Child Anxiety and OCD*, notes that anxious children naturally request more proximity and care. The attentive parent is simply responding to their needs and would likely respond less attentively if their child wasn't struggling with anxiety.

Dr. Lebowitz has developed a highly effective treatment for reducing childhood anxiety called Supportive Parenting for Anxious Childhood Emotions (SPACE). This program is designed to help *parents*, not the child (at least not directly). Dr. Lebowitz's research demonstrates that a child's anxiety can decrease significantly when parents make thoughtful changes in the way they support their child. Seeing a child struggle and responding in a way that might go against your natural instincts is understandably hard for any loving caregiver. But SPACE teaches parents how to engage with their child with supportive, positive, empathetic responses that help their child manage their worries and build their confidence.

Distress or Disorder?

One question we get asked a lot—and for good reason—is how to tell the difference between normal distress and an anxiety disorder. We all experience stress and anxiety, but we do not all have an anxiety disorder. Anxiety becomes a disorder when it regularly gets in the way of what we want or need to do. We don't all need to enjoy roller coasters, watch horror movies, or fall asleep easily, but we do all need to be able to go to school, make friends, and get a decent night's sleep.

In our professional capacity, we assess anxiety based on a person's ability to function well, focusing especially on three factors: intensity, duration, and recovery. Professionals are less concerned about the intensity of a fear or worry. We don't "treat" intensity, since it is likely a more fixed quality based on temperament (and we need our intense kids just as much as we need our placid ones). What we do focus on is duration (how long the feeling/physiological state lasts) and recovery (how quickly the child bounces back).

Another way to determine whether distress has started shifting into disorder is by looking for these common physical, behavioral, and emotional responses to chronic stress and anxiety, which can be mistaken for other problems:

* Frequent stomachaches or headaches
* Procrastination or disinterest
* Irritability, anger, and emotional outbursts
* Impaired memory and focus
* Restlessness or sleeping issues
* Social withdrawal
* Overeating or undereating
* Self-harming behavior
* Drug or alcohol abuse

WHAT DOES ANXIETY LOOK LIKE IN YOUR FAMILY?

Take a Look at Your Child

Family relationships: Does your child's worry seem to control family choices or activities? Are you preparing specific foods, answering or ordering for your child, staying with your kid at parties, hosting playdates or sleepovers so you are nearby, and/or staying with your kid until after they fall asleep? Do your kids ask repetitive or exhaustively detailed questions about future events?

Friendships: Do worries get in the way of friendships? Do worries limit your child's ability to socialize in certain settings, such as sleepovers, camp, birthday parties, and playgrounds?

Learning: Does your child struggle with worries or physical sensations that may accompany worries, such as stomachaches and headaches? Does your child ask you to intervene with the teacher to manage or make exceptions for them due to their fears or worries, such as switching to a teacher who is less "strict," needing to sit next to a certain friend, getting out of gym class, or skipping field trips? Does your child often panic about being called on by the teacher, taking quizzes and tests, or going to school in the mornings? Does your child often wish to be picked up early from school?

Sense of self: Does your child significantly struggle to fall asleep or stay asleep on their own? Can they sometimes manage worries on their own, or do they seem to need constant assurance? Do they tend to worry or focus on only the worst-case scenario and have trouble being open-minded to other outcomes? Do they have confidence that they can cope with most worries or feelings of panic, or do they get worried they *might become anxious later* (anticipatory anxiety)?

CONCERN-O-METER

Pick a color for each category. Draw a colored arrow for each to give yourself a visual picture of your child in this moment.

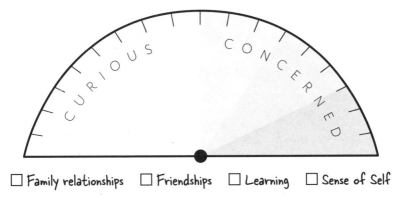

☐ Family relationships ☐ Friendships ☐ Learning ☐ Sense of Self

Take a Look at Yourself

How did you do during the pandemic?

We all experienced fear and anxiety with the COVID-19 pandemic. In many cases it exacerbated lower-level anxiety and made some people fearful in a way they had not been previously. It also revealed our individual methods for dealing with anxiety and uncertainty. How did you fare?

How do you feel right now?

If your closest friend asked you how you are feeling about your kid right now and you were totally honest, what words float into your mind? Is *worried*, *scared*, *concerned*, or *afraid* one of them? Chances are good that if you are anxious about your kid, your kid will pick up a message that there is something wrong with them or their environment. If your reaction to their anxiety is anxiety, this can launch a snowball effect.

Do you need help with your feelings?

If you are struggling with anxiety yourself, seriously consider getting treatment. This could include therapy, medication, or a combination of both. People can get so used to being anxious that they don't remember any other way to be. But anxiety is highly treatable, and treating it can improve your life and the life of your child.

How do you physically respond to your child's anxiety?
Think of a time when your child was worried and looked to you for reassurance. What did your face look like? What did your body look like? Were you unknowingly sending a worried message with your body? How could you move toward a more confident look and feel? What do you think that would be like for your child? What would that be like for you?

How might you be participating in your child's anxiety?
Anxiety is stealthy, and it takes effort and practice to spot it. Can you ask a loving friend or family member if they might see subtle ways you might be responding anxiously to your child's anxiety? Parents don't cause their kids' anxiety, but they are easily sucked into participating in it and can inadvertently worsen it.

HOW DO YOU THINK YOU TREND?

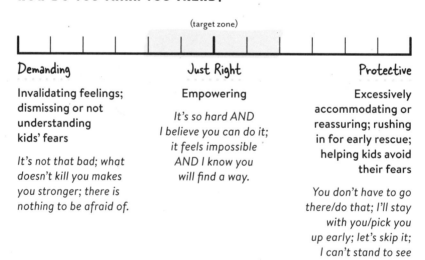

(target zone)

Demanding	Just Right	Protective
Invalidating feelings; dismissing or not understanding kids' fears	Empowering	Excessively accommodating or reassuring; rushing in for early rescue; helping kids avoid their fears
It's not that bad; what doesn't kill you makes you stronger; there is nothing to be afraid of.	*It's so hard AND I believe you can do it; it feels impossible AND I know you will find a way.*	*You don't have to go there/do that; I'll stay with you/pick you up early; let's skip it; I can't stand to see you upset.*

PLAYS FOR YOUR PLAYBOOK

If you want to support your child's ability to function well even when anxious, try out some of the tips below. See if you notice any shifts in your child's functioning (or your own). And as always, remember that sometimes the techniques that don't appeal to you are exactly the ones that you might end up finding the most helpful.

➔ **Gather your courage.** It can be hard to recognize that the best way to help diminish your child's anxiety is, paradoxically, to stop helping them feel better. It takes courage to make changes that initially might make your child more worried, not less. Remember to play the long game.

➔ **Anxiety is your frenemy.** Remind yourself that your child's uncomfortable feelings are useful and necessary. This works for all feelings, not just fears. Being scared they might fail a test can spur them to study harder. Feeling guilty that they hurt a friend's feelings can lead them to apologize or make reparations. Feeling lonely can push them through some social fears so they can reach out to a possible new friend. We tell kids that anxiety is their "frenemy"—they just want to make sure they are in charge of it, and not it of them.

CLIENT FILE
Be Careful with Your Kindnesses

Parents aren't the only ones who can get pulled into colluding with a child's anxiety. Heather recalls a wonderful first-grade teacher who was surprised to realize she was inadvertently adding to a student's anxiety. The teacher saw that this child was especially sensitive and, knowing it was hard for him, she was a little more enthusiastic when he shared something with the class. She often called on him first when he raised his hand. She would tend to stand nearby during recess. The teacher only realized she was being overly attentive when he approached her in the spring and nervously asked who his next-year teacher would be, saying that he needed the nicest one. Looking down at his little face, it dawned on her that her small and well-intentioned bits of "extra help" may have made him feel he would need extra attention from his next teacher and left him less confident in himself.

➔ **Be careful how you interact with anxiety.** Anxiety is like a dog that keeps begging for food at the table. Sure, if you give him a few scraps, he is happy, but what happens next? He is back for more, and this time might be pushier about getting it. In the same way, your child's anxiety wants attention and protection, even if you know your child is perfectly safe. By giving that reassurance, you are inadvertently training the anxiety that the only way to feel better is through your attention or protection. It's much better to lovingly but firmly refuse.

> *"That's your Worry Brain asking me for reassurance, but I already answered that question. Poor you, your Worry Brain sounds so upset and worried, but I don't want to feed it, so I'm not going to answer it again."*
>
> *"I know you are hoping to get assigned to Mr. Martinez's third-grade class this year. It's so hard to wonder for a few more weeks! And whatever teacher you get, the year is going to be a mystery, with all sorts of new things, some good, some bad, we can't even predict."*

➔ **But do not minimize feelings.** Minimizing feelings, especially in anxious children, is very tempting. Sensitive kids can invite invalidating responses from parents because we are just trying to get them to wake up and see that things aren't so bad! Giving them perspectives can feel like good parenting. But providing adult perspective on kid feelings can paradoxically have the opposite effect; when kids feel like you don't understand how hard it is for them, they actually ramp up their anxiety in order to feel understood.

➔ **Validate + express confidence + revalidate sandwich.** We are asking you to do something contradictory: help your child name and accept their scared emotions so they don't amplify further but not fix the situation for them. It's hard to both validate their feelings and express confidence that they can handle them on their own. Try our sandwich method.

Classic:

> *"Of course, you feel so hurt! I would, too! You know those kids so well [**validation**]. I know you'll figure it out [**confidence**], but man, I feel your pain right now [**validation**]."*

Advanced:

*"Oh man, you are deeply suffering [**validation**]. Who knows when this feeling will pass, but I know you won't feel like this forever [implied confidence that the feeling will eventually pass]. I am with you, but I sure can't take the pain away [implied **confidence** that we aren't worried they can't handle some pain in their lives, and implied validation that we also are NOT minimizing that pain, we know emotional pain is real, and, well, painful]."*

Be the Farmer; Embrace Maybe

There is a Taoist story of an old farmer who had worked his crops for many years. One day his horse ran away. Upon hearing the news, his neighbors came to visit. "Such bad luck," they said sympathetically. "Maybe," the farmer replied.

The next morning the horse returned, bringing with it three other wild horses. "How wonderful," the neighbors exclaimed. "Maybe," replied the old man.

The following day, his son tried to ride one of the untamed horses, was thrown, and broke his leg. The neighbors again came to offer their sympathy on his misfortune. "Maybe," answered the farmer.

The day after, military officials came to the village to draft young men into the army. Seeing that the son's leg was broken, they passed him by. The neighbors congratulated the farmer on how well things had turned out. We can all guess the farmer's response. "Maybe," he said with a shrug.

➡ Personify the worry. The science is clear: Separating a child from their anxiety allows the child to feel control over it. So ask your child to name their Worry Brain. Ask them to make it something silly or even a bit angry to shake up the worry system, like Butt Face. Have them pick a color for it or an animal shape. Have them draw it. Give it a funny voice. Give it a made-up theme song.

"Rats, this sounds like Mrs. Smoke Alarm is back, trying to tell us what to do. Should you sing her the 'Go Away' song? Or just ignore her? Or tell her to get lost, sister!?"

"Your worries are really yelling at us both right now. Poor guy. Mr. Pudding Head is so scared he wants to make sure we hear him!"

➡ Don't pretend you can be certain. Modern parents and children are especially uncomfortable with uncertainty. We all want to attempt to control situations to create the "best outcome." But try to reframe

uncertainty for yourself and your child. How do you know what the best outcome is? Recognizing we truly don't know can often help us be less interventionist in our children's problems or anxiety.

"It sounds like you aren't sure if you could get a solo in the choral concert, and it's making you wonder if you should even try out. I get it! Who knows what will happen? That's part of what can make trying out for things feel scary."

➡ Be prepared for your child to become loud. When parents stop being as accommodating with their child's anxiety, it can at first make them react even more frantically than usual. It's hard at first to stop helping with anxiety. Our friend Dr. Jonathan Dalton, a psychologist, tells parents to think of themselves as a vending machine. Your child is used to putting a dollar in and getting a bag of chips out every time. But if one day the machine stopped working, your child wouldn't just shrug and walk away. They might push the buttons over and over, try a different dollar bill, unplug and plug it back in, or bang

on the machine to get it to spring back to life. But eventually, over the following days, they will accept that the machine doesn't work like it used to, move on, and find another way to get a snack.

➡ **Kids can be angry with us.** When we don't help them face their own fears they can be both relieved AND quite angry with us at the same time. An anxious kid may demand extra support, but what we see over and over again is that same kid then blaming the parent for making them dependent on this help. Catherine recalls one teenager who had never learned to sleep alone: He was furious with his parents each day, although he relocated into his parents' room from his own in the middle of the night every night. Swings between enraged and needy are common in kids of all ages who are reacting to uncomfortable feelings of fear and powerlessness.

➡ **Be wary of walking on eggshells around your kid.** A giveaway sign of parents who are inadvertently engaging with their child's anxiety is when they tell us they are "walking on eggshells," working to avoid things they know will upset their kids.

➡ **Use accepting language and sounds when kids tell you about their anxious feelings.** Try "ouch" or "bummer," coupled with encouragement or even a gentle shrug of the shoulders (see our Shrug and Ouch techniques on pages 85 and 90). You want to send a message of sympathy but not distress. Your acceptance and empathy actually conveys that you believe your child can handle the uncomfortable feeling and can find their own way to cope with it. Kids recognize when you believe them, which gives them courage.

➡ **Reduce your own emotion when your child's emotional system is turned on.** Emotions are contagious, and they are looking to spread. Children seek to activate us emotionally so they can share some of our oxytocin. It is a tricky line, but the best response is validating their emotions without being too emotional. Matching their intense emotion increases their emotional brain activity and decreases their ability to think clearly. Being fully understanding and accepting about their feelings while modeling a much lower emotional tone can help kids get their "thinking brains" back online.

→ **A sympathetic face can be the opposite of helpful.** Be very careful of what your face looks like. Reduce the emotional valence of your facial expressions and body language because your child is looking to you for perspective. We love this example, again from our colleague Dr. Jonathan Dalton: Imagine you are an anxious flyer and there is turbulence. Who do you look to for reassurance? The flight attendants, whose body language will show you whether this turbulence is normal or scary. Now picture two different responses, both well intentioned: One attendant looks at you and, seeing your worried expression, mirrors it with a furrowed brow and sympathetic look, saying, "Oh, don't worry, this is totally normal, you are safe, your seat belt is buckled, it's all going to be okay." That seems helpful and kind, but now imagine that the attendant looks at you with a smile but a slightly bored expression and says, "Coffee or tea?" Which response is actually going to be more soothing? The message is the same, but the attention to the worry and the body language are different. Children can misread our sympathy as a reason to still be scared.

→ **Use fewer words.** The more we speak when kids are anxious, the more we appear to be trying to "solve" feelings—as if there was a problem to be solved, rather than a feeling to be felt and coped with.

→ **Share your oxytocin with them at other times.** Hug them, give them your undivided attention, laugh together, get creative together. Fortify them with good feelings in nonstressful times so that they have strength to draw from in difficult moments. Water the seeds, not the weeds. Your love and attention feed whatever behaviors they are engaging in at that moment you are giving your love and attention. Make sure you reward behaviors (laughing, being connected, relaxing) you want to see more of.

→ **Name a feeling for a child, and then ask them to look at the clock and notice what time it is.** Ask them to guess how long it might be before this feeling shifts. You can guess, too. (Pro tip: Make your guess longer than theirs!) This helps them see you aren't afraid of their anxiety, and you have every reason to expect the feeling to shift at some point in the future.

➜ **Take care of yourself.** Do everything you can to reduce and treat your own anxiety. Anxiety is contagious. The pandemic only heightened anxiety for many of us. Caring for yourself and reducing your anxiety is the best possible gift you can give an anxious child.

➜ **Ask the three magic questions:**

1. What's the worst that can happen? (This question often needs to be asked several times to get to the crux of the fear.)

2. How likely is that to happen? (Anxiety can make your child catastrophize or overestimate the likelihood of a bad outcome.)

3. Could you handle it if that happened? (This question orients your child toward their self-efficacy and can fortify them to face the fear.)

➜ **Children want to be understood more than they want to be rescued.** Surprisingly, kids' nervous systems will calm down just because they feel understood, even without a solution. Conversely, their nervous systems get revved up with problem-solving kinds of talk.

> "Oh my gosh, it must be so scary to be going to bed every night worrying about burglars!" [Say nothing more; just give a loving hug or touch on the shoulder.]

> "I can hear that you feel so left out." [Said with a mildly sympathetic face and slight shake of the head.]

> "You sound so lonely. It can be hard to even think about what to do next. Reaching out to people when you are in that frame of mind can feel so risky. I've been there."

> "It makes sense you feel you can't do it! It feels impossible to have to feel anxious all evening. Of course you just want to be saved somehow!" [Now shhhhh, don't problem-solve, don't reassure, don't say another word.]

➜ **Replace your own ideas and problem-solving with questions to help guide your child to problem-solve for themselves.**

> "It's so scary to go upstairs to brush your teeth by yourself. What do you think you will do to take care of yourself while you are scared?"

➡️ **Anxiety likes to play twenty questions.** When kids ask many detailed logistical questions in a row, see it as a warning flag that they might be feeling anxiety. Parents can get fooled by what sound like smart, mature-beyond-their-years questions. Often those seemingly insightful questions are smokescreens for bids for reassurance, and the subtext is *I'm worried about what might happen. Help give me certainty or let me lean on you for help, so I don't have to sit with my uncomfortable uncertainty.* In this situation, it's best to take an "asked and answered" approach, where you give an answer one time, and then gently refuse to continue responding:

> *"Terry, I already told you I don't know how the afternoon with the Smith family will unfold. It's really hard to not know. Scary even. But we're just going to have to wait and see what happens."*

➡️ **Don't let anxiety accumulate.** Early detection and treatment are most effective for anxiety. Studies show that it is more common for a child to be diagnosed with multiple anxiety disorders rather than only one, in part due to the amount of time it can take for parents to recognize and seek help for it.

➡️ **Acknowledge that this is hard!** It can feel almost impossible to convey two different messages to your child: I fully see you and believe in your deep struggle and pain right now—AND I believe in you and know you can manage it. The message you are sending to your child is that you recognize they're anxious. It can be painful to watch your child suffer—AND we know you can do it! Feelings are both deeply painful and completely survivable.

PRO TIP

Sawubona!

Are you having trouble not rescuing your child, and you want them to know you are truly present with them in a painful moment, even though you aren't rescuing them? Consider channeling and sharing the Zulu greeting "*Sawubona!*" It translates roughly to "I see you" or "I see the whole of you, you are valuable to me."

Jennifer Over Empathizes

My son Linus was just one year old when he fell and split the skin on his forehead. The bleeding was prolific. We promptly rushed him to the emergency room in a panic, but the triage nurse looked at me disdainfully and said, "Head wounds bleed." Good to know.

To immobilize small children for medical procedures, medical staff use a kind of straitjacket they kindly call a "swaddle." Not surprisingly, one-year-olds do *not* like this particular kind of swaddle, especially with the accompanying bright lights, strangers, smells, and everything else strange and uncomfortable about the situation. End result: a terrified baby.

Noting Linus's tears and my panicked face as he entered, our med tech sat down and said, "Hi Mom! My job today is to suture your son's forehead. I've done this thousands of times and I'm quite good at it." Then he smiled and said, "Does this seem like a safe procedure to you?"

"Yes, of course."

"Then would you please make sure you tell your little guy that, with both your words and your face, while I'm working?"

Oh. Suddenly, I got it. For the past hour, my fight-or-flight response had been on overdrive. I wasn't worried about the actual stitches—only that my son was in distress. And, of course, babies only pick up their parent's basic emotional tenor. This kind, experienced professional could see that my empathy was accidentally being transmitted to Linus as a message that this was an unsafe situation.

Taking a deep breath, I reminded myself that my child was in good hands and shifted my thoughts, and thus my voice and face. Smiling softly, I began murmuring his favorite changing-table game. "What does the cow say?" I softly asked. No answer, just tears. So I answered myself: "Moooo. And what does the monkey say? Ooh oooh oooh." I continued the little one-person game until finally, as the nurse was wrapping up, I asked "What does the crow say?" Through his tears, Linus looked up and volunteered a quick "Caw caw."

Jennifer's Loving Attention Backfires

Jennifer's son Milo was recovering from a major illness that had kept him out of school for over a year. They hired Adrian, a loving, energetic college student to babysit him and help him return to fifth grade and his regular activities. One day Adrian casually mused, "You know, Jennifer, it's weird, but Milo seems so much healthier when you aren't around." Ouch. Knife in the heart. But also, she knew what he meant. Milo was doing more when Adrian was around, and even though he still felt ill, the activity was helping him get back to his life and ultimately speeding up his recovery. Jennifer's heart, while loving, was unconsciously on the lookout for his symptoms, which made Milo pay more attention to his symptoms, too. So while it was painful for her to realize her presence was temporarily not healthy for her own kid, it was also incredibly helpful to have that kindly pointed out to her. She was able to add more hours to work, and trust Adrian to help Milo find a healthy balance between his real health symptoms and his drive to do more and recover faster.

→ **Ask for a Weather Report.** Help your child tolerate (but not avoid) their worry by mindfully tuning in to the present moment and into their own bodies using the outdoors. Ask them to step outside and tell you what the weather is like. Have them close their eyes and feel for a breeze, the sun, a raindrop, or a chill. Ask them to listen for leaves blowing or birds chirping.

WRAPPING UP

Anxiety can be deeply painful but is essentially harmless. The harm comes from our natural responses to the feeling, especially our tendencies to avoid or distract ourselves. We want to help parents to stop compassionately but inadvertently colluding with their children's anxiety. Instead, we encourage you to teach your child how to live with this highly human, natural feeling and function well regardless of their fears.

DEEPER DIVE

Breaking Free of Child Anxiety and OCD: A Scientifically Proven Program for Parents by Eli R. Lebowitz, PhD

> Dr. Lebowitz has written a parent guide for the SPACE (Supportive Parenting for Childhood Emotions) program. We consider this the new bible for parents who, finding they are unable to directly help their child reduce anxiety, focus on making parenting changes instead (the research shows it works!).

Freeing Your Child from Anxiety: Practical Strategies to Overcome Fears, Worries, and Phobias and Be Prepared for Life—from Toddlers to Teens by Tamar E. Chansky, PhD

> One of the most often recommended books on our shelves, this book provides parents with information ranging from what are normal worries versus something to be concerned about and proven, evidence-based methods parents can use to help reduce their children's anxiety.

For Kids

Guts by Raina Telgemeier

> This graphic novel presents the true story of a girl who had a stomach bug that turned into a fear of vomiting. Any kid who has physical symptoms when they feel anxious will connect with this book.

What to Do When You Worry Too Much: A Kid's Guide to Overcoming Anxiety by Dawn Huebner

> A terrific workbook to help kids understand and overcome anxiety—a classic.

David and the Worry Beast: Helping Children Cope with Anxiety by Anne Marie Guanci

> David is a character anxious kids can relate to as he learns how to overcome his "worry beast."

Staying Flexible

PSYCHOLOGICAL ADAPTABILITY

THE TAKEAWAY

✔ Kids crave certainty, which we can't always give them. What we can give them is the knowledge that they don't need to be in control to be okay.

✔ We can help our kids be open to new information, accept uncertainty as a more constant truth of life, and grow the ability to see themselves and others with flexibility.

✔ When we acknowledge the uncertainty and focus instead on our kids' growing ability to manage whatever may come, our kids in the end feel more secure because their security rests on themselves and their competence, not on their environment being perfect and constantly dependable.

THE SETUP

Nine-year-old Gabriel was stuck. He couldn't sleep after learning of a string of robberies that had taken place in his neighborhood. At bedtime, he would ask for constant reassurance that he and his family were totally safe, and for guarantees that no robbers could come in. But his parents' reassurance wasn't helping, and in fact made him feel less safe—he knew in his heart that his parents couldn't protect the house with total certainty, so why were they promising?

At Catherine's suggestion, his parents began a new conversation. They openly discussed with Gabriel the recent robberies, explained how they had improved their locks, and fully admitted that no adult can make things 100 percent safe. They even discussed the unlikely but terrifying possibility that someone could come in and hurt them. Bad things sometimes do happen; it's just a fact. The conversation was rough, with lots of tears. But after a few more hard nights, Gabriel was surprised to find he could fall asleep more easily again. He told Catherine, "My mind was so busy trying to make sure we were all safe, but we just can't be sure. So now, while I'm still super-afraid of robbers, my mind gives up on fixing it and I guess then I just fall asleep."

WHY IS THIS AN ESSENTIAL?

One of the most important psychological fundamentals for a mentally healthy life is developing a flexible mind. Young children naturally approach the world in black and white because it helps them begin to organize and make sense of the world. Thus, there are good guys and bad guys, yummy foods and yucky foods, fun activities and boring activities. And all of us, under stressful situations, tend to revert to this clear but limited understanding of the world. *I thought my boyfriend was the best, but now that we are breaking up, I realize he is the worst. I hate spinach, so all green foods are bad. My poor presentation in the reading group just confirms I'm a terrible reader.* As children grow, we want to help them recognize and make room for the many shades of gray, both in others and in themselves.

The brain also craves certainty. We all want to be sure, to feel a sense of control, and the uncertainty of not knowing is extremely

Bird on the Branch

Why does the bird not fear the branch breaking?

Is it because the branch cannot be broken? The branch will always be strong? No wind could ever damage or break this branch? The bird (or the bird's parents) could always work to make the branch stronger? No, of course not.

The bird is not afraid because the bird can fly.

When we work to reassure our kids that the branch (that is, their environment) is secure and steadfast, we are kindly, lovingly trying to reduce stress and uncertainty. But, unfortunately, the message our kids receive is *I need a strong branch to be okay.*

When we acknowledge the uncertainty of the branch and focus instead on our kids' growing ability to fly, the kids in the end feel more secure because their security rests on themselves and their competence, not on their environment being perfect and constantly dependable.

stressful. People of all ages can go to great lengths in their thinking to create a false sense of security to relieve their fear and suffering. But there is a price to pay. Achieving this calming mirage of certainty unfortunately requires our thinking to be closed and rigid.

One of the best gifts we can give our kids is the ability to see themselves and others flexibly: *I sometimes get really angry but other times can remain calm. I am sometimes very mad at my mother, but I love her all the time. My friend was mean yesterday, and I wonder what she will be like today?*

Another gift we can give our kids is the practice of feeling uncertain and the confidence that they can handle it. This is a difficult gift for many of us, as parents, to give. Most of us have the tendency to occasionally collude with our kids' desire for certainty; it soothes them (and us) in the moment. But even imagining the worst that can happen, and sitting together with that knowledge, subtly but powerfully communicates your belief that your kid can be okay no matter what.

We don't need to be in control to be okay. We don't know lots of things ahead of time. *I don't know if there will be a pop quiz in class today, but I can deal. I don't know if there will be a snake in the stream today, but I can handle feeling nervous. I don't know if I'll like the food at the birthday party, but I won't starve. I don't know if my best friends are going to the dance, but I'll survive the embarrassment if I don't find anyone to talk to. I don't know if I'll make the tennis team, but I can manage the feeling of failure. I don't know if my loved ones will always be here with me, but I know I can be okay even if I'm on my own.*

Psychological flexibility and the ability to tolerate the truth of uncertainty are the two main ingredients that create the life skill of adaptability. Moving from rigidity to curiosity, being open to new information, being aware that none of us are static beings, accepting uncertainty as the truth, and staying open to a generosity of thought about self and others is an easier, healthier, and more accurate way to move about the world.

Radical Acceptance: The Power of Tara Brach's RAIN

Meditation teacher, psychologist, and podcast host Dr. Tara Brach brought the term *radical acceptance* to the forefront in her popular book by that title. Radical acceptance is a core skill, based on the idea that our reality must be accepted, rather than fought against, and that fighting and resisting a situation causes much greater suffering than the situation itself. Radical acceptance means accepting everything about ourselves, our present situation, and our lives without any question, blame, or pushback. It is accepting yourself and your circumstances in order to better move through and past them. We are simply acknowledging our reality and what has happened or what's currently happening. Dr. Brach takes her definition of radical acceptance a step further: "recognizing what we are feeling in the present moment and regarding that experience with compassion."

Fighting reality only intensifies our emotional reaction. Research supports the idea that practicing acceptance not only improves general emotional well-being but is a powerful component in the treatment of multiple psychiatric conditions, including anxiety and depression.

In a *New York Times* article about using radical acceptance to cope with the COVID-19 pandemic, Dr. Brach said, "Life regularly and inevitably involves emotional stress, anger, fears around health, shame around failed relationships, but anything short of fully accepting our human experience will keep us caught in those emotions."

In weaving together the traditions of psychotherapy and Buddhism in her 2019 bestselling book *Radical Compassion*, she offers the marvelously simple pneumonic RAIN.

R—**Recognize** what's going on

A—**Allow** the experience to be there, just as it is

I—**Investigate** with interest and care

N—**Nurture** with self-compassion

We encourage you to visit Dr. Brach's website, tarabrach.com, to experience her marvelous lectures and meditations that she offers to all of the world for free.

CURIOUS ABOUT THE SCIENCE?

Renowned Harvard psychologist Dr. Susan David's concept of emotional agility describes a process that enables us to navigate life with self-acceptance, clear-sightedness, and an open mind. The process isn't about ignoring difficult emotions and thoughts. It's about holding those emotions and thoughts loosely, facing them courageously and compassionately, and then moving past them.

We need to be careful not to overvalue our rational mind and undervalue our emotional mind. Our brains take in and make sense of a vast amount of information relying on an intuitive ability to prioritize, categorize, and organize quickly and efficiently. These mental shortcuts are often helpful and allow us to do many things at once, but research shows us over and over that they also make us deeply vulnerable to thinking errors.

Dr. David's research shows that rigid thinking is correlated with poorer outcomes in terms of relationships, success, and contentment. In contrast, she demonstrates that emotionally agile people don't just use logic to solve problems, they also listen to their emotions—but without letting those emotions take over. Gently incorporating our emotions into our more logical thinking enhances our ability to pause, open our minds, remember our values, shift perspectives, and internally try on different responses to problems before acting on them. Flexible thinking and a tolerance for uncertainty are at the core of adaptability and our ability to align our actions with our intuition and values.

Psychological flexibility appears to be especially crucial in times of stress. Dr. Jennifer Daks and her colleagues published one of the first studies confirming that parental psychological flexibility—and inflexibility—appeared to directly impact families during the pandemic. More than job losses, illness, fears, isolation, or other possible stressors, they found parental inflexibility was predictive of greater levels of COVID-19-related dysfunction. A downward spiral also appeared to develop in these families: Inflexibility in a parent was correlated with other family members' increased stress overall, and increased fears about COVID specifically.

The Downsides of Mental Shortcuts

Our neurological makeup creates mental blind spots. However, when we become aware of and challenge these gaps or errors in our thinking, we can reduce their distortions of our judgment and decision-making. Here are a few particularly useful ones to know:

* **Availability shortcut.** Our brains give more weight to information that comes to mind quickly or is more emotionally charged. The first thought that comes to mind feels the most true, even if later thoughts refute it. Hearing about a plane crash can make you afraid to fly, even when you know driving is actually more dangerous.

* **Confirmation bias.** Our brains seek out and remember information that supports our preexisting beliefs and discounts information that does not support our beliefs. *Paulo has been quite clumsy with his water recently. Now we notice every time he spills something and don't even pay attention to the myriad times he doesn't spill.*

* **Negativity bias.** Our ever-alert brains are built to notice, retain, and ruminate on negative information more readily than positive information, giving it extra weight in our thoughts. We feel the sting of criticism more powerfully than the glow of praise. Insults are more "sticky" than compliments, and one frustration at lunch can lead to a kid recalling and describing the entire day as terrible.

* **Personalizing.** Our brains naturally tend to attribute our own actions to a situation but to attribute other people's actions more to their personality. *I didn't text Jamie back because I was in class, but Martha didn't text me back because she's a bad friend.*

Teaching our children to notice these mental shortcuts can allow them to override them and think more flexibly. Since these snap judgments can interfere with our ability to keep an open mind, they can also lead us astray as parents. Our kids change frequently, but parents can sometimes get frozen in time. Staying open to seeing our kids realistically, as they are right now, allows us to meet them where they are. It keeps us connected and helps our kids to feel seen and understood. Cognitive flexibility is an important part of this process.

Building a Flexible Brain

Trying to stay cognitively flexible is a lot like trying to become more physically flexible. The only way to become more physically flexible is to stretch. For example, anyone can eventually do the splits. If you rush it, you can pull a muscle and get injured, but if you are patient and persistent, pushing the edge of your flexibility a bit each time, you will eventually get into a split.

Similarly, developing cognitive flexibility requires us to get out of our comfort zone and stretch our thinking so we can be more open, but dramatic shifts do not serve us (or our children) well. Instead, try small but regular steps toward challenging your assumptions and becoming more mentally flexible.

Neuroscientist Dan Siegel describes mental and emotional agility as a river, with chaos on one side and rigidity on the other. Our job is to help our child steer their little boat so they can stay as best they can in the middle of the river, not stuck on one side, not stuck on the other, and not zigzagging back and forth from shore to shore.

The pandemic forced many families to respond to their kids with uncertainty. Will school be open next week? *I'm sorry, sweetie, I don't know.* How much longer will we be required to wear masks in this store? *It's hard to say.* When will Uncle Seymour come home from the hospital? *I'm sorry, we don't know.*

However, what if the pandemic forced us to get comfortable with uncertainty in ways we all needed? Much of the current mental health crisis in the country occurred well before the pandemic. From 2009 to 2021, the proportion of American high school students who said they felt "persistent feelings of sadness or hopelessness" rose from 26 percent to 44 percent, according to a CDC study.

Now signs are emerging that since the pandemic began, some kids may actually be developing new, more flexible thinking and better adaptability to changing circumstances. While some kids suffered deeply, a substantial number were largely unaffected, with some even possibly doing better during the pandemic. Long-term follow-up has shown remarkable signs of resiliency, with many kids displaying the ability to bounce back and adapt. It is possible the constant stress of uncertainty during the height of the pandemic may even have helped jump-start a process of becoming more used to living with uncertainty.

One way to look at the problematic effects of protecting the self from the discomfort of uncertainty is to look through the lens of how we as professionals understand and treat obsessive compulsive disorder (OCD). One of the main symptoms of OCD is the craving for certainty and attempts to create a more certain world through compulsions. Both people with and without OCD prior to the pandemic showed increased symptoms of OCD during the pandemic.

Let's consider a kid who is afraid of germs. He washes his hands, and his brain immediately feels better—he is now certain the germs are gone. A few minutes later, his hand brushes against the stair railing. Now he can't be sure he doesn't have germs. The discomfort of the worry drives him to wash his hands again, and for just a moment, he can again feel the (illusory) relief of certainty that every human craves.

The most effective treatment for OCD is to practice feeling uncertainty over longer and longer periods of time. In our example, we might challenge this boy to intentionally touch the railing and then wait one minute, then five, and then twenty-five, before washing his hands.

OCD can include a tendency toward magical thinking, another way to reduce the discomfort of uncertainty: *If I eat my peas in pairs of two, nothing bad will happen to my parents. If I check under my bed five times and wear my special pajamas, I can prevent a burglar from coming into the house.*

But even without OCD, many of us do this in life. We actually function well when we lie to ourselves, and it's awfully easy to lie to our kids. We tell ourselves, "I'm *sure* my kid is okay at school because I just dropped him off and he was smiling." Or we tell our kids, "Of course I'll be here right when you wake up." Yes, statistically, the chance of *not* being there may be 0.0001 percent. But that isn't zero chance. We can never be sure, and a part of our brain knows that, and keeps working to wring the feeling of risk down to 0.00000001 percent, and then perhaps to absolute zero—an impossibility. We need to train our brains to accept the natural uncertainty that is embedded in human life.

Flexible thinking and increased tolerance for uncertainty provide deep psychological benefits. Together, they are the necessary precursors to a kid who is comfortable in any environment.

WHAT DOES PSYCHOLOGICAL ADAPTABILITY LOOK LIKE IN YOUR FAMILY?

Take a Look at Your Child

Family relationships: Is your child flexible enough to flow with the needs of the entire family? How does your child manage when changes pop up within the family: a sibling falls ill, plans get canceled, the family has to leave early or stay late somewhere?

Friendships: Is your child able to shift or pivot when friends have requests or demands? For example, can they switch games during playdates, eat food served at a friend's house, and accept changing dynamics within a friend group? Can they tolerate their friends' small inconsistencies or mistakes or are they quick to label or judge them for their infractions?

Learning: Can your child manage last-minute changes in classroom activities or structure? Can they tolerate a substitute teacher or

Autism Spectrum Disorder (ASD)

All of us can become rigid from time to time. However, if you find your child struggles more intensely with rigidity, along with difficulties in picking up subtle social cues, you may want to get them screened for Autism Spectrum Disorder (ASD). Many people still associate ASD with severe, debilitating symptoms. But thinking on ASD has evolved considerably and ASD has been determined to be quite common; 1 in 44 people have ASD. Many austistic adults fly under the radar even to themselves, but may never have received a diagnosis, and people with ASD are all around us: a neighbor, a friend, a spouse, perhaps even ourselves.

Early diagnosis can be quite advantageous for kids. Families who become educated on ASD can help them develop self-understanding and workarounds that allow them to develop more flexibility, celebrate and maximize their strengths, and develop practical skills that help them understand and love themselves, and create deep and meaningful relationships with others.

music class on Thursday instead of Tuesday? Can they change focus quickly between subjects and classes?

Sense of self: How does your child manage the rhythm of their day? Can they get out the door on time in the morning? Can they miss school for a doctor's appointment or end a video game earlier than they had planned with relative ease? How does your child manage unforeseen circumstances, such as the loss of internet service or an unexpected houseguest? Do they see themselves in an open and changeable way, or do they see themselves as fixed and unchangeable (for example, "I don't eat vegetables, I will never like classical music, I'm a terrible writer")?

CONCERN-O-METER

Pick a color for each category. Draw a colored arrow for each to give yourself a visual picture of your child in this moment.

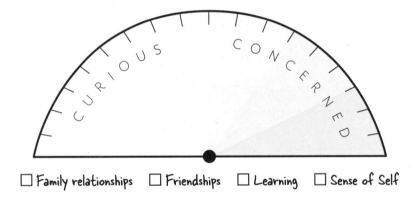

☐ Family relationships   ☐ Friendships   ☐ Learning   ☐ Sense of Self

Take a Look at Yourself

How flexible can you be?

Our kids need us to be flexible with them, to cut them some slack, and to sometimes set the bar lower—for ourselves and for them. It's our job as parents to prioritize and focus on the things that truly matter to our kids' well-being and to sometimes adjust our thinking to be responsive to our kids' needs. What might you let go of?

What are your gaps in understanding?

We *all* have blind spots—based in our own childhood experiences, our values and preferences, or our goals and expectations—that can interfere with our ability to support our unique children. Identifying your blind spots is crucial to mitigating them. Our children are (sometimes painfully!) good at helping with this, but if not, do some self-reflection or ask trusted loved ones.

Do you use rigidity as a crutch to remove complexity and uncertainty?

When children are young, parents learn that their kids benefit from some structure and routine. But some parents, in a desire to provide comfort and increase their sense of control, may accidentally become too unyielding and inflexible. Be careful. Know that a rigid mindset may create distance, while a flexible mindset often increases closeness.

How is your balance?

In parenting, as in life, balance is key. Trying to stay in that smooth-flowing spot between rigid and reactive can be tough, but by paying attention and making small adjustments when you begin to feel off course, you can find the flexibility that parenting requires.

CLIENT FILE

Finding a New Lens

Heather worked with the parents of Julie, a highly oppositional teen who would regularly sneak out of the house at night and take the train downtown. Heather asked the girl's parents to name some of their daughter's strengths, and they were so angry that they struggled to find any. But when they came back the next week, they had a list: Their daughter was resourceful, determined, and creative—all qualities they'd chosen based on the experience of her sneaking out. The parents were able to see their daughter in a more nuanced way than just difficult, argumentative, and rebellious, and looking at the positives allowed them to approach the unsafe behavior with more warmth and understanding.

Are you taking your kid's behavior personally?

The mental shortcut of personalization can lead parents to assume that their kids are intentionally trying to manipulate or misbehave. It can also lead parents to take personally their children's emotional outbursts or negative behaviors. Often the best gift we can give our children is a generous explanation for their difficult behaviors. When parents are unduly harsh in their assessments of their children's motives and behaviors, it can strain the connection and limit the child's motivation to improve.

Are you allowing your child to change?

Our kids need us to be flexible enough to meet them where they are right now, not where they used to be, where we think they should be, or where we wish they could be. Sometimes *we* have to let go of the past so *they* can evolve. Your daughter may have loved to dance when she was in elementary school (and you may have loved watching her) but in middle school she may decide to stop taking lessons. Her change is a loss for you, and in order to stay present you need to acknowledge it and let it go. Every parent of an older kid has had to grapple with the ways in which their child's preferences and path diverge from a parent's plans and expectations. Effective parents give their kids the freedom to become their authentic selves.

HOW DO YOU THINK YOU TREND?

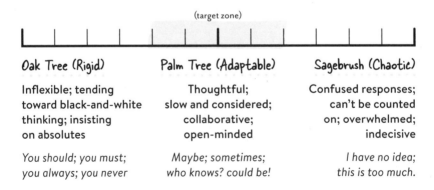

(target zone)

Oak Tree (Rigid)	Palm Tree (Adaptable)	Sagebrush (Chaotic)
Inflexible; tending toward black-and-white thinking; insisting on absolutes	Thoughtful; slow and considered; collaborative; open-minded	Confused responses; can't be counted on; overwhelmed; indecisive
You should; you must; you always; you never	*Maybe; sometimes; who knows? could be!*	*I have no idea; this is too much.*

PLAYS FOR YOUR PLAYBOOK

If you want to help your child increase their mental and emotional flexibility, try out some of the tips below. See if you notice any shifts in your child's functioning (or your own). And as always, remember that sometimes the techniques that don't appeal to you are exactly the ones that you might end up finding the most helpful.

➜ **Lean in to uncertainty.** Being adaptable and resilient requires us to be comfortable with a state of change and uncertainty. Help your kid recognize when things are in flux and model acceptance with it.

> *"Gosh, I don't know whether Aunt Nishi and Uncle Arvan will be coming this weekend. There are a few things they are sorting out before they know if they can visit. We will have to just wonder a while longer."*

➜ **Stay curious.** Ask your child questions without preconceived notions. What is life like for them now? Do not assume you know their answers. Listen with an open mind.

> *"I know you really loved soccer last year. How are you feeling about it this year?"*
>
> *"It sounds like you are not very interested in college right now. What did you have in mind after high school?"*

➜ **Reduce your use of the word *should*.** Challenge your own ideas about how things should or should not be.

➜ **Give second chances.** When kids act out in small ways, give them a little feedback and another shot at engaging in a more mature way.

Each Kid Is Different

"One size fits all" does not work, even within a single family. There is no single best way but rather many different ways to support different children. When you have multiple children in one household, it's your job to be flexible in your parenting to meet each child's individual needs. And remember the adage: "Comparison is the thief of joy."

Instead of "You shouldn't speak to me this way," maybe try "I was not allowed to talk to my parents this way, so this conversation bothers me. But I want to hear what you have to say—could you please speak to me differently so I can hear you better?"

➡ **Don't pigeonhole your own kids, and don't let them pigeonhole themselves.** Avoid seeing your child "as" something. Instead, describe the flexibility and variability you see in your child. For example, instead of saying "Jamie, you've got to stop being so hot-tempered," you could note that the moment is fleeting and flexible: "Jamie, you seem pretty mad this evening. And yesterday, you were cool as a cucumber at dinner. Isn't it funny how all of us are always changing depending on the situation?"

➡ **Be an exceptions detective.** Pick three adjectives you might use to describe your kid that bug or worry you a bit. Then actively look for exceptions that disprove that label so you can broaden your understanding of your child. Share some of these exception observations with your child.

> *For a child who is quick to give up: "Wow, look at you still working on that LEGO set, even though you made a few mistakes in the beginning. You can really stick with things."*

➡ **Teach kids about their memory's movie editor.** Our memory is biased toward cutting the boring and painful parts of our experiences, which can lead our memories to be overly positive. This "rosy retrospection" bias is why we tend to recall the fun we had on vacation while forgetting the flight delays, the long wait for a table at dinner, and the boring drive to the amusement park. It also leads us to make rosy projection errors, where we assume future events will be more enjoyable than they are, which can be upsetting when the inevitable bumps arise.

➡ **Come up with alter egos for the tough situations.** Some situations are likely to bring out the worst in us and our kids, such as those marked by stress, time pressure, or transitions. Try making alter

The Power of Both/And

One of the best ways to help develop more psychological flexibility is to construct thoughts using both both/and: *The chore is* **both** *boring* **and** *satisfying. The English assignment is* **both** *impossible* **and** *doable.* These are not contradictions. Both can be true.

egos for the difficult situations to give everyone in your family some extra space and grace for the less-than-ideal version of themselves. If getting your family ready for vacation brings out the worst in you, try labeling it:

"I think Airport Dad has come out to help the family not miss our flight. I'm grateful when Airport Dad bosses me around a bit; he's grumpy, but he gets us there on time! Once we are on the plane and Dad is back, I'm going to loan him my neck pillow."

If your kid has a known struggle point or a difficult transition, try using gentle humor to signal that you can tolerate their less-than-ideal self and have confidence it is temporary:

"Oh gosh, I think I'm talking to Concert Rashad. It's always stressful the day of, so I totally get why you might not want me reminding you about family obligations we have this weekend. I'll wait until Regular Rashad is back tomorrow before I bring it up again."

➡️ **Shake up their brains with a little humor.** Humor, surprise, and lightheartedness are perfect breeding grounds for flexibility. Injecting these qualities into the daily routine can be super-simple, like having dinner for breakfast or writing a joke on a sticky note and putting it on their computer at night.

➡️ **Activate the creative parts of the brain, where flexible thinking thrives.** Creatively thinking outside the box needs both hemispheres to be involved, but our adult reliance on language can keep us, and our kids, in the left hemisphere. Music, art, and comedy can all activate both sides of the brain.

→ Don't confuse consistency with rigidity. Consistency means kids can trust we will do what we say we'll do. But it is not an unbreakable promise. When it makes sense to be flexible, do it! Give a short explanation, even if it's just that you decided to be inconsistent ("I know I said no eating in the living room, but tonight we're going to break the rule."). Rigidity invites power struggles, which are typically unwinnable for parents.

→ Help your kid learn to see the gray. Caution: First test the waters to see if your kid's PFC—that boss of the brain—is ready to engage. If your kid is feeling emotional and can't think straight, they are not ready to discuss flexible thinking.

BLACK GRAY WHITE

"You are so disappointed with that C+ on your English paper. I feel for you. You worked so hard, and you care about your grades."

STOP. LONG PAUSE. Watch their reaction. If your radar tells you that your child's PFC thinking mode is turned on, and you are darn sure their emotional brain is not in charge, then you could add . . .

"Just wondering—do you feel like you got anything out of writing it in the first place? I know you love Dickinson." (If you're met with rolled eyes, you can always add with a twinkle, "Sorry, too soon?")

→ Model shifting from rigid to flexible. Kids are natural mimics, so show them how you shift your own thoughts.

"After that call from my boss, I'm just so annoyed. I want to blame her, but she might be right in her criticism of my project. I'm going to take a few deep breaths and try to remind myself she has good points, even if I don't love her tone."

→ Help children develop alternative explanations. Try to generate a lot of possible explanations rather than settling into a single hypothesis or judgment.

"I can see why you are so hurt by what Allison said to you. I know it seems like she was trying to hurt your feelings and that's quite possible. Can you think of any other reasons why she might have treated you that way?"

Jennifer Learns to Get Flexible

When my daughter Franny was little, she hated being helped out of the car. Each day she would scream-demand I go inside and let her get out of the car herself. Alone. Which seemed crazy, and frankly a bit neglectful on my end since she was barely three years old. The car trip would always end with me hauling her out, kicking and screaming.

My first two kids had taught me to parent with a pretty firm style—stick to the rules; don't offer too many choices. But Franny scoffed at my reasonable parenting. So I tried to validate and set limits, like I teach my clients. "You don't like this side. You want to be in charge. You have strong feelings. But this is the side we get out on." The more I stayed firm, the more she dug in her heels. I felt ridiculous—I do this for a living for heaven's sake! And I felt angry. Why was she in charge, like a tiny emotional terrorist?

I complained to my friend about my difficult and rigid child. "Well, you seem pretty rigid, too, Jen," responded my friend. "What do you care?" That certainly got my attention. I stopped and thought for a second. Why did I care? Was it a safety issue? We were parked in a driveway. She didn't have a habit of going into the street. She knew how to shut the door without smashing her fingers. While letting her get out of the car on her own without my supervision wasn't zero risk, it was pretty close.

"But what about limits?" I begged my friend. "Children feel more secure when parents stay in charge." My friend just shrugged and gave me a classic Dr. Phil "So, how's that working for you?" Touché. She added, "And maybe stop telling yourself she is so difficult. How about a more neutral phrase, like 'That Franny, she's full of beans.'"

So, the next day, I got a little less rigid myself. I pulled up to the house and said (through slightly gritted teeth), "Franny, you sure are full of beans! I'm going inside, so see you soon." I fake-calm walked into the house (then stalked her through the window). The car was silent, unmoving. Nothing. And then a door—on the scratchy tree side, of course—opened. Franny slid out, closed the door poorly but at least not on her hand, and walked right up to the house. An emotional terrorist, but a calm one. Not foolish enough to ruin the weird moment, neither of us mentioned what had just happened. Instead, I casually asked, "Hi, want carrots and hummus for a snack?" She, just as casually, answered, "Yes, please."

➡ **Play the "Benefit of the Doubt" game.** Come up with three alternative explanations for others' behaviors—the more generous (or wackier), the better.

> *"Ouch! That lady in the checkout line was so rude to me! I wonder why she did that? Can you help me play 'Benefit of the Doubt'? One: Her car just died and she's taking it out on me. Two: She can't help it because she was raised by rude monkeys, and she doesn't even know she's being rude. What's a good third option?"*

➡ **Moderation, and lots of it!** Balance is key. The one thing we don't want you to moderate is moderation itself. If you find you are in the middle between rigid and chaos, keep at it.

➡ **Help kids break the rigid habit of perfectionism.** Perfection in everything can become an accidental family value and create a lot of destructive mental habits in kids. Most things should be done well, but not everything. Add the phrase "good enough" to the family vocabulary.

> *"Well, I can see you didn't do a perfect job on your homework today, but do you feel you fully learned the new concept? Will your teacher accept it? Well then, good enough, let's get some sleep."*

➡ **Channel philosophical wisdom.** Whether you know it as the modern Serenity Prayer or ancient Greek Stoicism, parents can stay flexible by following this mantra: "Let me find the serenity to accept the things I cannot change, the courage to change the things I can, and the wisdom to know the difference."

WRAPPING UP

A less commonly known pillar of good mental health is a flexible mind. One of the best gifts we can give our kids is the ability to see themselves and others flexibly, and to keep that ability even under duress. There is a danger to both rigid thinking and rigid feeling. Parents can actively help kids move from rigidity to curiosity, from a limiting sureness about others to generosity, and from black-and-white thinking to rainbow colors.

DEEPER DIVE

Radical Acceptance: Embracing Your Life with the Heart of a Buddha by Tara Brach

> We will never get enough of Tara Brach, an internationally known psychologist and teacher of mindfulness, meditation, and emotional healing whose straightforward, accessible practices are grounded in both modern brain science and ancient wisdom.

How to Talk So Kids Will Listen & Listen So Kids Will Talk by Adele Faber and Elaine Mazlish

> This 1980 book is a classic for a reason—it is an outstanding parenting resource, as relevant today as when published, as is the authors' book *Siblings without Rivalry: How to Help Your Children Live Together So You Can Live Too.*

Thinking, Fast and Slow by Daniel Kahneman

> A fascinating walk through decades of groundbreaking research on how we think and the biases we are vulnerable to.

For Kids

My Day Is Ruined! A Story for Teaching Flexible Thinking by Bryan Smith

> A children's book offering four steps to more flexible thinking.

For Teens

Conquer Negative Thinking for Teens: A Workbook to Break the Nine Thought Habits That Are Holding You Back by Mary Karapetian Alvord and Anne McGrath

> Totally readable, this concise workbook helps teens break free from nine common negative thinking habits that get in the way of developing psychological adaptability.

Letting Go

BUILDING INDEPENDENCE

THE TAKEAWAY

✔ Our goal as a parent is to work ourselves out of a job—often through leaps of faith (not certainty!) in our kids' abilities.

✔ When we do too much for our kids, it sends the message that we don't think they are capable of doing it themselves.

✔ We can practice getting out of the way while our kids work—and sometimes stumble—to do things on their own.

✔ An increasingly high number of kids aren't mentally prepared for the independence of leaving home, and experience high rates of anxiety and depression as a result.

THE SETUP

eather was working with the parents of Jordan, age 7, who was struggling with separation anxiety, including not wanting to be left alone at her beloved hip-hop dance class. Before recommending any specific ideas for anxiety, Heather took a quick inventory of the daily routine, and one of her initial suggestions was to give Jordan some more chores, including emptying the dishwasher. At their next appointment, Jordan's parents gleefully shared their amazement that Jordan had decided on her own to go to her dance class. When her dad asked her what made it easier that week, she replied, "Now that I'm old enough to empty the dishwasher and put away all the sharp knives, I'm old enough to be by myself the whole dance class."

WHY IS THIS ESSENTIAL?

Building independence in kids is one of the most important and difficult parenting jobs. It's the ultimate version of playing the long game, entailing a gradual transfer of knowledge and power across the years, often with leaps of faith rather than of confidence. Parenting is about working yourself out of the job, moving from supervisor to consultant to mentor and beyond. If we fail to prepare our kids to

BUILDING INDEPENDENCE

succeed without our involvement, we risk making our kids dependent on us, which will limit their future happiness and success. Also, when we remain too involved, doing things for our children that they are capable of doing for themselves, we send a subtle but clear vote of "no confidence" that can affect children's self-esteem, their coping skills, and our parent-child relationship.

As parents, we have millions of daily opportunities to help grow independence in our kids—we just have to take advantage of them. But there are a number of trade-offs. Any time we ask our kids to take something on, it's temporarily harder on us as parents, since it won't be done quickly or well. And, the more we create opportunities for building independence, the more we must give up on our deep craving for perfect safety, for certainty, and for control. The stakes are high, as we are seeing ever-increasing numbers of young adults who are struggling to launch and parents who wish they had better and sooner understood how to prepare their kids to leave the nest. No matter the age of your child, we encourage you to always be on the lookout for opportunities to shift ownership of meaningful responsibilities and grow your child's independence.

CURIOUS ABOUT THE SCIENCE?

What does the science tell us about helping build independence? Let's start with chores. Harvard's Grant Study, spanning more than seventy-five years, found strong support for chores as a path to develop work ethic. Another study from the University of Minnesota found the single best predictor for future relationship success with family, friends, and romantic partners was doing chores at 3 and 4 years of age. Both studies support the idea that encouraging independence is a key to healthy growth and development. Dr. Richard Rende's research at Brown University has also shown that chores, increasing at specific ages, are strongly correlated with a decreased risk of alcohol and drug abuse, increased school engagement, and increased family connectedness through a sense of shared responsibility. Children are built to learn experientially, and they suffer when they are not given enough opportunities to work.

We know that compared to past generations, American parents have less tolerance for the trade-off between increased independence and safety. Dr. Roger Hart, an environmental psychologist, observed eighty-six children between the ages of 3 and 12 daily for two and a half years in a small town in Vermont in the 1970s. He mapped the distance each child was allowed to go by themselves and created averages for each age group. He found that by age 10, most kids had the run of the town, including the neighboring lake. Dr. Hart returned to this same town one generation later to document the children of his original subjects. He found that the scope of kids' free rein had shrunk down to their own properties, despite the town being essentially unchanged physically, demographically, and crime-wise. When he interviewed the new parents (whom he had interviewed when they were free-range kids), to ask why they had so drastically reduced their own children's freedom to roam, he found that the overwhelming reason was fear. It can feel scary out there.

A frequent companion to a lack of child independence is parental overinvolvement (after all, if the child doesn't yet have ownership over a task or responsibility, the parent does!). And parental overinvolvement can actually do measurable harm. A recent study led by Stanford University professor Jelena Obradović examined parents' behaviors when their kindergarten-aged kids were playing, cleaning up toys, learning a new game, and discussing a problem. They found that when parents stepped in more often to instruct, correct, or question, even when the child was on task, the children had more trouble regulating their emotions and behaviors at other times. These same children also performed worse at delayed gratification and other executive functioning tasks. It appeared that parents unnecessarily assisting their kids was related to their children having worse

A Letter from Catherine—College Rebounders

High school students and their parents devote immeasurable energy, time, resources, and support to pave the way for the greatest possible college opportunity. Tutoring, SAT prep, AP classes, extracurricular activities—given the competition, expense, and stress of applying to colleges, we get it. The three of us have personally walked this walk and, speaking for myself, not always gracefully. However, I want to bring you into my vantage point as a psychiatrist "raising" kids in my practice for nearly twenty-five years.

Each year, I am utterly stymied by the number of students in my practice who need to press the pause button during or after starting their first year of college. Our colleague Kathy Essig dubbed this group the "college rebounders."

I always reserve the day before Thanksgiving just to see college freshmen in my practice. And as depressing as this sounds, I reserve the day after Thanksgiving to see their parents to "drop the bomb" that I will need to help their college freshman withdraw due to mental health issues. I find that both students and parents feel a quiet shame about this. There is an eerie kind of silence in a family when a kid is just not quite ready, functionally or emotionally, for the independence required in college life.

Our colleagues Dr. William Stixrud and Ned Johnson explain why the transition to college is treacherous for some kids in their book *The Self-Driven Child*: "As we see it, there are two critical issues at hand. First, college life is a highly dysregulated environment with inconsistent sleep patterns and diets, little structure, and an abundance of binge-drinking, pot-smoking, and abuse of stimulants like Adderall. Second, students haven't been given control of their own lives until way too late. You wouldn't tell a kid to merge onto the freeway the first time he gets behind the wheel of a car, and yet that's essentially what we do in expecting students to go from parental control to near-total freedom."

We dedicate so much energy into parenting our kids, but we can accidentally neglect the most important work of all: equipping our kids to live without us.

behavioral and emotional control, and this finding held across the socioeconomic spectrum.

Some consequences of not equipping our kids to function without us often don't appear until they have left home for the first time. As many as 30 percent of first-year college students don't return for their sophomore year of college, even though many of them are fully academically prepared for college content and rigor. The First-Year College Experience survey found that 60 percent of first-year college students said they wished they had more help getting emotionally ready for college. "Emotional preparedness was a major factor in determining whether a student had a successful 'freshman' year or not," the researchers noted. Their survey of more than 1,500 first-year college students showed that those who felt less emotionally prepared for college when compared to their peers had lower GPAs and were four times more likely (22 percent versus 5 percent) to describe their first-year experience as "terrible/poor." Half of the students said they felt stressed "most or all of the time,"

Becoming Interdependent

When we talk about the importance of independence, we do not mean to imply we want to develop a bunch of lone wolves—in fact, the opposite is true! Research pretty much universally finds the single most important variable linked to happiness and longevity is the quality of one's relationships. Being able to form and maintain close connections with other humans is truly essential to wellbeing. So as our children become increasingly *independent* of us, we hope they are simultaneously becoming increasingly *interdependent* with others: good friends, siblings, teammates, teachers, relatives, or neighbors. Parents can help by giving kids the freedom to choose their own friends, modeling how we tend to our own adult relationships, and by regularly encouraging them to reach out more as they grow a widening circle of other amazing people in their lives. One of our main jobs in helping kids develop independence includes helping them increase their emotional independence from us—to make more and more space for others.

Collaborative Problem-Solving

A critical but often overlooked type of independence is the ability to solve problems. Parents tend to be very good problem-solvers and may enjoy doing it, and may accidentally skip past teaching this skill to their kids. When your child faces a problem at any age, we suggest using these five steps:

1 Brainstorm potential solutions together (let your kid take the lead as much as possible).

2 Agree on a solution to try.

3 Let your kid test the solution.

4 Together, evaluate how effective the solution was (including acknowledging that what might have worked for them might not have worked for you, and vice versa).

5 If the solution was not effective, they can pick another solution to repeat the test/evaluate cycle.

and more than a third felt they did not feel as if they were "in control of managing the stress of day-to-day college life." The majority of college students surveyed reported that they needed to improve their time management and independent living skills.

A thought leader in this area is the witty and wise Julie Lythcott-Haims, former Dean of Freshmen and Undergraduate Advising at Stanford University. She cites a 2013 study in which a whopping 95 percent of college counseling center directors said the number of students with significant psychological problems is a growing concern on their campus. Seventy percent of directors believed that the number of students with severe psychological problems on their campus had increased in the past year. At the top was anxiety, appearing in 41 percent of college students, followed closely by depression at 36.4 percent. Bottom line: We need to teach, but also let experience itself teach, our kids to function independently throughout their childhood and adolescence in order for them to thrive as adults.

WHAT DOES INDEPENDENCE LOOK LIKE IN YOUR FAMILY?

Take a Look at Your Child

Family relationships: Does your child have regular responsibilities around the house (pet care, laundry, setting the table, or other chores)? Do they feel a sense of ownership and care toward their household and other family members?

Friendships: Does your child play independently with friends, or do they want your attention or ideas for playing? Does your child have the freedom to choose their own friends? Is your teen making their own plans with friends?

Learning: Does your child feel responsible for their own schoolwork and homework? Are they able to advocate for themselves with teachers, coaches, and other adults, or do they often lean on you to "fix things" for them?

Sense of self: Does your child appear confident in managing their responsibilities and in caring for themselves (getting dressed, packing their backpack)? Can they tolerate boredom and figure out how to fill their free time?

CONCERN-O-METER

Pick a color for each category. Draw a colored arrow for each to give yourself a visual picture of your child in this moment.

☐ Family relationships   ☐ Friendships   ☐ Learning   ☐ Sense of Self

Take a Look at Yourself

How does it feel to see your kid become more independent?
Is it a huge relief? Bittersweet? Do you feel it as a loss when your
child does not need you to do something for them? Are you
prepared for the inevitable pulling away that comes with your
adolescent's increasing need for privacy? Are you emotionally
ready to be less involved? Or are you possibly too quick to pull
away when you're not feeling needed, creating an accidental
cycle of failure? As children grow up, parents need to prepare
to exchange the quantity of involvement for the quality of the
relationship.

Do you find yourself getting frozen in time?
Increasing independence is a constant process of stepping back
and letting go, but it is extremely easy to get stuck in place
as parents. Ask yourself two key questions: What am I doing
now for my child that they are capable of? What are the next
responsibilities I want to prepare my child to take on? Determine
what realistic gaps in knowledge, skills, or motivation currently
exist. Create a plan to address these gaps and nudge your child
toward increasing their independence.

*What stands in your way of encouraging more independence in
your child?*
Resist the urge to do for your child things that they are capable
of doing just because it's easier or faster for you to do it. Kids can
take a million times longer than you to do any task, and still do
it poorly. Fight the inevitable frustration we all sometimes feel at
our children's lack of skill and speed and, instead, use your love
for your child and your goal of building their independence to
grow your patience. Avoid letting your own time stresses keep you
from letting them do the job.

Are you a perfectionist? A control freak?
If so, be forewarned: Allowing your child to gain independence
may be difficult. Keep your larger goals and values in mind as you
decide how much freedom and responsibility to give them.

Do you accidentally make adulthood look like a drag? Do you find yourself complaining about being on an adult treadmill of overload and stress, without describing or living a balance of downtime and pleasure? Some kids have said that parents make adulthood look unappealing, which disincentivizes them from wanting to grow up. How do you think your kids feel about being an adult?

One of the notable trends in parenting over the past few decades has been parents' increased reliance on their children as sources of company. Many parent-child relationships are now characterized less by authority and more by friendship. While there are some true positives to parenting from a less authoritarian stance, there are some hidden dangers in parents' overreliance on their children as social and emotional outlets. It can confuse boundaries, erode influence, reduce their sense of security, limit growth into full independence, and make parents dependent on their children. Do you worry this could be you?

Will your child worry about you when they leave home?

Many teens express concern about how their parents will fare without them. How do they see the quality of your adult relationships? Do you find yourself unwittingly leaning on your child socially or emotionally? Do they see your life as full and fulfilling even without them living at home?

HOW DO YOU THINK YOU TREND?

(target zone)

Indifferent	Empowering	Overinvolved
Little or poor communication; being out of touch; lack of attunement	Age-appropriate expectations, ongoing transfer of power to child, encouragement for stretching and growing	Doing kids' work for them; oversharing; micromanagement; using "we" instead of "they"
Kids should be able to do this. It's not that hard! Figure it out.	*Let me know if you need help. Let me show you, and then you can try it.*	*You might need me. We have a science project to finish. You aren't ready for that. Be careful!*

PLAYS FOR YOUR PLAYBOOK

If you want to work on helping your kid develop independence, try out some of the tips below. See if you notice any shifts in your child's functioning (or your own). And as always, remember that sometimes the techniques that don't appeal to you are exactly the ones that you might end up finding the most helpful.

➜ **Answer the key question: What is something I am doing for my child that they are capable of doing for themself?** What tasks and responsibilities are they ready to learn? It may feel loving to ask less of your kids and to do more for them, but kids don't benefit from, or even appreciate, being overly cared for over the long term. Make a plan for skills and responsibilities you will teach and transition to your child over the next few months, and then reevaluate and build the list.

➜ **Have a collaborative conversation.** Brainstorm about what new responsibilities your child might be interested in and share your own priorities. Find the sweet spot between too much/overwhelmed and too little/demoralized. Remember that when your child chooses a chore, it has a little motivation built in.

➜ **Ask for real help.** Kids know when parents are inventing chores versus when parents actually need help. Look for opportunities where the chore is meaningful to you; it will help the job be more meaningful to them as well.

"I'm in a pickle with this leak under the sink. Can you help me this afternoon? I feel really confident in asking you to drive to the hardware store on your own to buy the gasket, but I want to know how you feel about it."

➜ **Know when to do nothing.** Keep yourself honest. If you say you won't interfere, don't interfere! Nothing is as demoralizing as giving your child a new responsibility and then micromanaging and critiquing them while they do it. Encourage a growth mindset by focusing on the effort to learn, not the end result.

➜ **Watch videos of young children doing amazing things.** If you are wondering what a 3-, 7-, 11-, or 14-year-old is capable of, just take a browse online to see kids from other cultures cooking over fires, caring for younger siblings, biking to school, and more. Some of these kids come from circumstances where they're required to work due to economic necessity, and in some cases hardship. But much of it is also simply cultural. It can be perspective-shifting to see the natural capability of kids at different ages around the world.

→ **Assign your child tasks they are terrible at.** Give them the opportunity to practice. If they are often careless, give them the chore of clearing plates after dinner. If you worry that your teen is a terrible driver, don't reduce their driving responsibilities; instead, encourage more driving, at least in lower speed limit areas.

→ **Give your kids some "dangerous" jobs and chores.** Balance your fears about risks to bodily harm with risks of feeling incompetent. Push yourself to let them bike to the grocery store to get that loaf of bread you forgot for dinner or let them put boxes up in the attic even though it's tricky to walk only on the joists. Let your toddler carefully put the dinner knives in the dishwasher. Kids feel proud and build self-confidence with "dangerous" jobs and are often especially careful with the added responsibility.

→ **Don't watch your kids practice.** When parents observe their kids practicing for a sport or artistic endeavor, it can add an evaluative performance element that is countereffective. Practice is for making mistakes, self- or coach-correcting, and improving, and parents are much more likely to interfere with rather than help this process.

→ **While you are at it, don't attend every single game or performance.** Kids' activities are primarily meant for the kids' enjoyment and development. While you want to be engaged and supportive, be a little late sometimes, or miss a few, so that you don't accidentally send a message that their activities are designed to entertain you. And when you aren't there, there is an extra benefit: Your kid gets the opportunity to tell you all about it.

→ **Once a year, have a Yes Day.** Based on a children's book of the same name by Amy Krouse Rosenthal, a Yes Day is where parents *have* to say yes to their kids. Scared yet? You start with some ground rules, such as: on a weekend; only for today; safety first; must be free or under ten dollars or whatever fits your budget. Then, within that safety net, you allow the kids to be in charge. Why does this help with independence? While it sounds easy, many kids actually end up struggling with this day. They truly aren't used to making many decisions. When a child is in charge of a day, it can help develop reasonableness, responsibility, and confidence. Your kids can also enjoy the feeling that even if you aren't thrilled with their choices, you fundamentally trust them. Bonus: It can be delightful for you as the parent to give yourself permission to relax, live in the moment, and be carefree, without for once having to be the director of your family's weekend day.

➡ **Self-advocacy skills are crucial!** Help kids learn to communicate with authority figures on their own, like talking to teachers, coaches, bosses, and doctors. Remember, you as parents won't be able to call their college professors or future employer.

"I know it can be hard to ask your coach about playing a different position. Would you like to practice on me first?"

➡ **See one, do one, teach one.** In medical school, students are taught daunting procedures with this mantra. Pick a task, and show your child how you do it, then have them do it, and then suggest they share how it went with Grandma, a friend, or another trusted person. This encodes the new skill in the brain in three different ways.

"I know you have never made a doctor's appointment before. Why don't you watch me call my doctor? Then next time you can call yours to make an appointment while your little sister listens."

Don't Jump to Solutions

Separate the solution from the requirements. Help your child identify the requirements of a problem, and then give them a chance to develop their own solutions.

"Your doctor said you need fresh air and exercise every day. What ideas do you have for how and when you want to do that?"

➡ **Make a list of the skills needed for "adulting."** Think about the practical knowledge your child will need to live away from you and make a master list. Over the months or years, help your child learn to do these day-to-day tasks.

➡ **Be a good sounding board.** Try to listen actively, which can be harder than it sounds. Let go of your assumptions about your child, ask good open-ended questions (when in doubt, just ask "What do *you* think?"), and listen to their responses with an open mind. This is not something that can happen when you feel rushed, so be direct and let your kids know when it isn't a good time for you to listen well.

CLIENT FILE
Operation Free Rein

By the time Marina's child Hector was in fourth grade, going to the school where Jennifer worked, he and his mother had walked the mile home from the school at least a hundred times. Still, when he asked to do it alone, Marina was hesitant. He had to cross a number of busy streets, the buses and cars didn't always follow the speed limits, and he had no cell phone if anything went amiss. But deep down, Marina believed he could manage these everyday dangers. So together they agreed on a plan. For a few days they walked together, but Hector was in charge—he would say which way to go, when to cross the street, or what he might do if a stranger approached him, and he would narrate his thought process throughout. They called it Operation Smart Hector. Then he moved to phase two, Operation Mom Might Be Watching, in which he did the walk home solo, but with Marina sometimes hidden somewhere along the way to "catch him" following the safety rules (and to give Hector the playful challenge of trying to spot his mom). Phase three was Operation Free Rein. Marina knew she had made the right decision when an elderly neighbor asked her, "Was that your son I saw walking home alone the other day? He was walking so proud, like he was ten feet tall!"

➡ **Embrace the mistakes.** Trial and error is our best way to learn, so don't forget to embrace the error! When your kid comes up with a solution for a problem, let them try it out, if possible, even if you think it won't work, or won't work as well as your remedy. Your job is not to prevent the mistakes; it's to help your kid learn from mistakes.

➡ **Encourage your child to "phone a friend."** You may be your child's first stop for questions, but it's not ideal to be their only, or even first, resource. So, when it seems appropriate, encourage your child to ask their friends for help or advice. You want your child to develop a network of resources (and to hear other points of view) as they hone their own thinking. Just as you want to move from supervisor to consultant, you want them to build a whole network of consultants, especially smart and kind peers, separate from yourself.

> *"That problem with your friends at lunch sounds complicated. Can you talk to your cousin Ellie? She might have some good ideas for you."*

➡ **Remember Chutes and Ladders when you see your child struggling.** Kids tend not to be consistent when they change. It is often two steps forward, one step back. We think of it like a game of Chutes and Ladders. Sometimes there's a big developmental bump. Other times things go awry, and it feels like sliding backward a few steps. Don't freak out if your kid seems to be temporarily slipping; it's all part of growing up.

➡ **Be a good boss.** Try this thought exercise: Imagine your kid is your employee. Are you a micromanager, or do you trust your employee to do their job? Are you a harsh critic, or are you encouraging? Do you clearly communicate expectations, roles, responsibilities, and consequences? Would you want to work for you? It can be a helpful litmus test for parents to consider whether they would want to have their parental self as a boss, and if not, why?

➡ **Online academic tracking programs are a blessing and a curse.** Many schools give parents a day-to-day online view of their students' grades, homework, and assignments. These tools can be great for students who genuinely need help tracking and completing assignments, but they can also be obstacles to encouraging independence in kids.

Heather and the Mismatched Socks

When my youngest child, Henry, was a toddler, I gave him near-complete freedom to choose his outfits. While I was prepared for these outfits to be mismatched, I failed to anticipate that he would prefer his clothes to be inside out and backward. Literally. I tried to encourage him to "right side" things, but he was adamant that he liked it his way. I was stuck between two unsatisfactory choices: rescinding some of that newfound independence or sending him out into the world each day wearing clothes that were inside out and backward (and mismatched to boot). I chose the latter, which required me to endure many curious, often overtly judgmental, looks and comments from what felt like every single person we encountered for the several years that this trend lasted.

At the age of 8, having been charged with putting away his own laundry, he decided that matching socks was a waste of time and instead just threw all his socks into a drawer and randomly pulled two out each day. Of course, they were never the same—not even close. He delighted in the arbitrary combinations of color, length, and style, which were of course highly eye-catching (especially since he chose to wear shorts as often as possible).

Despite knowing better, I tried subtle forms of parental interference: I would move the dress socks to a different drawer, or I would "help" him sort his laundry and zero in on the socks to furtively match pairs, or I would encourage him to wear different colors of the same-length socks, hoping it looked a bit more intentional. He saw through all of it and became ever more determined to keep his socks as different as possible. Or at least that's how it felt to me as I quietly lived the power struggle.

The bottom line—again—was that my caring about how he looked was in direct conflict with his freedom to be independent. I finally came around when I heard him tell someone that it was his "signature style" and that he had calculated how much time he saved over the course of a year by not bothering to match his socks (5.5 hours!). The logic was undeniable, but the gut punch was realizing that he was comfortable in his own skin and proud of his way of doing things, and I was trying to undermine both for the sake of appearance. Honestly, I was ashamed that I had not seen it sooner.

6

BUILDING INDEPENDENCE

In our view, they should be used sparingly and with a goal to work yourself out of the monitor role—and always approach your child about their work with curiosity rather than frustration; it may well be that the tracking program is wrong.

➡ **Don't fish for your child; teach them how to fish.** Like a good mentor, recognize the importance of growing your child's problem-solving skills rather than just solving their problems.

➡ **Expect to be disappointed.** As kids grow into their unique selves, they will inevitably be different from us, and from our dreams for

Use the Independence Formula

Greater dependability = more freedom
Less dependability = less freedom

Freedoms and responsibilities should rise (and fall) together. Help your kids see that when they are dependable with their responsibilities, it allows you to more comfortably increase their freedom and independence. Thus, kids who (mostly) come home on time will be allowed to stay out later in the future.

Kids who are not behaving dependably should experience a temporary reduction in their freedoms. When this happens, give your kid other chances to be dependable and reward them with greater independence when they are. By pairing what they crave—freedom and independence—with responsibility, you help your kids develop the ability to govern themselves according to the rules of the wider world.

MAKE DENTIST APPOINTMENT
TAKE OUT THE TRASH
COME HOME ON TIME
WALK THE DOG
STAIRWAY TO FREEDOM

Whose Problem Is It?

It can be really hard to turn off the parent problem-solving brain and to make way for your child to take charge. When a specific challenge arises, one useful framework is to ask yourself who owns this particular problem. You might be surprised how rarely the answer is you!

Child Owns if: *natural consequences are tolerable*

Joint Ownership if: *child can take the lead but needs some support, coaching, practice, or other help.*

Parent Owns if: *natural consequences are too severe or safety concerns exist*

them, in ways small and potentially large. If we are prepared for this to happen, it can help us still support their independent growth even when we don't prefer it.

➜ **Transition "parent" from verb to noun.** As your child gets older, you should be reducing how much you are doing for them and increasing how much they are doing for themselves. See your role as shifting from director to audience, or from coach to fan. Move from parenting (verb) to being a parent (noun).

WRAPPING UP

Building independence can be hard in the moment, but the payoff is huge. It takes heart and effort to continuously assess our children's current capabilities and challenges. Remember, the road is often bumpy, with fits and starts. But keep aiming for a gradual transfer of knowledge and power as they grow. Parenting is about working yourself out of the job so that you can eventually enjoy the pleasure of seeing your child manage life's struggles, and thrive all on their own.

DEEPER DIVE

How to Raise an Adult: Break Free of the Overparenting Trap and Prepare Your Kid for Success by Julie Lythcott-Haims

This former Stanford Dean of Freshmen felt compelled to write her first parenting book when she observed with alarm how her Stanford students increasingly struggled to live independently. Yet as a mom, she found herself falling into the overparenting traps. Her 2015 book is a thoughtful, funny, empathetic look at modern parenting and how we can do better.

Middle School Matters: The 10 Key Skills Kids Need to Thrive in Middle School and Beyond—and How Parents Can Help by Phyllis L. Fagell

Middle school is a crucial developmental stage, an optimal time to help kids build character and key skills to thrive. Fagell, a professional counselor, offers an invaluable guide for parents of middle schoolers.

For Kids

All by Myself by Mercer Mayer

A sweet and timeless picture book for young kids celebrating independence.

Trusting the Spark

MOTIVATION

THE TAKEAWAY

✔ Every child has sparks of motivation in them. Our job is to nurture it and fuel the fire (which may mean accepting that what motivates your child might not be your first choice!).

✔ We want motivation to be intrinsic, not based on rewards (which can actually diminish intrinsic motivation).

✔ Motivation is fueled by three key ingredients: competence, connection, and autonomy. Parents can have positive—and negative—effects on their kid's motivation.

THE SETUP

Heather was working with the mom of a fifth grader who often failed to finish his homework, and when he did, it took him three hours instead of thirty minutes. His homework became a nightly game of tug-o-war. The more his mom pushed, the less inclined he was to work on it, and each night involved yelling and tears (for both mother and son!), followed by hard feelings on both sides. The mom became even more convinced that her involvement was crucial as their battle raged. She tried many ways to boost her son's motivation—reasoning, begging, guilt-tripping, and bribing. Nothing helped.

Then this mom deliberately changed her approach. She reached out to the teacher for help and they worked together on a plan where the teacher took the lead. She then told her son she was feeling too responsible for his work, and she was going to let him figure it out with his teacher. While he still struggled with managing his work, he stopped struggling so much with his mom. In the end, he asked to set up a schedule where he did his homework while his mom cleaned up dinner, and then they would watch a favorite TV show together.

WHY IS THIS ESSENTIAL?

Helping our kids learn how to motivate themselves is an important parenting job, with long-term repercussions, and can be extraordinarily

7

MOTIVATION

hard to do. Motivation is easily misunderstood, and so many popular notions about how to motivate kids are ineffective. We see many struggles in families resulting from motivation mismatches. Our goal as parents should be to protect and build upon our kids' natural intrinsic motivation—to nurture its spark so that the fire can grow, without inadvertently extinguishing the flames. Our kids need us to create the conditions for self-motivation—and to avoid the temptation of trying to bribe or coerce them with external rewards and punishments. It's well worth the effort: Intrinsic self-motivation is a renewable resource our kids will carry with them for the rest of their lives.

Warning: This chapter isn't designed to help you motivate your child to do what you believe will be best for them. It's designed to help you support and grow your child's self-motivation toward activities, goals, and values that are meaningful to them. In the end, truly motivated kids become who they really are, not who their parents want them to be. And this makes for purposeful, engaged, and generative young adults who thrive and are interesting to be around.

CURIOUS ABOUT THE SCIENCE?

Dopamine is one of the brain chemicals at the neuroscience core of intrinsic motivation. We receive blasts of dopamine, the feel-good neurotransmitter, when we experience pleasure. Whether we are having a cupcake, winning a game, or acing a test, dopamine gives the brain's reward center a big *YES*. But dopamine does not just passively arrive with pleasure—it also makes us go after it. Science is beginning to revise its understanding of dopamine; it may be that this neurochemical is not only about experiencing pleasure but also about giving us the motivation to seek out pleasure and reward. "Low levels of dopamine make people and other animals less likely to work for things, so [dopamine] has more to do with motivation and cost/benefit analyses than pleasure itself," explains dopamine expert Dr. John Salamone.

Vanderbilt researchers found differences in dopamine levels among individuals throughout the motivation spectrum. They used brain imaging to compare individuals seemingly driven to work hard to those generally preferring to take it easy. We call them go-getters and sackers, in humble agreement that even among the three of us authors, we have at least one of each. The go-getters' group had higher levels of dopamine in brain areas related to motivation, including that brain boss, the PFC. In contrast, the slackers' group had dopamine releases in a different part of the brain, the anterior insula, which is related to emotion and risk perception.

So how do we get more dopamine to the parts of the brain where it will do the most good? Many motivation professionals rely on

PRO TIP

The Power of Mindsets

Carol Dweck's groundbreaking research on mindsets has revolutionized how we think about potential across many domains, including intelligence and talent. Many parents are familiar with the general concepts of the growth mindset (the belief that your capacity to do something can grow through effort) and the fixed mindset (believing that your capacity to do something is innate and unchangeable). One reason we focus heavily on encouraging parents to pay attention to both their child's and their own internal dialogue is because it is through how we talk to ourselves that mindsets can be changed, and there is very good reason to foster growth mindsets.

Dweck's research illuminates how mindsets can affect motivation and resilience. Under a growth mindset, mistakes are seen as opportunities to learn and improve, which leads to increased motivation and effort. Under a fixed mindset, mistakes can feel shameful, indicate lack of ability, which leads to decreased motivation and effort. The effects of mindsets are profound. Whether or not we believe we can improve from mistakes affects our attention and brain power, which affect our subsequent behavior. In other words, *believing* you can improve leads to improvement. So follow Dr. Dweck's excellent advice: Focus on the process of learning, and praise effort over achievement.

What Keeps Us From Changing?

Heather worked with one dad who was very self-aware in describing how his own parents' reliance on "tough love" and strict focus on work ethic had become deeply ingrained in him. Those lessons he'd absorbed in his childhood propelled him to coax and badger his own daughter to work harder and get better grades, unsuccessfully and worse, at great expense to their relationship. Though he saw the distress his approach caused, he was finding it really difficult to change. This dad was able to honestly admit he felt better when he nagged his child. It gave him an outlet to vent his own frustration and fears and made him feel like he was doing something. Only when he recognized that it was about him more than his daughter was he able to begin to try a different way.

Edward Deci and Richard Ryan's landmark self-determination theory, which they laid out in 1985, but others have confirmed decade after decade, to explain the complex relationship between our motivation, personality, and functioning. Deci and Ryan identified three innate, universal needs that make people intrinsically motivated: feeling competent, feeling autonomous, and feeling connected to others. In this internally motivated state, people take actions that are driven by their goals. They feel control over these actions and responsible for their outcome.

We also know something that gets in the way of intrinsic motivation: rewards. Hundreds of studies have demonstrated that when children are rewarded for doing a task they find inherently enjoyable, they tend to lose interest in doing the task for enjoyment's sake. When external rewards crowd out internal motivation, psychologists call this the "overjustification effect." It seems the result of providing a reward for kids doing things they naturally enjoy has the paradoxical effect of turning play into work.

Edward Deci first showed this happening in an experiment with college students working on a puzzle. Researchers told half the students they would be paid for participation, and then observed what all the participants did when given extra time. The "volunteer" students worked on the puzzle for longer than the "paid" students, supporting the idea that giving an extrinsic reward reduced students' intrinsic motivation.

It's true for younger children as well. Another landmark study with young children by Mark Lepper, David Greene, and Richard

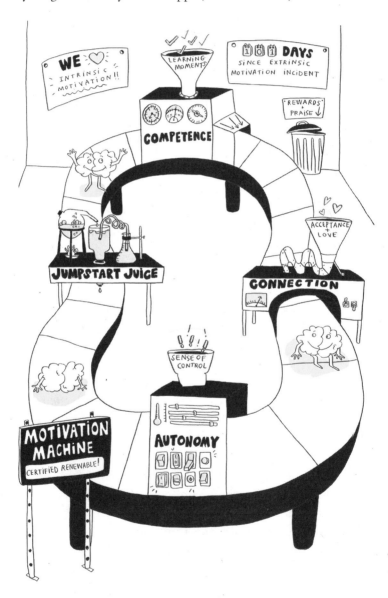

Nisbett in 1973 involved a drawing task with children who already loved to draw. One group of kids was told they would receive a reward for drawing, another was surprised after the fact with a reward, and a third group didn't get a reward at all. The kids were then observed to see how much drawing they spontaneously engaged in over the next

Be Careful with Rewards and Punishments

It's no wonder parents are confused about how to help motivate their kids! This is an area where it's best not to rely on popular wisdom, as much of it is ill-founded. Here are some pointers regarding rewards and punishments:

* A reward creates a new short-term behavior, not a long-term internal change.

* A reward loses potency over time as kids get used to it. Eventually kids will require an increased or different reward just to maintain an extrinsically rewarded behavior.

* Rewards are best for learning new skills that have no intrinsic motivation (aka toilet training). When using rewards, be sure to have an exit strategy!

* Natural consequences are your friend—they show kids how the world works (cause and effect). Do not impose your own unrelated punitive consequences when natural consequences are enough.

* Avoid giving punishments after the fact with no advance warning. Instead, lay out consequences ahead of time, which can be motivating for learning and changing behavior.

* When possible, outsource the consequence-imposing "bad guys" to other people (aka teachers or coaches) or inanimate objects (timers or printouts of the House Rules). Kids are better able to receive consequences when they're not wrapped up in their relationship with their parents.

* Motivation is not additive; you don't get more by adding extrinsic rewards to intrinsic motivation. Instead, extrinsic rewards cancel out intrinsic motivation.

few days. The kids who had expected and received a reward actually drew less compared to the other groups. Perhaps even worse, their drawings were rated by judges as being less aesthetically pleasing. The expectation of a reward appeared to have a detrimental effect on both the quantity and quality of drawing. The takeaway: Parents should be wary of using rewards when even a seed of internal motivation already exists in their child.

Intrinsic motivation is a precious resource that can be nurtured, perhaps even increased, but not usually through direct or heavy-handed ways. Instead, the research suggests focusing on supporting the ingredients of internal motivation: competence, autonomy, and connection with others.

Getting Started: Jump-Start Juice

Intrinsic motivation is a powerful force, especially once the motivation machine gets going. But what turns on the machine? It turns out that no matter how motivated we may be to engage in a task, we cannot always depend on that same motivation to get us started. Sometimes intrinsic motivation needs a jump-start!

Even when motivated, many of us cannot wait around until we are "in the mood" to start working on what we care about. Moods are fickle and can often be a mix of positive and negative (I might truly want to work on this chapter and enjoy it once I get going, but I still don't feel like sitting down at my desk). And feelings such as fear—of failure, of the idea that we should be doing something else,

How Do They Do It?

How do people with what appears to be amazing self-discipline do it? Turns out, they don't, exactly. Research has shown that seemingly self-disciplined people simply avoid putting themselves into situations where they are required to use any self-regulation in the first place. Those who are best at exerting self-control are actually best at setting up situations in which they do not need to exercise self-control. Rather, they know how to prevent their own access to temptation.

of not being the "best" at something—can sabotage the discipline we need to get our motivation machine started. There are no perfect conditions and no perfect moods.

So, for some of us, even when we have the powers of competence, autonomy, and connection that build our intrinsic motivation, we still have trouble getting started. We find that we have to rely on self-discipline to get us going—and when we lack structures and routines to support that effort to initiate, we can drain our willpower.

Developing our own internal structures, rituals, and routines will help jump-start our motivation. These systems, when used regularly, become habits, and habits bypass the need for continual willpower and discipline over how we spend our time. The more systems and routines we set up, the fewer last-minute decisions (re: willpower) we have to produce. Habits can short-circuit our need to "feel" ready. If we can use habits to get us started, even before we feel like it, the intrinsic motivation that's already inside can awaken and bring us the dopamine we need to keep going.

These routines only work when set up ahead of time and then intentionally practiced until they become habits. Systems to jump-start intrinsic motivation should include at least some of the following:

➜ A predetermined time

➜ A predetermined place

➜ An almost painfully detailed set of steps, ideally written down

➜ An extremely easy first step that is mindless, pleasant, even a bit goofy

➜ Physical movement of some kind. For example, think of the difference between walking through the kitchen and considering doing the dishes versus lying on the couch and considering doing the dishes.

➜ Creating a pattern from the elements above, in an almost robotic sequence, repeating it until it is a habit.

Everyone knows how dreadful some chores can feel at first, but once automatized, they can feel neutral or even pleasant. Think of when you were a little kid, and brushing your teeth felt so exhausting and you would avoid it and put it off. But now, it's a habit so deeply ingrained that the brain takes over. You just stand there at the sink and take the cap off the toothpaste, get your toothbrush, and begin.

WHAT DOES MOTIVATION LOOK LIKE IN YOUR FAMILY?

Take a Look at Your Child

Family relationships: Does your child rely on your engagement and energy when they aren't feeling motivated? Do you have to constantly prod your kid to get started on homework or chores? Do you find yourself begging, bribing, lecturing, threatening, or criticizing in an effort to get your kid to do their work? Does it feel like your involvement, even nagging, is actually getting in the way of your relationship, or of even liking each other?

Friendships: Does your child constantly compare themselves to their friends in terms of accomplishments, rather than being driven by their own interests? Does your child appear motivated to pursue friendships and peer engagement? Do they have friends who also have passions or interests, and appear to have some motivation themselves?

Learning: In what areas is your child already motivated? Does your child feel equally unmotivated in every subject, or do some school subjects seem to spark some interest? Do they get excited about learning (at least some) new things, in school or outside of school? Do they sometimes delve a little deeper or get a little curious about learning more? Do they have hobbies or outside interests that they choose to pursue?

Sense of self: Is your kid able to initiate action toward their goals? Does your child request or demand rewards for doing things? Does your child seem to feel satisfied or proud of themselves when completing a task? To what degree does your child choose what they do and how or when they do it?

CONCERN-O-METER

Pick a color for each category. Draw a colored arrow for each to give yourself a visual picture of your child in this moment.

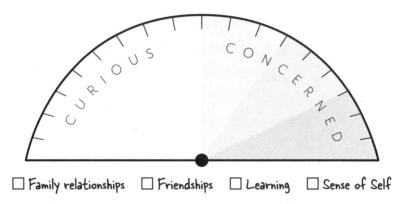

☐ Family relationships   ☐ Friendships   ☐ Learning   ☐ Sense of Self

Take a Look at Yourself

✻ *Do you expect more of your child's motivation than you do of your own? Do you allow your child to feel unmotivated sometimes?*
Most parents have figured out hacks for the times when our own motivation may be hard to tap into. And adults tend to have more motivating responsibilities and freedom of choice than a child. We understand in ourselves the way motivation waxes and wanes, yet we often become concerned when our child appears unmotivated. And keep in mind, school demands a specific kind of motivation to study and be tested on a wide array of subjects that's rarely required elsewhere.

✻ *Are you trying too hard to control your child with praise?*
Remember, the way we communicate has a big effect. Praise can have an element of control. It can limit children's ability to self-evaluate and feel autonomy. It can also damage your trustworthiness as an evaluator. Some children react negatively to excessive praise due to this subtle control element.

✻ *Do you try to create motivation in your kid?*
Do you rely on rewards and punishments to change your child's behavior? Do you have the flexibility of mind to see that what motivates your child might be different from what motivates you?

Do you take the time to approach your child with curiosity and have the room to be surprised by what they say?

Posing open-ended questions—and listening actively—shows your genuine interest in what your child thinks. It supports their autonomy and stimulates a collaborative problem-solving process between you and your child. Together, you and your child can generate solutions to their problems, and their participation increases their intrinsic motivation.

Is your ego wrapped up in your kid's performance?

Do you feel like your child's successes or mistakes reflect upon you as a parent? Consider whether this inclines you to respond in ways that may undermine their intrinsic motivation.

What is your personal threshold for your child's mistakes?

Do you find it difficult to tolerate their inevitable shortcomings? Examine what this says about your own insecurities (we all have them) and your personal need for perfection. To develop their continual intrinsic motivation, our children need our unconditional love and acceptance more than our rigid behavioral standards to achieve. All parents are influenced by their own upbringing, though we sometimes struggle to recognize it.

HOW DO YOU THINK YOU TREND?

(target zone)

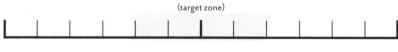

The Judge	The Facilitator	The Cheerleader
Criticism; frustration; threats; punishment; guilt trips; power struggles	Open-ended questions; curiosity; lack of agenda; trust	Rewards; bribes; overuse of praise; cajoling; guilt trips; power struggles
	What are you into these days? What was	
You don't seem to care about anything. Why are you are so lazy? Where is your passion?	*fun about your day? What was hard about your day?*	*If you practice every day, you'll earn a prize! You want to do this; you just don't know it. I think you will love this!*

PLAYS FOR YOUR PLAYBOOK

If you want to work on supporting your child's own natural motivation, try out some of the tips below. See if you notice any shifts in your child's functioning (or your own). And as always, remember that sometimes the techniques that don't appeal to you are exactly the ones that you might end up finding the most helpful.

➡ **Don't confuse motivation with self-control.** Being motivated is one thing; finding the willpower to start and sustain hard tasks is another. Building the self-discipline to ignite and sustain work that your child is already motivated for is a different skill, one of managing impulses and self-control. Read about Essential #2 (page 61) to learn how to help a motivated child put that motivation into action. Motivation is the spark, while self-control is the tool to fan the spark into a flame and keep it burning.

➡ **Be a motivation seed spotter.** Catch your child being motivated in little ways or by things you may not be able to relate to. Nurture and highlight the motivation itself; don't focus on the current source of the passion. Intrinsic motivation to get a high score on a video game is the exact same intrinsic motivation needed to study for a test. Notice what your kid is already doing instead of what they aren't, even if they aren't always doing it reliably.

> *"Oh my gosh, you spent the last hour working on your Minecraft village! How did you stay so focused and motivated? Show me what you did! Walk me through how you decided on building a moat here instead of your usual waterfall."*

➡ **Be a competence seed spotter, too.** Highlight what your child is capable of and good at, not what they are struggling with. This is not praise but observation and description. Sometimes kids benefit from us repeatedly noticing what they are doing well, especially when they are feeling low. Hold up the mirror, and don't worry about being redundant so long as you are sincere and authentic.

> *"Look at this photograph! I can see how carefully you chose your angle so that the tree branches framed the shot."*

➡ **Offer new opportunities for your kid to gain competence.** When kids feel a new bit of competence, it gives them confidence, setting off a powerful chain reaction to increased self-esteem. Parents can't praise their kids into feeling better about themselves, but they can give their kid lots of opportunities to learn new skills and then recognize their growth.

➡ **Good communication nurtures connection, competence, and autonomy.** Ask your kid what they think about their daily life and the world around them. Give them some say in what happens to them. These communication-based connections build competence and autonomy, pulling together the three building blocks of intrinsic motivation.

Parent Trap: Praise

Praise can be tricky. Sometimes it implies an element of control that many kids are sensitive to and reject; the subtext can read, "You please me when you . . ." But not all praise is problematic. The goal should be providing information, not motivation. Praise as information uses feedback to hold up the mirror so kids can see themselves in a new way. This kind of feedback can be very motivating, and it's more self-driven, which is the goal. To use praise effectively, follow these principles:

✔ **DO** describe what you see: "I noticed you hung your coat up when you came inside."

✔ **DO** appreciate when you can: "Thanks for putting away the groceries. I really appreciated the break."

✔ **DO** orient the praise toward self-evaluation: "What a shot! You must have felt so proud of yourself."

✔ **DO** ask your kid to consider praising themselves: "I saw your painting right in the school display case today. Wow. How did you feel when you saw it there?"

✘ **DON'T** use generalizations: "You are always so helpful."

✘ **DON'T** evaluate your kid through praise: "You did a great job putting away the groceries!"

✘ **DON'T** create "praise junkies." Too much praise can be demotivating. Don't feel the need to praise your kid for everything they do every time they do it.

➡ Opt for an authoritative parenting style. Research shows combining high responsiveness with high demands is a powerful parenting approach. Find the middle path between being too strict and too permissive. Provide some structure and guidance while also being responsive to your unique child's wants and needs. Give your kids freedom, but within limits.

➡ Use the fresh start effect with your kids. Researchers have found that people are better at making changes when they tie them to a special occasion or key date, like the start of a new school year or semester, a birthday, a holiday like New Year's, or other significant event.

➡ Stay current on your kid. Kids keep changing, and they need to be seen for who they are right now. Nurture your connection. Show curiosity about what your child thinks and observe them to see what they seem to most enjoy doing.

"What do you think about chess club? Do you still enjoy it? Do you want to sign up for it again this semester?"

➡ Channel your inner Jeopardy contestant. When you have ideas for your kids, phrase them in the form of a question rather than telling them in a declarative statement. Kids need the opportunity to consider suggestions and decide for themselves whether to follow them in order to feel autonomy. And take their answers seriously; they often intuitively know better than you what might work well for them.

"How do you think your teacher would respond if you asked for extra time on that assignment?"

➡ Let natural consequences do their job. Natural consequences are a parent's best friend. Empathize with your child's disappointment or frustration when tough consequences happen, but don't intervene to prevent the consequences. Kids are experiential learners, so be sure to allow them the experience of messing up and/or the natural harshness of the real world.

"Gosh, it must have been tough to be benched for the whole first half. It's a rough punishment for being late to practice last week." (Loving shrug.)

Too Much Information

Georgia's mother, who was deployed overseas, registered to use the parent view of the online academic tracker for Georgia's new middle school so she could be more involved while she was away. She would check the tracker every few days, but often when she looked, she would see that Georgia had a D or F in one class, or another. So her evening calls with her daughter became dominated by her questions, worries, and frustrations. Georgia always had an explanation for a poor grade: They didn't complete a test because of a fire drill; the teacher posted the quiz but hadn't graded it yet so the system gave her a zero. It all seemed kind of fishy—how could that many things go wrong? But over time, her mom discovered that Georgia's grades would eventually pop back up to her usual A or B, just as Georgia said they would. The grade tracker was stressing them both out, so her mom stopped using the app and followed her school progress the old-fashioned way: by letting Georgia work things out with her teachers and seeing her grades at the end of each quarter.

→ **But don't pile on.** When kids are suffering from natural consequences of their own making, this is a perfect opportunity for you to be a (mildly!) sympathetic ear, rather than another voice of disappointment or added punishment.

→ **Longing can be good.** Let your kid work for and wait for the things and events they desire. You don't get the same emotional payoff from something that comes quickly and easily as you do from something you wait for and work for. The feeling of satisfaction from finally getting something you've been waiting for is the payoff for delaying gratification. If we do too good a job of providing for their every need and desire, our kids can miss out on that sense of longing that naturally rewards patience and hard work.

→ **Give meaningful choices.** For a choice to be motivating enough to spur action, a kid needs to care about the decision at hand. Children

Don't Get Trapped in a Dad- or Mom-ologue

We often want our kids to understand our reasoning, but many kids tune us out when we explain, defend, suggest, nag, or advise too much. Make sure you are having a dialogue, not a monologue. In important, logistical, or limit-setting conversations, keep your talking short and to the point, and don't forget to actually listen to your child's point of view!

are not fooled by nonmeaningful choices like "Do you want the big fork or the little fork?" Instead, provide choices that matter to them: "Do you want to empty the litter box before or after the swim meet?"

➔ **Don't offer freedom you don't intend to grant.** Encouraging autonomy, a driver of intrinsic motivation, doesn't just mean asking kids questions and giving choices; it means truly listening to their responses and making changes as needed. If you give your child a chance to say no to something and they take it, don't then try to change their mind.

➔ **Reduce options.** Too much of a good thing is no longer a good thing. Don't give more choices than your child can comfortably manage. Limits provide a sense of security for kids. Kids who crave autonomy fight for more freedom than they actually can handle, and parents need to judge how much is enough. Transfer power and autonomy gradually.

➔ **Walk away from power struggles.** Kids' need for autonomy propels them toward power struggles. It's a natural response to craving more power than they have, not an intentional act of disobedience or disrespect. Power struggles are unwinnable for parents. Just getting a reaction from a parent can encourage a kid to keep up the fight. Our best option is to disengage from power struggles in order to end them.

➔ **Recognize how little autonomy kids often have.** We parents can sometimes focus on all the freedoms kids have: no stress of having a full-time job or worry about paying bills, lots of downtime to do

How to Set Effective Limits

When kids don't follow the rules, parents often blame their lack of motivation. But sometimes the problem is the rules, not the kid. Effective (and motivating) limits have three characteristics:

1. **Rules are CLEAR.** A limit should be a clear behavioral expectation that is understood in the same way by both you and your child. If there are any loopholes, kids will find them! When you first set a limit, ask your child to explain what it means back to you so you can spot the gray areas and clarify.

   "You may stay at the playground without me while I run to the pharmacy. But you may not go beyond the playground fence and you may not speak to any adults you don't already know. Can you explain the rules to me so I know we both agree?"

2. **Consequences are KNOWN IN ADVANCE.** Kids need to know what the results of their choices will be up front if these consequences are going to be motivating factors in their decision-making.

3. **Parents are CONSISTENT.** Parents need to dependably:
   * Remember the limits they set
   * Follow through with any planned consequences

   A limit is a promise from you to your child, so make sure you stay trustworthy! Parents don't have to be 100 percent consistent, but we should own up to those times when we forget or don't plan to hold the limit. Each parent may have somewhat different limits, and that's fine; kids are pros at naturally adjusting to different expectations.

BONUS TIPS

* **Explain.** Give a short version of the "why" behind your limits.

* **Collaborate.** What do your kids think the limit should be for someone their age? What do they think is a good consequence if a limit is broken? You would be surprised how strict kids can be when asked.

* **Post.** Write down and post your agreements. When a kid breaks the agreements, you can simply point to those posted rules.

* **Treat it as a living document, not a one-and-done.** Limits must change over time as children grow and develop.

whatever they want, fun sports and activities to participate in, and plenty of socializing opportunities. With our adult lens, we romanticize childhood as a carefree time. Yet kids have little control over much of their day-to-day lives, and they lack the life perspective to appreciate the freedoms they have. Treating them as ungrateful for how good they have it is harmful to connection and motivation.

➜ **Create some novelty.** Kids' brains respond to novelty with a little hit of dopamine, which increases motivation. Kids who are caught in a rut of sameness can become demotivated. Shake up some routines or tasks for which your kid seems particularly unmotivated. For example, consider having a family draft for chores or put the chores into a hat and let your child draw some out each week.

➜ **Consider giving in on struggles that are not mission critical.** If you value a certain task or achievement but your kid doesn't, is it worth the cost to your relationship to fight with them about it? Accepting your child's point of view even while disagreeing with it helps build their feeling of autonomy and competence, which are natural motivation drivers.

➜ **Teach your kid to consider their Future Self.** Instant gratification rewards are intrinsically motivating because we get a little happy hit of dopamine when we do them (ice cream tastes good!). But our brains don't have a chemical reward for delayed gratification tasks (studying doesn't usually feel good while you're doing it). It can help to teach kids to talk to their Future Self to bring the future reward into focus.

> *"I know you would rather take a nap than research that term paper right now, but think how grateful Future Dahlia will be the rest of this weekend."*
>
> *"I know you really want to play on the iPad, but you also have to feed the cat. Future Alex will be relieved to have that job off his chore list—and so will his cat!"*

➜ **Describe times when you have felt unmotivated.** Kids need to know that motivation can be hard for everyone at times and that motivation does not magically happen. Show them ways you have adjusted your expectations and been compassionate and flexible with yourself.

Catherine and the Outfield Toad

"Practice what you preach." This phrase guiltily repeated over and over in my head when my son Tommy was young as I worked to get him interested in sports. Of course I wanted my son to be internally motivated, but secretly I wanted him to be motivated to do the things *I* love.

One thing I had dreamed of as a parent was attending his Little League games, so I signed him up as soon as he was old enough. But despite my wildest cheerleading, he simply had no interest in the game.

His happiest game was when he unearthed a little toad while digging in the outfield, and for a while he looked forward to practice with great delight, hoping to see the little amphibian again.

We tried every sport. I'm sure I even tried some bribes, despite knowing—as a professional—that bribes often decrease motivation. I'm not proud of how I pushed him, and certainly not proud of the internal loss I was experiencing. When he was about 10, he finally refused to play any more sports and the vision of my son playing sports in high school faded away.

It was about that same time that Tommy had a field trip to the National Zoo in Washington, DC. He was captivated, mesmerized by the frog aquarium tanks, and suddenly my dreamy son got focused. He comfortably engaged the zoo "frog man" for over an hour, learning all about the serious risks to endangered frogs. He raced to his room when we returned home and made a paper flyer to raise awareness at his school. He also mailed his flyer to the frog man at the zoo.

He soon received a return letter. Little did we know, the frog man was one of the world's leading experts on amphibians and renowned for his groundbreaking research regarding their risk of extinction and climate change. As Tommy grew up, this expert became his mentor. Long story short, my son never gave up his disdain for baseball or his passion for frogs. And his internal motivation has continued to grow, driving him to pursue his interests in the natural sciences in college and beyond.

Share with them times when you had to accept your own naturally waxing and waning motivation.

"I really don't feel like going for a run right now, but I know if I do it, I'll be glad I did. So here I go."

"I hate to sort the laundry, but it has to get done. So, I guess it's better to do it now than have it hanging over my head. I know I'll be relieved and glad that I did it an hour from now."

➜ **Teach your kid that action can inspire motivation.** Like the Nike slogan, sometimes the best way to get motivated is to Just Do It. Waiting for motivation to come can be a dead end for tasks that aren't intrinsically motivating. Our thoughts, feelings, and behaviors are interconnected—if we change our behavior, our feelings can follow. Help your child learn that sometimes you need to start doing something in order to feel like doing it.

➜ **Help your kid find their flow.** Psychologists have identified a state of energized focus, or "flow," in which the activity is so engaging that you lose all sense of time. You're "in the zone." Activities that produce flow are highly enjoyable and intrinsically motivating. They are not the screen-time "junk food" that manipulates our dopamine response but rather the low-tech activities that create intrinsic satisfaction. Look for times when your child is deeply engrossed in an activity and (later!) talk to them about that satisfying feeling of immersion. Encourage your child to find their flow activities.

WRAPPING UP

Motivation is a complex and often misunderstood topic that can be affected by many parenting choices, including expectations, praise, rewards, and consequences. Parents need to remember that no human can or should be motivated by everything all of the time. Intrinsic motivation can be boiled down to three surprising and perhaps counterintuitive key ingredients: competence, connection, and autonomy. Parents can influence intrinsic motivation by wisely contributing to these three ingredients, allowing kids to adjust the dials of their own motivation machines.

7

MOTIVATION

DEEPER DIVE

The Self-Driven Child: The Science and Sense of Giving Your Kids More Control Over Their Lives and *What Do You Say? How to Talk with Kids to Build Motivation, Stress Tolerance, and a Happy Home* by William Stixrud, PhD, and Ned Johnson

> Our close friends and colleagues Dr. William Stixrud and Ned Johnson have written two outstanding books about how parents can nurture intrinsic motivation in their kids.

Mindset: The New Psychology of Success by Carol S. Dweck, PhD

> To learn more about the power of mindsets, we encourage parents to check out Dr. Dweck's excellent book.

The Price of Privilege: How Parental Pressure and Material Advantage Are Creating a Generation of Disconnected and Unhappy Kids by Madeline Levine, PhD

> Madeline Levine's 2006 book was a wake-up call to many parents with the drive (and financial means) to pay for their children's activities. Her book is intended to help parents living in the "rat race" be informed and intentional about raising psychologically healthy kids.

For Kids

Your Fantastic Elastic Brain: A Growth Mindset Book for Kids to Stretch and Shape Their Brains by JoAnn Deak, PhD

> An excellent book about growth mindset and motivation.

The Girl Who Never Made Mistakes: A Growth Mindset Book for Kids to Promote Self-Esteem by Mark Pett

> A great book for tackling perfectionism in kids.

For Older Teens

Where You Go Is Not Who You'll Be: An Antidote to the College Admissions Mania by Frank Bruni

> We love recommending this book to older teens (and their parents). With real data, it breaks down the myth that success can happen only if you get into certain colleges. Instead, Mr. Bruni shows how students can make the most of a college education at any school, and how to develop passions, interests, knowledge, and skills no matter what the name of the institution.

Being Human

COMPASSION AND GRATITUDE

THE TAKEAWAY

✔ The skills of compassion and gratitude are hugely important for overall well-being, and are linked to increased happiness, better health, and greater life satisfaction in all people.

✔ A conscious development of gratitude leads us to look outside ourselves and toward others, which grows compassion and social connection.

✔ Compassion and gratitude can increase our sense of well-being and contentment, which can replace our impossible desire for a constantly happy life.

THE SETUP

Twelve-year-old Spencer, who identified as nonbinary, had always been a bit shy. But since middle school, they had also become highly irritable and withdrawn from their friends. Jennifer recommended group psychotherapy, but also that Spencer add a volunteer activity to their schedule. Based on Spencer's interest in animals (they already had a hamster and a fish), their parents helped them engage with an animal rescue program. Soon, Spencer was fostering some kittens who had been separated from their mother—and started inviting friends over to visit with the animals. Their mother overheard a friend ask Spencer why they hadn't hung out as much, and Spencer replied, "I'm sorry. I guess I used to feel really mad about stuff and didn't want to be around anyone. But when I see these kittens don't even have a mother, I realize I'm actually really lucky, and I don't know . . . I just don't feel so mad anymore."

WHY IS THIS ESSENTIAL?

Evolutionarily, we are not wired to be balanced, happy, or satisfied—we are wired to be scared. Recall from Essential #4 (the one about anxiety) that the content lizard is not our ancestor—she was likely eaten eons ago. Her worried lizard cousin may not have been happy, but he stayed alive to pass on his genes to us. This makes our worried thoughts sticky in the brain, while happier, more balanced, bigger-perspective thoughts can slide right off like Teflon. But we can evolve beyond our instincts.

The skills and mindset of compassion and gratitude are hugely important for overall well-being. These traits have been linked to increased happiness, better physical health, and greater life satisfaction in kids and adults. We can all become more grateful and compassionate, more appreciative of our blessings and less focused on our disappointments, and kinder in how we think and act toward ourselves and others starting at the earliest ages. By prioritizing and encouraging gratitude and compassion, we can put into practice concrete and effective ways to help our kids, as well as focus on our broader family values.

Like mindfulness and meditation, gratitude is a dual practice of attention and intention, of consciously noticing, then choosing to shift the mind away from thoughts that are worried and thus evolutionarily sticky ("What if I'm not included?"; "Maybe I failed that quiz."; "Is my mommy okay?") to thoughts that highlight contentment ("I'm lucky to be invited to this picnic."; "I'm thankful my friend was waiting for me when I missed the bus."). In gratitude, as with mindfulness, we "turn the mind." And a gratitude practice, much like a meditation practice, helps train the mind to stay a bit longer on these less sticky but more balanced thoughts. Thus gratitude, like mindfulness, takes up time and space that might overwise be occupied by worries.

A conscious development of gratitude also leads us to look outside ourselves and toward others—a necessary condition for compassion. We are evolutionarily wired for compassion, and it is one of the traits that can keep us well liked, well fed, and more likely to spread our DNA. Practicing gratitude, turning the mind toward others, can lead us to feel more compassion for others. And compassion is a value that, when lived, brings deep fulfillment and social connection, increases oxytocin (that feel-good chemical), helps us make social connections, and binds us more closely to others who may love and care for us.

Mindfulness is about turning inward. It can calm our feelings, but it also may separate us. A gratitude practice or loving-kindness meditation, with the accompanying increase in compassion for others, knits us back together socially and emotionally.

Compassion is Empathy Plus, a practice that improves the life of not only individuals but also families, communities, and our world. Nobody says it better than the Greater Good Science Center: "Compassion is not the same as empathy or altruism, though the concepts are related. While empathy refers more generally to the ability to take the perspective of and feel the emotions of another person, compassion is when those feelings and thoughts include the desire to help."

CURIOUS ABOUT THE SCIENCE?

What Science Says About Compassion

What is the use of compassion and how has it helped our species evolutionarily? Compassion is the emotional response that arises when we are confronted with suffering (another's or our own) and the desire we feel to help relieve that suffering. Dr. Dacher Keltner, founding director of the Greater Good Science Center at the University of California at Berkeley, is an expert on the science of compassion. His research has helped show how the human "compassionate instinct" has ensured our survival as a species.

Physical pain activates a part of our brain called the anterior cingulate. That same brain region lights up when we see somebody else's suffering. In Dr. Keltner's words, "We have the same pain response to other people's pain as we do to our own experience of pain. We are wired to empathize." He also directs our attention to an ancient part of the mammal brain related to nurturing behavior, the periaqueductal gray, which also lights up when we feel compassion—a sign that we have the instinct to relieve suffering by nurturing. The vagus nerve—our nervous system's longest wandering nerve, which stretches from the brain to the abdomen—also shows activity when we feel compassion. The stronger our compassion, the stronger our vagal response. Research by Keltner and others suggests that we are evolutionarily wired to care about other people and that compassion may have ensured our survival because of its massive benefits to our species as a whole.

The science indicates that compassion makes us more resilient to the effects of stress, strengthens our immune response, and even may improve longevity. It also increases our social connection to others. Dr. Martin Seligman, an expert on the psychology of happiness, has shown how meaningful social connection improves both our mental health as well as recovery from disease. Cultivating compassion has been shown to increase daily positive emotions, reduce depressive symptoms, decrease the amygdala response, improve emotional regulation, and increase life satisfaction. Social scientists James Fowler of the University of California at San Diego and Nicholas Christakis of Harvard have shown that kindness behavior spreads from person to person to person. When people benefit from kindness, they "pay it forward" by helping others, creating a cascade of kindness and trickle-down effect in a social network. To put it simply, compassion is contagious.

What Science Says About Gratitude

There's empirical support for the idea of a "set point" to happiness, meaning that we each tend to have a default level of happiness that is determined by a combination of temperament, mood, and emotions, and not by life circumstances. For example, in the spectrum of completely life-changing experiences, studies have shown that people who have had life-altering lottery wins, after an initial bump in euphoria, reported no more baseline happiness that those who have had life-altering spinal cord injuries.

The Happiness Trap

We encourage you to view happiness as a transient state of mind, not a goal. None of us is entitled to be happy. As the Buddha says, life is suffering. If we can accept suffering as an expected and natural part of life, it helps us feel grateful for what we do have and compassionate toward ourselves and others as we suffer. Through compassion and gratitude, a sense of well-being and contentment can grow, replacing our (impossible) desire for a constantly happy life.

How can we better manage our expectations of happiness so that we might be able to experience more of that transient but delightful feeling no matter our circumstances? One key is gratitude, which is a way of maintaining perspective and not getting stuck at our current set point. Gratitude has been shown to be an effective method for increasing well-being and contentment, both day-to-day and by nudging our set point for happiness upward.

Many studies have shown the benefits of gratitude for kids of all ages. Research has linked gratitude to happiness in children by as early as age 5. A study of middle school children, from ages 11 through 13, showed that children who expressed gratitude were more optimistic, had better social support, and were overall happier. These more grateful kids wanted to give more social support to others as well. And an adolescent study (ages 14 to 19) showed that grateful teens were more satisfied with their lives, more likely to want to improve their communities, and overall more engaged with and successful in their schoolwork. They were also found to be less envious, less emotionally down, and less materialistic.

Studies of adults and gratitude have found similar effects. Gratitude has even been linked to better physical health in adults. Several studies have found that people who feel more gratitude also experience better sleep, less fatigue, and lower levels of cellular inflammation. In one study of heart failure patients, participants who kept a gratitude journal for eight weeks had reduced signs of inflammation afterward, giving evidence of the direct effect of gratitude on health.

We hear from parents who are worried that their children are not particularly grateful, and research backs that up. A national poll conducted in 2021 asked parents of kids aged 4 to 10 if their kids are "grateful for what they have." Eighty-one percent of parents worried that they were not, and almost half also described feeling embarrassed by their children's selfish or entitled actions.

What if your kid does not appear to be wired as particularly grateful? One study found that writing daily gratitude lists for just two weeks increased positive mood, happiness, and life satisfaction and reduced negative moods and depression symptoms. Research suggests there are actions we can take, even short term, that can increase our own and our child's feelings of gratitude.

WHAT DO GRATITUDE AND COMPASSION LOOK LIKE IN YOUR FAMILY?

Take a Look at Your Child

Family relationships: Does your child consider the needs of other members of the family? Do they notice and respond to other family members' moods and stress levels? Do they pay attention to what is happening in their family members' lives? Do they try to provide comfort or show compassion if someone is distressed? Do they ever express appreciation for what they have and what people do for them?

Friendships: Does your child notice when a friend is being left out or did not get their "fair share"? Is your child able to share with friends when they have less (cake, toys, adult attention, and so on)? Does your child pick up on cues about friends' needs or emotional well-being?

Learning: Do your child's teachers or coaches ever describe your child as supportive of their classmates, generous with the ball, cheering on others in group work, reveling in other kids' successes, or other acts of support for classmates? Does your child express appreciation to teachers or coaches? If your child is older, do they show interest in and satisfaction from volunteer or service work?

Sense of self: Does your child express compassion regarding news about people's suffering? Do they recognize and appreciate the privileges in their life? Do they have a desire to help others? Are they open to conversations about what other people might lack or need? Are they kind or harsh toward themselves? Do they express self-compassion or self-criticism when struggling?

CONCERN-O-METER

Pick a color for each category. Draw a colored arrow for each to give yourself a visual picture of your child in this moment.

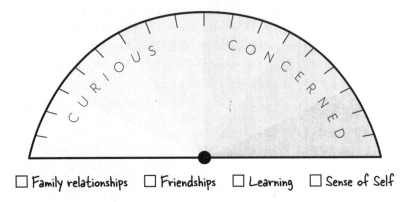

CURIOUS · CONCERNED

☐ Family relationships ☐ Friendships ☐ Learning ☐ Sense of Self

Take a Look at Yourself

❋ *What are you thankful for?*

What are your silver linings these days? Is it easy for you to consciously think about what is good in your life when asked? What have you taken from the pandemic or other adversity that you are grateful for?

❋ *How would your children describe you?*

Would they say that you are a thankful person or that you tend to take things for granted? Would they describe you as compassionate toward others, and yourself?

❋ *Do your children feel you appreciate them?*

Do you try to highlight their strengths and show kindness for their struggles? Do you share with them your optimism and confidence in them?

❋ *What is your inner monologue about yourself and your life?*

Are you compassionate or critical? Do you tend to appreciate what you have? How would you feel if others could listen in to your inner dialogue? Is this how you hope your kids will talk to and evaluate themselves?

COMPASSION AND GRATITUDE

8

HOW DO YOU THINK YOU TREND?

Gratitude

(target zone)

Entitled	Grateful/Balanced	Guilty
A victim	Grateful	Unable to fully enjoy good things
Jealous	Open-hearted	
Envious	Can see self in context to the larger world	Sees oneself mostly in the context of those who are suffering more
Sees oneself mostly in comparison to those who have more	*Things aren't perfect but we have more than enough.*	Worried about appearing entitled
I deserve more! Why do bad things only happen to me?	*I feel lucky.*	*My problems don't count.*
	We may not have X but we sure have lots of Y and Z.	*I don't deserve to feel sad when so many others suffer more.*

Compassion

(target zone)

Narcissism	Self-compassion	Self-hatred
Overly fixated on the self	Less focus on rating self (looks, money, skills, intelligence)	Constantly rating self compared to others and coming up short
Overly high self-esteem	Less focus on comparisons with others	Imposter syndrome
I'm the best!	Lack of harsh judgment about the self	*I'm the worst. I don't deserve to be treated well. If only people knew how bad I was.*
Why don't people treat me better?	Willingness to see the self as imperfect	*I have everyone fooled.*
	I am worthy just as I am, just as others are worthy.	

PLAYS FOR YOUR PLAYBOOK

If you are looking to increase your child's gratitude and compassion, try out some of the tips below. See if you notice any shifts in your child's functioning (or your own!). And remember, sometimes the techniques that don't appeal to you are exactly the ones that might be the most helpful.

➤ **Model gratitude and compassion out loud.** Lead by example. Consciously focus on what you are thankful for. Count your blessings. Start a daily gratitude practice. And don't just enumerate your blessings; savor and reflect on them.

> *"Guys, I'm having a rough day, and have to get out of my head. I think it will help to think about someone else for a while. Mrs. Nelson just came back from the hospital. I'm going to pick a few flowers from the yard and bring them over. Anyone want to help? Would one of you find some ribbon and the other a pretty jar? It won't take long to do this, and I really think it will help me get some perspective about my situation."*

➤ **Gratitude is contagious.** Engage your child in discussions of gratitude. Create some gratitude rituals, such as a dinner or bedtime conversation where you all share. Or make a gratitude jar in which all family members can drop written notes about things they're grateful for and read them together as a family at the end of the week or month.

➤ **Focus on people.** Research shows that focusing gratitude on human beings, not just things or events, is more impactful.

> *"I sure feel grateful to have Mrs. Davis for our crossing guard. She knows how to keep us safe and she's always so friendly."*

➤ **Record gratitude in a shared space.** Leave notebooks in strategic places for you and your family to capture specific moments of gratitude (handwriting can be more powerful than typing). If your family members appear annoyed by this practice, offer to be the permanent scribe. Reread these gratitudes in difficult moments to remind each other that tough times pass, and we are all stronger than we sometimes feel.

The Compassion Paradox

Did you know that beating ourselves up for a mistake makes us more likely to repeat it? In contrast, having compassion for our current self leads to growth of our future self. Numerous studies show that judgment, frustration, and lack of understanding toward ourselves leads to making the same mistakes over and over. Paradoxically, having self-compassion actually increases our chances we will improve next time.

➡ **Have your kids catch you writing in a gratitude journal.** Leave it out so they can see. They might even take a peek and find you are grateful for them. Heather had a client who was struggling to connect with his two teenage daughters. When he tried to have conversations about gratitude, they rolled their eyes. Nonetheless, he recorded his positive feelings about his daughters in a gratitude journal that he left out where they could look at it. It seemed like they did not touch it at first, but he learned a week later they had been reading every word.

> *"I am so grateful that Jamie had the insight and care to notice her sister really needed more help with that school project. I'm so glad she mentioned it to me. Our lives are so much nicer with her around."*

➡ **Find the gratitude in the tough times, not just the good times.** Show your kids how to search for something good in the difficulty.

➡ **Ask for help.** We all have moments where we struggle to find our gratitude.

> *"I'm feeling sorry for myself today. Can someone help me remember three things I could feel grateful for right now?"*

➡ **Go beyond saying "thank you."** Studies show most parents focus on kids saying "thank you" but pay much less attention to the feelings or thoughts of thankfulness. Politeness is important, but connect these social manners with the actual deeper feelings. Use "thinking and feeling" questions to help cultivate a deeper sense of gratitude.

"How did it feel when you opened your present from Aunt Jill and saw that backpack you have been wanting?"

➡ **Make a habit of demonstrating thanks with your kids.** This can take the form of service to others (running errands for an elderly neighbor), acts of kindness (cookies for first responders), being

The Ancient Philosophers Were the World's First Therapists

While our parenting tools are designed to fit a modern world, many ancient philosophers wrestled with the same questions we face today and came up with insights that are still highly relevant.

Plato, for example, described our rational self as a charioteer struggling to keep two flying horses (our noble spirit and our passionate, irrational nature) moving together in harmony. Homer wrote about Ulysses preventing his crew from seeing or hearing the Sirens' songs and keeping himself restrained so he could not join them—not so dissimilar to turning off your email notifications when you're trying to finish a term paper.

Aristotle had the idea of virtue as the middle way, counseling people to seek the moderation between extremes. He proposed taking small steps toward the middle as a way to create meaningful change. For example, if you want to become braver, act the way a brave person would and it will manifest. By acting bravely, you are reinforcing being brave, and you will become braver as a result.

Epictetus, an influential Stoic, was a fan of giving practical advice based on his philosophic ideas and wrote one of the first self-help books. Stoicism called for a somewhat surprising way to cultivate gratitude and appreciation: by practicing negative visualization. Stoics would start their day by imagining worst-case scenarios. Just thinking about an awful thing provided a moment of relief and gratitude that it wasn't true. And, as the day progressed and the negative events did not happen, they felt more grateful for their circumstances, knowing how it could be worse.

charitable (donating time, talent, goods, or money), praying before meals, or writing notes of thanks and appreciation to family, friends, teachers, coaches, and so on.

➡️ **Think like a museum curator.** Kids—and all humans—have a finite capacity for attention and appreciation. If there are too many objects or choices competing, the value of each is diluted. Consider how a museum curator helps us appreciate the art by hanging it far apart and rotating the collection rather than putting it all out together. We can do the same for our kids by reducing their access to all their possessions at once.

➡️ **Replace judgment with empathy.** Model how to give grace and the benefit of the doubt. Help children come up with generous, situational explanations for others' behaviors. Recognize that children notice how you talk about others. If you are really harsh or judgmental about others' mistakes, your kids will use that to gauge how approachable you are.

> *"I can get so frustrated and judgmental when someone is driving too slowly or is too hesitant. But then I try to think, 'Maybe it's a new driver or an elderly person.' I remember what it was like being a new driver and worrying that people were mad at me for going so slow. And I would want someone to treat Mama Betty with respect even though she is getting a little slower."*

➡️ **Be kind to yourself, too!** Practice self-compassion out loud. Identify things you can do to recharge your emotional batteries and prioritize doing them. Remember that emotions are contagious. Set an example for your children of how to show yourself compassion for your own shortcomings.

> *"I have had a rough day. I know you guys need dinner, but I have to take care of myself for a bit, or I won't be any good to anyone else tonight."*

➡️ **Ask them to join you in compassion for you.** Kids need you to give them opportunities to be compassionate toward you, and they often love rising to the occasion.

> *"Would you guys mind laying out some apples, cheese, and crackers while I go take 30 minutes to have a nice, relaxing bath? I know it is not a great dinner plan, but I think I could use you guys feeding me for a change, is that okay?"*

Heather Finds Light in the Darkness

The summer my son Will was 15, he was diagnosed with a rare and massive brain tumor. As a parent and a person, I have never felt so helpless and afraid. In the blink of an eye, we found ourselves on a long and terrifying journey.

Even in this shocking and sudden darkness, we found comfort in unexpected places: the nurses who joked with Will while caring for him. The techs who made an extra effort to brighten difficult moments. The doctors who compassionately explained the grim prognosis. And in the outpouring of love and support from our family and friends—even from friends of friends. This "village" reminded us of all that was good and filled our hearts with gratitude.

Will survived surgery and recovered remarkably well. But then came complications and a vicious cycle of re-hospitalizations and more surgeries. One Friday the 13th encapsulated this awful roller coaster. After an emergency neurosurgery, we felt relieved and hopeful—until we found out that Will had contracted a brain infection and was rapidly becoming incredibly sick. I raced into the ICU room to the most devastating moment of all, which was when my critically ill son did not recognize me.

This was my purest moment of terror, and it was one of the few times when I could find no gratitude to comfort me. My son's life was in danger and all we could do was wait. That weekend, time moved agonizingly slowly.

Now, as I reflect with the considerable hindsight of knowing there was a happy ending, I can see how much the practice of gratitude helped. Will maintained a remarkably positive attitude throughout, but at times I struggled not to be angry and resentful at the universe for what he was going through. It wasn't easy to find silver linings some days, and I learned that I had to find compassion for myself in the dark times when gratitude failed me. It took effort to balance the fear and uncertainty of what else could go wrong with the appreciation for what was going right and the awareness that it could always be worse.

I was profoundly changed by this experience. I suspect I will always be a bit haunted by the most harrowing moments, but those memories are fleeting. Mostly I am thankful for all we gained. I got better at parenting out of pure necessity, learning to tolerate uncertainty, working to manage my own fear and anxiety, trying to trust in the strength of my children and to appreciate the growth afforded by the adversity.

➡ Ask for forgiveness to help kids have opportunities to provide grace and empathy toward you.

"Justin, can you forgive me? I really lost my temper there. I had a rough day. I know it's no excuse, and I know I ended up taking out my frustration on you over something really small like socks on the floor. I'm very sorry."

➡ Help your kid shake free from the trap of constant mild griping. For teens especially, it's socially common to complain and exaggerate. To help them balance their memories of the day, use the validation sandwich (see page 111). And watch your own griping! We can all be caught in that trap.

Self-Esteem vs. Self-Compassion

Many parents tell us they wish their kids had better self-esteem. When asked what they are hoping for, they describe the desire for their child to have a stable, generally positive sense of themselves, regardless of any particular achievement or how others are doing. They also wish their child could listen to feedback or criticism without feeling devastated. Turns out, most parents' ultimate goal for their child is actually self-compassion, not self-esteem.

SELF-ESTEEM: *Evaluative*	SELF-COMPASSION: *Connective*
Judging our self-worth	Assuming we have worth
Seeing ourselves as "special" or better	Seeing all individuals as worthy
Fragile ("Someone could be better than me.")	Stable ("I know I am valuable, even if others are better at some things than me.")
Based on perceived success	Based on our values
Separating us from others	Connecting us to our community
Criticism or feedback often feels dangerous, making a child more resistant to the information.	Criticism or feedback has no bearing on a child's essential sense of themselves, so they are able to accept and learn from the information.

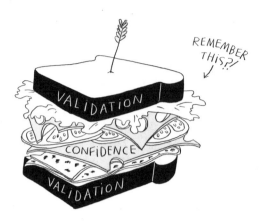

"How was your day?"

"Terrible. I'm sure I failed my chem test."

"Bummer [validate]! I imagine your day was a mix of good and bad, just like mine [confidence], but I know it's hard to remember anything else when you don't do well on a test [validate]."

➜ **Use the "rose, thorn, and bud" interview questions.** At the end of the day (or week, month, or year), ask your kids for something terrific (their rose), something not so great (their thorn), and something that could be the seed of something getting better (their bud). This reminds kids to expect good, bad, and hopeful things to be happening in their lives at all times. The good can be enjoyed, and the bad does not need to be fixed, just accepted.

➜ **Model acceptance for good enough.** Show them you can provide grace to yourself. It will remind them that you can give them grace when necessary as well.

"Man, I know I am not grading these papers as carefully as I usually do. But honestly, it is all I have in me right now. I hope my students will be understanding."

WRAPPING UP

Gratitude is closely tied to happiness, and it can and should be cultivated. Compassion, the flip side of the gratitude coin, is equally important to psychological health. And looking ahead to our next Essential, gratitude and compassion are fuels for resilience.

DEEPER DIVE

Greater Good Science Center

We encourage you to check out the many resources and wonderful research available at the Greater Good Science Center, based at the University of California at Berkeley. You'll find everything you need to know about well-being, including the latest scientific findings about happiness, gratitude, and compassion; engaging videos and articles; and podcasts and quizzes. The Center has resources geared to parents and a newsletter and online magazine to keep you current.

Self-Compassion: The Proven Power of Being Kind to Yourself by Kristin Neff, PhD

A broad view that focuses on self-compassion over self-esteem. While her book is written for adults to focus on themselves, Dr. Neff has numerous activities and action plans that provide particular focus on teaching kids self-compassion as well.

The Good Enough Child: How to Have an Imperfect Family and Be Perfectly Satisfied by Brad Sachs, PhD

Dr. Sachs is a psychologist and prolific author of a treasure trove of parenting books written with compassion and humor.

For Kids

Listening with My Heart: A Story of Kindness and Self-Compassion by Gabi Garcia

A gem of a book for young children that reminds kids to have compassion for themselves as well as others.

Have You Filled a Bucket Today? A Guide to Daily Happiness for Kids by Carol McCloud

A book for young kids with a concrete and catchy theme for generosity and gratitude.

The Boy at the Back of the Class by Onjali Q. Raúf

A book for older kids centered on a Syrian refugee that builds compassion and empathy.

Bouncing Back

RESILIENCE

THE TAKEAWAY

✔ Our capacity to manage stress is directly linked to resilience, a crucial element of long-term thriving and mental health. We can intentionally wire our brains to become more resilient. Building resilience is a safeguard against developing anxiety and depression.

✔ For children to develop resilience, they must learn how to handle setbacks and failures and recognize their own strength in surviving them.

✔ Resilience is a kind of psychological superpower, built upon the foundation of all the Essentials working together.

THE SETUP

Imani, age 14, struggled with isolation, rigidity, and perfectionism. She was a straight-A student and involved in lots of clubs. Her parents said she seemed "perfect" to her teachers, relatives, and friends, but at home she would often fall apart, cry for hours, or demand that her parents help her. She told them she was lonely even at school and didn't feel she had any real friends.

When Jennifer met with Imani, they agreed that her perfectionism was bringing her down. Imani decided to start a daily habit of what she called "The World Tour of Small Mistakes." She assigned herself the job of making at least two small mistakes every day. She started *very* small, spelling her name with two *n*'s on her homework, or tearing a tiny corner of an assignment. She moved up to texting a friend with just half of a message and then waiting two minutes before finishing the text, changing her order at the last minute at the coffee shop, and wearing a T-shirt with a small ink stain on it.

Jennifer knew Imani was finished with therapy when she had not only intentionally messed up a line during the dress rehearsal of the school play but, more importantly, had told two different friends about her struggle with wanting things to be perfect, even sharing

her attempts to break free with her small mistakes. By opening up to her friends—not a part of the assignment at all—she had been able to push through the barrier of isolation she herself was creating and began to feel a true sense of being accepted for her authentic, if perfectionistic, self.

WHY IS THIS ESSENTIAL?

Resilience is the ability to bounce back from negative events—to struggle and persevere despite the challenges. Resilience directly increases our capacity to manage stress. It is one of the characteristics most strongly linked to long-term thriving and is an essential ingredient to mental health. When we prioritize the development of resilience, we help ensure our kids' long-term well-being.

While chronic stress unintentionally rewires the brain, we can deliberately work to rewire our brains instead for resilience. Parents can provide the foundation for developing resilience in our kids via three factors: unconditional love, security, and connection. A key ingredient for resilience is the ability to fail. Since we ourselves are models for our children, and our own displays of resilience affect the growth of our children's resilience, it is crucial for us to welcome failure in both our lives and our children's lives. This Essential comes near the end of the book because all the other Essentials are building blocks to resilience.

CURIOUS ABOUT THE SCIENCE?

Behavioral epigenetics is a fascinating field of study pioneered by Drs. Michael Meaney and Moshe Szyf. They demonstrated that emotional traits, both positive and negative, can be passed down through generations. This is especially true in the case of chronic stress arising from neglect. Their groundbreaking work with rats

demonstrated that maternal neglect experienced by one generation of rats was genetically encoded into the next generation of rats, causing this new generation to neglect their young. In other words, the impacts of trauma can be passed down genetically to future generations.

Subsequent research has found support for the idea that not just trauma but resilience may be genetically heritable. Until recently, very little was known about the mechanisms underlying resiliency, but exciting emerging research has found specific genetic variants that contribute to the human capacity for psychological resilience under trauma and stress.

Regardless of any inherited inclination toward resilience, research has also found that resilience can be developed. And, in fact, recent research shows that increased resilience was one of the outcomes of the COVID-19 pandemic. Researchers looking at a group of several thousand military veterans found that one year into the pandemic, 43 percent of them had experienced COVID-19-associated post-traumatic growth (a type of positive psychological change resulting from a traumatic situation), including a greater appreciation of life, better relating to others, and greater personal strength. Veterans who also experienced COVID-19-associated post-traumatic stress disorder (PTSD) had an even greater prevalence of post-traumatic growth. The veterans who experienced post-traumatic growth also had a significant reduction in suicidal ideation.

Many of our Essentials have been linked to increasing resilience, such as sharing emotions openly and regulating emotions effectively; having mental flexibility, self-control, motivation to succeed, and self-efficacy; feeling connected with others; having a positive outlook; and using collaborative problem-solving. The most significant of these factors has consistently been connectedness: Having a stable and committed relationship with at least one adult, no matter the environmental stressors, strengthens a child's resilience.

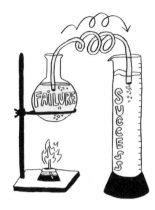

Another key to resilience lies in failure. Northwestern University researcher Dashun Wang calls failure "the essential prerequisite for success." His team's analysis of data sets from three diverse fields—scientific research, entrepreneurship, and terrorism (!)—found the same pattern: People who eventually succeeded and people who eventually failed did not differ in sheer persistence (they had nearly identical numbers of attempts). Instead, the critical differentiator between eventual success and continued failure was the ability to learn from previous failures (such as adapting their methods or approach to a problem).

The lesson? We must face adversity in order to develop resilience, and once we have acquired it, resilience allows for recovery and growth in the face of failure.

Resilience is linked to greater psychological and physical well-being, improved learning and academic achievement, and reduced risk-taking behaviors (such as excessive drinking, smoking, and drug use) and it is well documented as a protective factor against anxiety and depression. Resilience is well worth fostering both through its composite parts and as a whole.

WHAT DOES RESILIENCE LOOK LIKE IN YOUR FAMILY?
Take a Look at Your Child

Family relationships: Does your child have the ability to roll with the punches in your family? Can your child hear constructive criticism and grow from it? Can your child cope during family crises or tragedies?

Friendships: Can your child manage the ups and downs of peer relationships? Can your child make new friends or bounce back with complicated friendships? Can they recover from an unkindness? Would your child have the capacity to shift friend groups if necessary? Can they apologize?

Learning: Can your child accept when teachers or grading do not seem fair? Do they continue to work even when faced with difficult assignments? Can they handle being cut from the team, not chosen for the play, or not selected for an academic award?

Sense of self: Does your child give up easily? Can they learn from their mistakes? Do they blame others for their failures and disappointments? Can they shift directions, or do they get stuck when something doesn't turn out the way they had hoped or planned? Does your child feel brittle or fragile to you?

CONCERN-O-METER

Pick a color for each category. Draw a colored arrow for each to give yourself a visual picture of your child in this moment.

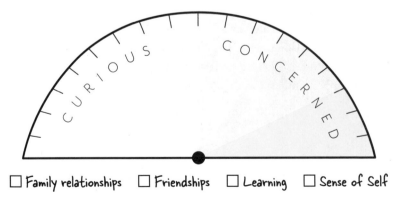

☐ Family relationships   ☐ Friendships   ☐ Learning   ☐ Sense of Self

RESILIENCE

9

Take a Look at Yourself

How does fear interfere with your ability to manage difficult situations?

Do you have optimism that your child is strong enough to bounce back from adversity? Are you afraid of your child's reaction to failure? Can you recognize the gift that each setback brings?

Would your kids notice the coping skills you use?

Could they describe them? Would they be able to tell someone else how you cope during tough times?

Are you modeling resilience when things get tough?

Keep assessing and asking yourself how you are reacting to your own natural failures, as well as those of your children. Do you get stuck on the setbacks? Do you remain accepting of yourself and your kids even when circumstances are discouraging or when mistakes are made?

When your kid has failed, what was your reaction?

Did you try to do something about it, such as softening the blow in some way, or were you able to tolerate their pain and disappointment? Do you think you can welcome more failure into your children's lives in the future, seeing the benefits it brings?

HOW DO YOU THINK YOU TREND?

(target zone)

| | | | | | | | | | | | | | |

The Doubter

Fragile; brittle; fearful;
risk averse; easily frustrated;
barely surviving

*You aren't strong enough;
I'm worried this will damage
you; I worry this failure could
ruin your future.*

The Believer

Willing to take risks;
participatory;
persevering; thriving

*You've got this; I know you
will bounce back from this;
I've seen you manage worse;
look at you do hard things!*

PLAYS FOR YOUR PLAYBOOK

If you want to support your child's growing resilience, try out some of the tips below. See if you notice any shifts in your child's functioning (or your own!). And remember, sometimes the techniques that don't appeal to you are exactly the ones that might be the most helpful.

➜ **Express a vote of confidence in your child's resilience and abilities.** Our authentic belief in our children's strength can bolster them in tough times. They need our optimism, not our worry and doubt.

➜ **Attitude is everything.** Shifting our mindset about how we approach stress can change our stress response. Focus your attention on the process, and view setbacks as temporary speed bumps, not stop signs.

➜ **Send healthy messages about failing.** Failure is an essential part of learning and should not be feared. Failures are what build character and strength. Share your past failures more than your successes. Celebrate them, even—not as eventual happy endings, but as ways to build toughness.

> *"Your problem is reminding me of the time I failed chemistry in college. I could not wrap my head around some important concepts, and the teaching assistant told me to drop the class. I didn't listen and ended up with an F. I honestly didn't leave my room for days after that. It was a hard time for me, but after surviving that week, I figured I could handle any more F's that might come my way."*

➜ **Share some current everyday failures as well.** It is a gift to your kids to be authentic and to share your own humanity. That is the best model for resilience you can provide.

> *"I can't believe I told everyone in the neighborhood meeting about the break-in I had heard about. I rambled on and on about my worries, only to be told it was a rumor and hadn't happened. Oh man, I felt like I was going to sink into the floor. I could barely listen to the rest of the meeting. I feel like now everyone sees me as some kind of nervous, foolish person. It will be interesting to see how I'm going to make myself go to the next meeting next month."*

9

RESILIENCE

➜ **Teach goal setting.** A good goal is one that stretches your current ability. It should be something you can already do, sort of, at least occasionally. Kids need to learn how to set goals that stretch them, and how to break bigger goals into smaller, doable parts. So while your child's goal may be to ride a bike, their first goal might be to coast on it without peddling for five seconds.

➜ **Celebrate effort, not outcome.** Encourage a growth mindset and discourage perfectionist thinking. Get out of the habit of evaluating your child; teach them to judge themselves according to their own goals. Make sure your child is harboring realistic expectations; don't let them fall into the fixed-mindset trap of believing their abilities are innate and predetermined. And don't let them assume that they should be good at everything—most kids are specialists, not generalists.

➜ **Highlight examples of resilience in the wider world.** Use current events, books, TV, movies, and music to start conversations about people who have rebounded from failure and overcome the odds.

> *"Did you see that interview with Miss Teen USA? She completely froze up and sounded really silly in her answer. But man, in the end, she held her head up high, smiled, and admitted she lost her place. And then she came back out for the talent portion! Impressive!"*

Welcome the Hard Experiences

Psychologist Hara Estroff Marano makes a compelling case for what she calls "experience deficit disorder" in her book *A Nation of Wimps: The High Cost of Invasive Parenting*. She argues that by overprotecting our kids from the difficult parts of life, we deprive them of the ability to learn how to cope—we accidentally make our kids less resilient.

Remember: Talk to the Brain That's Listening

Words from parents are rarely neutral. Instead, they are generally either helpful or not helpful. And timing is *everything*. To make sure your words are helping the situation, first notice which part of your child's brain is turned on. If your child is upset, most likely their PFC is turned off and their amygdala is turned on. Remember, the amygdala doesn't process complicated language—you might as well try talking to a fish. So instead, say as little as possible, make comforting murmuring sounds, and use only words of empathy and validation: "This is hard." "Ouch." "You are upset." "Bummer." A time of high arousal is a terrible time to use words to reason, explain, instruct, or defend. Later, when your child's PFC is back on, you can use more words—and feel free to add some ice cream to that talk to keep the amygdala happy while you and your kid's PFC confer!

➡ **Name the hardness of things, instead of the ease.** And model acceptance that sometimes life is hard. We can't always thrive. Sometimes it is more useful to just survive.

> *"Ooh my gosh, that hockey game was brutal. 0 to 12. Man, I can't imagine the morale on the bench."*

➡ **Avoid pump-'em-up comments.** Sit in the hardness with your kid for a while. Rather than adding the usual "but you tried so hard," just keep quiet and listen. This allows your child to have some space to share their own resilience. After a bad game, for example, your kid might end up responding, "Actually, we did okay. It was awful, sure, but we started making jokes about how we can use a video of this game to prove our toughness when we want to go pro."

Catherine Finds That Attitude Is Everything

My daughter Kate went through grade school as the shy kid. By the time she reached high school, however, she had decided enough was enough; she vowed to break free from this label. She studied how to face her social anxiety and deal with the amygdala fight-or-flight response that happened when she tried to speak in class. It didn't go so well.

She applied for a school mentor position, but she was declined. She tried out for captain of an extracurricular activity but was passed over. She applied time and again for various internship positions, summer scholarship programs, and student helper positions—all of which resulted in a big fat NO. Having to interview, to assert herself with eye contact, and use a stronger voice was physically exhausting and scary. But she kept trying, despite rejection after rejection. It seemed like she never caught a break.

I felt my own emotional regulation and clarity unravel. It was absolutely gut-wrenching to witness her tears hiding behind fake smiles. I was powerless. It didn't matter what I said—real confidence is earned through experiences.

The rejections and failures took a toll on Kate's self-esteem. So she made it a game where she set about applying for anything that came her way. She even sought things she knew were unattainable so she could chalk up more failures.

With quiet determination and wide-ranging efforts to land a job, internship, or any type of position, things suddenly began to change. She applied to give lessons for kids and adults at the National Air and Space Museum in Washington, DC, and was accepted. She was invited to intern with a computer lab at a local university. And thanks to her weird wide net of risk-taking and applications, a local company she hadn't even contacted offered her a coding internship.

Kate retained a humble perspective. She understood the suffering it sometimes takes to succeed. Despite her personal achievements at the end of her high school year, what I am most proud of is her determination to not be afraid of failure. I just recently moved to my office the note she made for herself with her self-created mantra that had hung for years over her bed. In colored crayon capital letters, it says: "ATTITUDE IS EVERYTHING." I see it every day.

➡ If you are itching to praise, suggest to your child that they might praise themself. Try turning that urge to praise on its head and put the focus on your child's self-perception.

> *"You pushed through that class speech despite your embarrassment. Wow, I bet you are impressed with yourself there."*

➡ Describe the details back to your kid (without praise!) when they show resilience. Help them notice their own strengths and integrate this idea of themselves into their identity.

> *"Sounds like you really powered through that speech even though your hands were shaking the whole time. You felt really embarrassed, but somehow you just kept going."*

➡ Ask questions about how your kid managed, like an interviewer on a talk show. This helps them solidify their own strength and makes it more likely they can draw from their experience in the future.

> *"How did you do it? Did you know you had that kind of fortitude going into it? What was your brain saying to you during this time? What did your friends tell you after the fact?"*

➡ Don't be afraid to ask your kid more about the hard parts. Asking about and accepting the hard parts or pieces of failures shows that you know they can handle difficulty and pain. Your implied message is that you deeply believe in them.

> *"When your friends said they had noticed your shaking hands and quivering voice, did you feel embarrassed? Did you admit you felt humiliated by the speech, or did you act like it was no big deal? Are you dreading next time?"*

WRAPPING UP

Resilience is the aggregate of most of the other Essentials, and it determines how well we respond to life's challenges. It is a psychological superpower, connected to a wide range of positive mental and physical health outcomes. To develop resilience, kids need to experience a variety of failures and learn they can survive. In this way, over time, survivors become thrivers.

DEEPER DIVE

Scaffold Parenting: Raising Resilient, Self-Reliant, and Secure Kids in an Age of Anxiety by Harold S. Koplewicz, MD

> Written by the founder of the Child Mind Institute, *Scaffold Parenting* provides solid, well-written, exquisitely compassionate parenting advice.

The Blessing of a Skinned Knee: Raising Self-Reliant Children by Wendy Mogel, PhD

> Dr. Mogel's parenting books are full of great advice and good humor. She uses Jewish teachings to provide valuable lessons and timeless wisdom to parents.

The Gift of Failure: How the Best Parents Learn to Let Go So Their Children Can Succeed by Jessica Lahey

> This book is a bit of a manifesto for allowing mistakes that build resilience, especially where school is concerned, and will help any parent struggling with overparenting.

For Kids

The Most Magnificent Thing by Ashley Spires

> A lovely book for young children about flexible thinking, frustration, failure, creativity, and perseverance.

The Undefeated by Kwame Alexander

> This award-winning book is a beautifully illustrated poem highlighting many moving examples of the resilience and perseverance of Black Americans.

Mistakes That Worked: 40 Familiar Inventions & How They Came to Be by Charlotte Foltz Jones

> Filled with fun stories and funny illustrations, this book provides abundant examples of "successful failures."

All Together Now

LIVING THE
PLAYBOOK

THE TAKEAWAY

✔ Kids are mimics—if they see us living these Essentials ourselves, they will learn without much interference from us.

✔ We can model living well—and be open and transparent with our kids when we fall short (and we will!)

✔ Everyone benefits when parents take the time and energy to grow and self-actualize alongside their children.

THE SETUP

You are reading this book. You have come this far. So now we are going to share with you a shortcut to all of this parenting stuff. The singular, underlying secret to this whole parenting gig is that you only truly need to focus on the last Essential: Live the playbook for yourself.

WHY IS THIS ESSENTIAL?

If you can do the Essentials for yourself, you don't need to work hard to proactively provide them for your children—it'll happen whether you try or not. Evolution has made children and adolescents natural mimics. They will do what you do. Conversely, children and adolescents have an extremely sensitive hypocrisy meter. So, no matter how much you tell them about the importance of sleep or expressing gratitude, if they don't see you prioritizing sleep and gratitude yourself, they will tune you out.

There is no need to magically master all these Essentials at once—good luck with that! The truth is we are all works in progress. Instead, your goal should be twofold: work to live the playbook, and make sure your children see your work. Narrate both your victories and failures and share your continued striving. You can provide both a model of healthy living and a model of resilience to your kids. Living well is hard but living well is worth the effort.

10

LIVING THE PLAYBOOK

CURIOUS ABOUT THE SCIENCE?

Research shows that how well parents are faring is a major determinant of how our kids are doing. Dr. Suniya Luthar, who has led decades of groundbreaking research on the mental health of children and adolescents, surveyed a diverse group of more than 46,000 students in sixth through twelfth grade beginning in 2019. She found that the strongest predictors of depression and anxiety in the kids were, first, their perception that their parents were dissatisfied with them and, second, their parents' mood.

The Ultimate Parent Trap—Selflessness

Among the three of us, we have worked with more than ten thousand families over the past twenty-five years. And one thing we have discovered is how often parents are willing to do whatever it takes to help their children—unless and until we recommend that they take better care of themselves. Certainly, many parents take this professional advice. But many other parents (equally as loving) will answer with some variation of "Yes, I'm planning to get treatment for my own anxiety down the road, but right now I have to stay focused on my child." Or "I see where starting a meditation practice, gratitude journal, medication, or anger management program could be helpful for my child, but I personally don't need that kind of thing." Or even "I hired you to help my child, not me."

There is no substitute for leading by example. And there is no statute of limitations on emotional evolution and psychological well-being. Think of it this way: By living the playbook yourself, you are gaining a twofer for you and your family. Trust us—as professionals and parents of adult or near-adult children—the finish line of active daily parenting arrives much faster than you expect. Each year seems to speed up, and when a child leaves the nest, we are all left wondering whether we have focused on the right things and done what we could to prepare for that child to thrive as an adult. If you live the playbook yourself, you can know you have done all you can.

PLAYS FOR YOUR PERSONAL PLAYBOOK

1 Take a Pause

Kids' needs are a moving target, but parents don't need to be in constant action. You will have to keep adjusting your aim to stay current with what your child needs—but don't forget the value of doing nothing, too. It's crucial for parents to sometimes pause, take stock, recalibrate, and rest. We encourage you to find compassion for yourself as you move through the ages and stages with your child. You're not going to get parenting "right" all of the time—or maybe even a lot of the time. And that's okay. In fact, sometimes that's great! You've got the opportunity to model some of the most valuable essentials when you blow it: how to feel difficult feelings, how to have grace for your mistakes, how to recover from them, how to adjust your approach, and how to try again. Hit pause, breathe deeply, recenter yourself on what truly matters to you, and keep going.

2 Be a Gardener, Not a Sculptor

It can be tempting to see your kid as clay and you as the sculptor. But that conceptualization places too much pressure on you to make a perfect someday-adult. It also puts too much pressure on your kid to be something that might not be their natural best state.

Instead, see yourself as a gardener planting a mysterious seed. You don't know if your kid will be a tomato plant, a rose bush, a maple tree, or even some kind of plant you've never heard of. All you know is that you want to cultivate the earth and environment around your kid for optimal growth, so they can be the healthiest and most fruitful . . . whatever plant they can be. That means amending the soil, making sure your plant has the right amount of water at the right times, and doing other caretaker—not creator—duties.

 **VS...**

These are all things that can be achieved if you are working on caring for yourself. Because guess what? When it comes to your child, you are the soil. You are the water. You are the gardener.

3   Turn the Essentials on Yourself

We recommend you go back and apply the tips, tricks, and plays to yourself. We know it's hard. We struggle, too. We also aspire and fail, aim and fall short, stumble and get up and give up and complain and get frustrated and feel sad and lose hope only to eventually try again, just like you. But your kid wants and deserves to have a thriving parent. So here at the end, to help you live the playbook, we have some bonus questions to help you nurture yourself, as your child's loving gardener. Here are our final tips, framed as questions rooted in each Essential for you to ask yourself just about *you*.

POINTS TO PONDER

Essential #1
Rest, Recreation, and Routine

Are you living the basics? Prioritizing your sleep, exercise, and nutrition? Making time for fun and actually having fun? Both with and without your children?

Essential #2
Attention and Self-Control

Adult PFCs get overloaded, too, affecting the balance of adult attention and self-control. When our energy gets depleted, we need to use our own tools to rejuvenate our PFC fuel tank.

Most people can juggle and thrive to a point, but then they collapse. Do you know where your personal line between thrive and collapse lies? Can you stay on the thrive side of the line?

Have you taken our advice to identify your stressors and maybe even make your own stress bucket (see page 62)? Great, but now what are you actually going to do about it? Make one change at a time so you do not get overwhelmed and so you gain some positive momentum.

Essential #3

Feeling Uncomfortable

Do you struggle with feeling uncomfortable feelings? What's in your way?

Do you need a new approach to your difficult feelings? Could you use some help? If you do, can you admit it to yourself? How will you get it? What's the first step?

Remember the goal to "feel the feels": Know your feelings, name them out loud, and tolerate them. Do you find yourself being judgmental and self-critical about your feelings? We all need to accept a range of tough emotions as human.

Essential #4

Anxiety

Do you avoid your own anxiety? Do you have the skills necessary to approach the things you are anxious about?

You know anxiety is contagious. Instead of always looking to see if your anxiety is affecting others, take a moment to look and see where you are being affected by others' anxiety, perhaps by your kids, other family members, a colleague, or a friend. How can you lovingly create boundaries for yourself so that you can protect yourself from the detritus of other people's raw emotions?

Essential #5

Flexibility

Do you use rigidity as a crutch to remove complexity and uncertainty from your life?

Do you try to control too much as a way to cope? Remember that rigidity distances us while flexibility brings us closer, and if you're living the playbook, you're trying to stay open to change in order to grow. Develop your flexibility so you can stay humble, welcome failure, be resilient, and thrive under any conditions.

Independence

Are you tending to your own interests and adult relationships? Do you show your kids that you can have fun without them sometimes?

Live a full and balanced life. And make sure you're maintaining your own emotional independence. Remember that you are trying to work yourself out of a job. Beyond parenting, what other "jobs" fulfill you and give you purpose?

How are your adult relationships? If you are in a committed relationship, how is the health of that relationship? How are your friendships? Are you tending to them?

Kids feel responsible for adults who still need them. What do you need to continue to do to build your own vibrant, independent life?

Essential #7

Motivation

What more do you want to learn? In what areas? Be your own seed spotter—find what makes the fire of motivation burn inside you.

Recall the concept of flow, the highly motivated state in which an activity is so intrinsically enjoyable that you lose yourself in it, with no awareness of time passing. What activities bring you flow? Is there a way you can do more of them?

The spark and pleasure of intrinsic motivation doesn't have to happen through a job. Many of us work to pay the bills but find deep satisfaction and motivation in other parts of our lives. In what realms are you highly motivated?

Where do you feel passion? A sport? Your religious community? Art, dance, music, reading, nature?

Do you tend to approach life as a series of *have-tos*? Do the things you think matter to you actually motivate you? If not, do they really matter to you?

Essential #8
Compassion and Gratitude

What do you expect from yourself? Are you your toughest critic? Do you give yourself grace? Do you treat yourself like you would your best friend?

There is so much talk about gratitude, but how many people actually walk the talk? Do you?

Think of the most authentically happy person you truly know (not just the person who seems happiest in your social media feed). What are their defining characteristics? How can you learn from them?

Essential #9
Resilience

Resilience is the sum total of the other Essentials. It is both a benchmark and an outcome of psychological health. Your resilience has no doubt been tested by many life circumstances over the years. How have you fared?

What can you change or accept? What's in your way? Where can you continue to grow in building up your own resilience?

Essential #10
Live the Playbook

Have we convinced you to put on your own oxygen mask first? You can parent your children with these Essentials *and* evolve yourself simultaneously. We can learn so much from our children, and, if we let them, they can reveal to us truths about ourselves. There is no one in this world watching you more closely or wanting your love and attention more than your children (unless you have a dog; then maybe it's a tight contest). The proverb "Physician, heal thyself" is worth considering as you weigh whether to do the work of living the playbook. **Parent, parent thyself.**

10

LIVING THE
PLAYBOOK

WE ARE ONLY HUMAN, AFTER ALL

Like every parent (and human), each of the three of us has certain Essentials that are incredibly hard for us. We try—but definitely do not always succeed—to practice what we preach in our own lives. As we worked on this book, we adopted "live the playbook" as a mantra to remind ourselves that it is natural to struggle and to fall short. We try to remember the goal is perseverance, not perfection. The concept grew more and more powerful to us as we grappled with our own challenges in life, and what started as a joke became a profound, fundamental truth.

We also used this mantra to encourage each other. We know firsthand how hard it can be to share our parenting insecurities, vulnerabilities, and fears. We have benefited tremendously from each other's support in difficult moments. The considerable time we spent together writing this book became a way to make space for our friendship and our adult selves—and we and our families are better for it. While we love helping parents professionally, we firmly believe there is unique power in parents sharing their hopes and fears with trusted fellow parents in an authentic and vulnerable way. We encourage you to consider developing some of your own "In the Trenches" stories or just questions and concerns to share with people whom you know will support you without judgment.

The bottom line is that we believe that *Raising a Kid Who Can* is not just about parenting and it is definitely not just for our children. Being parents helps us grow as individuals. The more we try (and fail, and try again) to demonstrate to our children the qualities we hope they will adopt, the more self-actualized we become ourselves. The less we focus on them and the more we focus on ourselves, the better our children end up. It is with humility and solidarity that we offer to you the hope that you will not only find ways to help your children with this book, but you will find some nuggets of wisdom for your own life.

RAISING A KID
IN THE DIGITAL AGE

We have come to a pivotal point in recent history, one that has affected almost every aspect of modern life and child development. It is, of course, the electrically charged and lightning-speed transformation of the digital revolution, and most especially, the rise of portable, highly connected digital devices.

Why is this important? The digital age is moving so fast in real time that the research about its impact on brain development can't keep up. Evidence-based research requires an approach that is slow and steady and stands the test of time. But given what modern neuroscience investigation already shows about the digital world and brain development, we feel we can't wait to act until the evidence tells us whether we should have heeded the warning signs. Teachers, doctors, and, yes, mental health professionals already see concerning indicators of damage in kids.

In this book, we are sharing information that is backed by the science. But for this topic, we are deviating from our strict, evidence-based playbook protocol to share concerns that are not—as yet—scientifically validated. There is serious potential vulnerability in developing brains from this new digital age, and we worry that if we wait for research to fully catch up to real time without speaking out, it may be frighteningly too late.

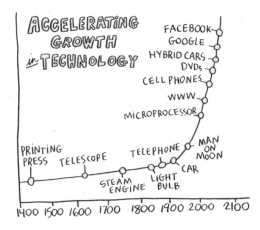

We believe that the ways in which we use technology is harmful to many aspects of human development. Most especially to our two superpowers as a species: to be consciously present to one another, and to be able to think deeply within ourselves. The technology journalist Johann Hari, after interviewing numerous "attention engineers" at Google, Twitter, Facebook, and others, came to the conclusion that the addictive quality of interactive technology is a public health crisis, just like the lead in paint in the 1970s that created (and in some areas still creates) brain damage in children.

Throughout this book, we have highlighted specific risks to kids and offered ideas for how to counteract those concerns. But in this section, we want to highlight some emerging evidence that our constantly available, addictive digital devices may be actively damaging development in children, and to give some guidance on how kids and parents might work together to protect themselves.

OUR ATTENTION SPANS ARE SHRINKING

You may have heard the statistic that the average human attention span has decreased from twelve seconds to eight seconds, less than that of a goldfish (which clocks in at an impressive nine seconds, by the way). It came from a headline-grabbing Microsoft report that appeared in dozens of news stories in multiple countries. Yet the nuance—that the statistic was cited in the Microsoft research paper but was NOT actually a finding of the Microsoft study—was completely lost. This saga illustrates the problem. We are in a world where information and entertainment are always available in quick-hit, bite-sized chunks, little morsels that keep our eager brains occupied and coming back for more.

So, has the average human attention span actually decreased? This is hard to answer. It turns out it's pretty difficult to study attention spans in general because our ability to sustain attention depends on a bunch of constantly changing variables, such as our mood, our health, the time of day, and of course the specific task that we are doing at that moment. Attention is not something that researchers can measure as a whole. If we are watching a riveting movie, we are less likely to have any urge to glance at our Apple watch. But doing taxes? For many of us, the buzzy call of the notification breaks through our concentration much more easily.

Dr. Gloria Marks is a leading expert on attention and the impact of digital media on people's lives. She has been tracking people's attention for two decades, curious about how attention spans may be changing with the rise of digital technologies. Starting in 2004, she shadowed people with a range of work, professions, and workplaces, measuring precisely how much time they spent on one activity before switching to another. Her thousands of hours of meticulous data collection tracked people's attention spans as they moved between email, spreadsheets, web pages, and other screen tasks that fill many people's typical workday.

In 2004, her earliest study, Dr. Marks found that people averaged about 2½ minutes before switching from one task on a computer screen to another computer screen. In 2012 it went down to 75 seconds. Her studies show a continued decline to an average time of 47 seconds per screen by 2021. Other researchers have replicated her results, giving alarming evidence that our individual attention spans on our various screens are declining over time, all in concert with the rapid rise in technology usage.

Many people are feeling a clear change within themselves. A 2021 large-scale survey of British adults found that half of respondents felt their attention span had gotten shorter. Two-thirds of survey participants, including 58 percent of the youngest (18- to 34-year-old) respondents, believed that young people's attention spans are worse than in the past.

And there is data that already hints that kids' attentional capacity may also be affected by their digital media use. The *Journal of the American Medical Association* reports a large-scale study that followed more than 2,500 high school students. These teens did not have ADHD symptoms at the beginning of the study and were asked how much they engaged in fourteen different types of digital media usage. These students were then screened for ADHD symptoms every six months over two years. There was a statistically significant relationship between the frequency of digital media use and symptoms of ADHD: Heavy users of social media were significantly more likely to have ADHD-like symptoms two years later than teens who were lower-frequency users. In short, heavy digital media users showed increased difficulty with sustaining attention, similar to ADHD symptoms.

Perhaps the most compelling evidence to date verifying that our ability to pay attention is compromised by our devices comes from research into people's ability to concentrate on specific tasks when their smartphones are nearby. Numerous studies have found that the mere presence of a smartphone impairs attention and cognitive capacity. A smartphone within sight, even if it's turned off and upside down, appears to reduce the ability to focus and perform tasks. The closer the device, the more performance is weakened. Why? Because, like someone newly sober trying not to drink while inside a bar, a tiny part of the brain is actively working to not pick up or use the phone, leaving less brainpower for the task at hand.

MULTITASKING IS A MYTH

One delightful and delusional belief that wreaks havoc on human focus is the idea that we can multitask. The hard truth is that our brains are wired to focus well on only one thing at a time and distractions overwhelm our human thinking capacity. The human brain evolved over these past 40,000 years to be able to think about a maximum of three or four things at the same time, and to sustain attention and focus well on only one. Thus, multitasking is, technically speaking, neurologically impossible. While it might feel like we can pay attention to two things at the same time, this is not what is actually occurring in the brain. Instead, we are rapidly "task switching."

MIT neuroscientist Dr. Earl Miller is one of the leading experts in task switching. Miller explains that when we think we are multitasking, we are actually switching from one task to another very rapidly and incurring what is called the "switch cost effect"—the expense of cellular energy required to switch between multiple tasks. On top of these switch costs are additional energy costs needed to return our focus to what we are doing. But it feels good to task switch! By flipping from task to task we get novelty and stimulation, and with it the dopamine feel-good pings in micro-addictive doses. And then, thanks to these dopamine hits, our brain gives us the false feedback that we are totally rocking it, when in reality we are spread thin and doing a mediocre job.

Additionally, Stanford researchers are finding evidence that heavy multitaskers have reduced memory, reduced overall concentration, and less creativity over time. It's become clear: Our brains were not built to multitask. Attempting to do so makes us less productive, more worn out, fuel depleted, less efficient, and less attentive. And in the bigger picture, constant electronic interruptions and distractions have potentially devastating implications for learning and developing brains.

Another problem of this mythical "multitasking" (aka task-switching) is that it's associated with increasing anxiety and burnout. Dr. Marks and other researchers have highlighted how rapid task switching costs us brain energy and resources as it keeps pulling our attention back to what we want to be doing. Worse, it has the added potential to set off our physiological stress response and increase anxiety. Remember how uncontrollable stress can shut down that brain boss PFC's functioning? This nasty combination of too much stress making it hard to think, plus the poor actual concentration that naturally results from volleying between different tasks, leads to a double whammy that exhausts our brain and executive function . . . which further reduces our attention and cognitive fuel, spiraling into even more anxiety. And, perhaps ironically, once we are anxious and exhausted we go to our devices for easy dopamine comfort food, since we're too depleted to pay attention to things that are more difficult. Like a codependent death spiral, our digital lives and our anxiety seem inextricably linked.

And this is just what happens to adults. As mental health professionals considering these same effects on our kids' maximally vulnerable, still-developing brains, we begin to feel panicky. It is highly likely that kids' brains are being harmed by the myriad of information streams begging for their immediate attention, and likely stunting the hugely important life skill of self-control along with it. From a neurobiological perspective, it seems clear to us that a childhood filled with hours of switching from screen to screen will likely lead to future adults with reduced capacity to sustain attention and manage their impulses. We fear the serious, long-term, negative impact on the permanent wiring of young brains in this digital age.

A MIND NEEDS TO WANDER

Daydreaming may be a dying art, yet there are important developmental and cognitive reasons for letting our minds roam. Dr. Jonathan Smallwood, a leader in the study of mind wandering, has shown that under low-stress conditions these self-generated thoughts serve several critical functions; allowing us to connect our past and future selves together; to make goal-directed, long-term plans; and to access the gateway to creativity. Smallwood explains that although mind-wandering may sometimes be unpleasant for the individual who experiences it and disruptive to the tasks we need to attend to, it offers freedom from the here and now and in doing so may reflect a key evolutionary adaptation for our brain. Smallwood even believes that spacing out is important for human survival as a species: "It could be at the crux of what makes humans different from less complicated animals."

Technology threatens our ability to let our minds wander by crowding out that daydreaming space, replacing our built-in moments of downtime with constant stimulation, forcing our willing minds to keep working and push aside new ideas and insights.

WHAT CAN WE DO?

We cannot yet prove it but we sincerely believe that closely restricting digital devices when kids are young, and teaching them how to manage their own device use as they get older, can make a real difference for brain development. As parents we all know how to do this—we do it all the time. In theory, it should be as simple as helping kids manage consumption of their own Halloween candy. But what are we supposed to do when not just every day, but every SECOND is Halloween, and the candymakers continue to add more and more addictive substances to every piece?

While we need to be vigilant, we also need to be compassionate toward ourselves and our children. We want to continually work to engage in the best of this global digital world, while keeping its addictive qualities to a minimum. This is parenting at its most difficult, and the challenges are shifting daily, sometimes hourly. As former Google design ethicist Tristan Harris stated in testimony to the US Senate in 2019, "You can try having self-control, but there are a thousand engineers on the other side of the screen working against you." It's not a fair fight, and we agree with the conclusion of journalist Johann Hari and the attention experts he interviewed across the globe: It's not your fault.

Here we offer you a mini-playbook—parenting plays to help you help your kids manage their screen time when it gets in the way of the Essentials.

Essential #1

REST, RECREATION, AND ROUTINE
Technology Is a Sleep Stealer

Sally's 10-year-old daughter Daisy had recently seemed out of sorts, irritable, exhausted after school, falling asleep at dinner, and less focused on homework after the winter break. Then, late one night, Sally noticed a faint blue light coming from under Daisy's closed door. Daisy had been pretending to go to sleep, and then taking out her iPad and watching YouTube videos of cats and crafts (and who knows what else!).

Does your family use screens to wind down at night? If so, you are not alone. However, there is emerging evidence that screens inside bedrooms can be disruptive to both the quality and quantity of sleep. Kids can fall down TikTok or YouTube rabbit holes that take away all sense of time. Social media use can trigger emotions that interfere with sleep. And there is evidence that the blue light of the screen suppresses the melatonin cue that triggers sleepiness.

What You Can Do

PRESCHOOL: *Do It for Them*
Avoid screens of any kind after dinner. Use sensory and analog activities to create wind-down routines such as baths, story time, and snuggles.

ELEMENTARY: *Limit and Teach*

In the evenings, transition from interactive tech, such as gaming or social media, to more passive screen time, such as watching a TV show, and watch the show together if possible. Create—and follow—consistent rules, such as no screen time starting at least one hour before bedtime. Help kids shift their brains from the stimulation of the screen back into their bodies.

TEEN: *Gradual Transfer of Power, With Curiosity*

Don't let them charge or store their phones in their bedrooms. Create an "electronics garage" where kids dock and charge their devices in a central location at night. Model this behavior yourself. Defang the standard arguments we hear kids give for needing a device in their rooms by buying everyone an alarm clock and some way to play music. Help teens tune in to the effects of tech on sleep by asking (curious, nonjudgmental) questions: "So you tested out playing *Fortnite* right up to bedtime this weekend. How did you think it went?" It's okay if you don't like the answer; we are trying to get them thinking for themselves.

Essential #2

ATTENTION AND SELF-CONTROL
The Death of Reading

Unfun fact: A recent study found today's teenagers now focus on any one task for an average of 65 seconds (for adults, it's 3 minutes, also not awesome).

Ask a parent of an older kid when their kid stopped reading "for fun," and, if they have stopped, many of them will say, "The day we got them a smartphone." This isn't a parent's imagination. Reading initially requires the ability to decode letters and sounds, but once that is learned, reading simply requires increased attention spans to match the appropriate cognitive content. And there is emerging evidence that technology can reduce attention spans in children—and adults.

Your Attention Is for Sale

Technology is here to stay, and it will continue to be designed to be maximally appealing—and addictive—to kids' developing brains. Like most of the professionals and parents we know, we've struggled with how to balance the use of technology with our kids' healthy development.

One approach we have found to be effective is to teach kids that their attention is a commodity, and it's being bought and sold without their consent or awareness. We let them know that many of the masterminds who created the apps and games they love do not allow their own kids to use them. We encourage parents to have regular conversations with their kids about technology, listening without judgment to their kids' points of view, and to use the appeal of technology to motivate growth in other helpful areas (such as self-control).

What You Can Do

PRESCHOOL: *Do It for Them*

Avoid hypnotic content, of just colors, shapes, sounds. If you do allow some shows, choose slower, more story-based content with a natural beginning, middle, and end.

ELEMENTARY: *Limit and Teach*

Watch longer, slower, older movies, driven by character rather than action, to harness technology to expand attention span. If you are using audiobooks, make sure to also provide physical books your child can use to follow along.

TEEN: *Gradual Transfer of Power, With Curiosity*

Help kids use smart technology to counteract the insidious nature of interruptions. Ask them how they prefer to use their "do not disturb" settings, batch notifications, and mute when they need to use technology for schoolwork to help them manage and reduce the additional technology vying for their attention.

FEELING UNCOMFORTABLE
Technology "Saves" Us from Feeling the Feels

Jennifer had a teen client who told her one day, only half joking, "I've been putting my phone deep in my backpack so I wouldn't be tempted to text and drive, but then I started to feel my feelings at the stoplights, so I had to take it back out."

Technology is a quick fix, an immediate distraction that feels (ha!) like a solution to the distress of uncomfortable feelings. It becomes a convenient escape hatch that is available when we most want an out. This strategy is highly effective in the short run. However, technology robs our children of learning that feelings come and go naturally. If you always have your phone or iPad available in your pocket, you never have the opportunity to experience that a feeling has a beginning, middle, and end.

Recent studies have shown how screens can negatively affect the development of anxiety and emotional regulation in kids. One study linked screen time to higher rates of pre-teen obsessive-compulsive disorder. Another study showed how the use of screens to calm kids during emotional outbursts may calm them in the short term but inhibits their ability to learn to manage their emotions in the long term. Furthermore, by rewarding tantrums with something fun, parents may inadvertently reward the frequency of tantrums.

What You Can Do

PRESCHOOL: *Do It for Them*
Avoid using screens to help young kids manage upset feelings, especially tantrums.

ELEMENTARY: *Limit and Teach*
Pay attention to when your child wants screen time. Is it often when they are feeling scared, angry, or hurt? Could you sit with them a bit instead? Play some mellow music? Take a walk? Don't let kids use screens for mood management.

TEEN: *Gradual Transfer of Power, With Curiosity*
Create open conversations about how you as an adult also find yourself using this super-handy technology to avoid uncomfortable

feelings. It is easier for teens to share their own struggles with screens when they have an adult who can honestly relate.

ACCEPTING ANXIETY
Don't Be Digitally On Demand

Heather worked with a loving mother whose daughter Dara had lots of safety worries. In the hope of helping Dara stay in school, the mom had purchased a smartwatch that was designed just for younger kids. Dara could text her mom (and only her mom) a little heart if she was feeling a bit unsteady, and her mom could text a little heart back. This worked beautifully for a few days, until Dara's mom was in a work meeting and didn't get the text. The lack of instant response put her daughter into a frantic tailspin and resulted in, ironically, her mom being called to school to pick up Dara early.

If there is one feeling that all of us most commonly manage through technology, it's likely anxiety. Anxiety seeks avoidance like a heat-seeking missile, and technology is only too happy to oblige. While we all can sometimes benefit from a little respite from the hard stuff of life (vegging out to a favorite show after a long day), we should be cautious about the role tech can play when our kids feel anxious. After all, if tech becomes an accomplice to anxiety, it will make the anxiety grow, increasing the demand for digital distraction, and creating a vicious cycle.

What You Can Do

PRESCHOOL: *Do It for Them*

Name, out loud, when you notice your child using technology to try to avoid feeling scared or worried. For example, you might say, "You are hoping that I will FaceTime Grandma so you won't have to be worried if she is safe. I get it, it's really hard to feel worried." Then *don't* FaceTime Grandma for a little while. Teach your child it's okay to be worried.

ELEMENTARY: *Limit and Teach*

Teach children that you aren't always digitally available to help them manage their worries. This tells them implicitly that you know they can do that on their own.

TEEN: *Gradual Transfer of Power, With Curiosity*

Be "busy" and miss some calls; respond slowly to some texts, and then follow up later to ask them how they managed the situation (without you!). A healthy parent is a not-always-accessible parent. And even though it can sometimes be tempting, make sure *you* don't check in with *them* too often either!

Essential #5

PSYCHOLOGICAL ADAPTABILITY
Mind Wandering: The Essence of Creativity

Each workday before the pandemic, Catherine dragged her early morning zombie-like self to an exercise class at a local gym. Catherine's drill-sergeant instructor had zero tolerance for cell phones or other glowing devices in the darkness of the spin classroom.

But during the pandemic, the class had the privilege of continuing the daily spin ritual through the screen and virtual world. But the virtual experience had a screen full of distractions: the trainer cheering, members competing, pinging stats, and virtual high-fiving. Catherine was shocked to realize she had been using the pre-pandemic gym spin time not just to exercise, but to let her mind wander in a non-distracted cycling zone. With the virtual version, she noticed what was missing: the no-screens-allowed classes had been a wonderful gift of time and space that allowed her to generate her creativity.

Staying mentally and emotionally flexible requires allowing space for the mind to wander. But tech is designed to keep feeding us more of what we have already looked at, and it can constrict rather than expand our thinking. There is emerging research on the topic of allowing the mind to wander and the value of keeping your attention unoccupied by external factors—in fact, it is a requirement for creativity. This has been true forever. If you are in Times Square, it's hard to mentally "hear" anything beyond the neon-flashing billboards, even as you people-watch and have a little whisper of an idea that could make a terrific short story for English class.

Social Media: It's Complicated.

The social media landscape is changing so radically and so quickly that it's outpacing steady and measured research. Therefore, we have yet to find consensus among experts—but we have examined the research that exists and can offer some practical suggestions for how to help your older child manage and thrive within this tricky, lightning-fast digital environment.

THE RISKS

Research clearly shows correlations between social media use and depression in some teens. Teens who used social media more than five hours a day were found to be twice as likely to be depressed as nonusers. And girls appear to be disproportionately affected. Even Facebook's own research found that heavy Instagram use was linked to depression and body image issues for girls. (After hearing early statistics at a medical conference in 2017, Catherine went straight home and attempted to rip the phone out of her own teen daughter's superglued grasp. As you might imagine, the impulsive "conversation" was not particularly pleasant—or effective.)

Newer, larger studies show that social media use is perhaps only mildly harmful to most kids, with some notable exceptions, such as kids with depression, anxiety, and ADHD. In fact, these preexisting conditions may actually *cause* increased social media use, rather than the other way around. Social media is psychologically rewarding by (evil?) design, and we are incentivized to stay engaged. Individuals with poorer self-regulation or who are struggling are especially vulnerable to developing a bad feedback loop of using social media to cope, leading to even worse mental health, leading to even more social media use.

There appear to be specific ages when teenagers are most vulnerable to the negative effects of social media (for girls between 11 and 13; for boys between 14 and 15; for all genders at age 19). These are ages where many kids go through major social upheaval—experiencing body changes, beginning a new middle or high school, going to college, getting a new job, or living independently for the first time—that might change the way they interact with social media and make them particularly impacted by social media feedback.

It appears the risks of social media are specific to each individual child, based on constantly changing variables of biology, genetics, environment, and developmental stage. Some brains, and some ages, are simply more vulnerable to the negative effects of social media.

THE BENEFITS

It's not all bad news. Some newer data show some kids may be building deeper friendships through texting and social media. And social media can open a world for kids who previously would be limited by their geography or their economic opportunities, or who have social anxiety, autism, or limiting medical disorders, or who have been ostracized by their in-person peer group. Social media allows for creativity, identity exploration, and global networks for building a community that was simply impossible a few decades ago. Teens can interact with humans on the other side of the planet, with the potential to share their passions and ideas for a better world. And thanks to the web-based connection, including social media, most every human did not need to be completely alone during the worst of the pandemic.

HERE TO STAY

The internet and social media are here to stay—and there are risks with not allowing social media use as well. Like it or not, online platforms are a significant part of many kids' social lives. They can connect with friends, be in group chats, find out about homework they missed, and be in on the latest joke or meme. For many kids, online connections are also the only way they might be able to be included in activities that take place IRL. Especially for older kids, we have seen how parents' attempts to limit access to online socializing can have two inadvertent results: kids who have fewer social connections and fewer opportunities to be invited to in-person social experiences; and kids who find work-arounds, hide, or deceive their parents in order to be online.

When parents try to fully limit access to social media, they are missing a rich opportunity to help their kids, with their guidance and guardrails, learn how to manage their consumption of social media. Kids grow up quickly, and parents cannot externally control their social media use in perpetuity. Kids have to learn, practice, struggle to limit, and figure out their own needs. With our support, they can practice, make mistakes along the way, and learn how to recover from those mistakes.

BEST PRACTICES

So what's a parent to do? We recommend that timeless parenting approach: Use your values along with your knowledge of your specific child and life circumstances to guide you. In light of what we know and especially what we don't yet know about the effects of social media, here is what we advise our parent clients:

Practice communication and transparency. All of us struggle to have a healthy balance of technology in our lives. Be open with your kids and share your own struggles and methods. This is new territory for all of us, and it's an opportunity to connect and commiserate, rather than just worry and lecture.

Approach slowly and with caution. It's easier to add in than take away technology. Employ significant oversight in your child's younger years, with increasing privileges as they prove themselves to be generally responsible in their online life. Don't let your kids be early technology adopters. The parent advocacy organization Wait Until 8th (waituntil8th.org) has some great resources for parents.

Raise informed consumers. Teach your kids that, just like nutrition for our bodies, we all need to be careful about the content we put in our brains. Educate kids on how social media is designed to be addictive and raise them to become informed consumers. Take social media vacations so they can feel the contrast of actually being unplugged. And don't shy away from discussing difficult topics such as hate speech, sexting, and sending or receiving naked pictures. Today's kids have the internet in their collective pockets.

Take pornography, for example. A 2019 British survey of more than two thousand parents and young people found a huge gap between parents' knowledge of their kids' exposure to online pornography and their kids' actual experience. Three-fourths of parents thought their child would not have seen online pornography, but more than half of 11- to 13-year-olds reported that they had, and that number rose to two-thirds for 14- and 15-year-olds. The majority of these young people reported that their initial viewing of pornography was accidental.

So don't avoid these hard conversations; be direct, compassionate, and collaborative. Remember, your kid's brain can't fully grasp the permanence of the online world. We all need reminders that you can't erase the internet.

Teach kids to know themselves. Are they more impulsive than some of their friends? Then they need more guardrails, such as keeping phones out of their rooms. Are they in a sensitive period in which seeing pictures and stories of others seems to make them feel worse about themselves? Help them to design rules for themselves on how and when to use social media (for example, never text when angry, never use social media after X o'clock each night). Help them learn to identify their own yellow and red flags in terms of when they need a social media break.

Prioritize in-person connection. Human beings still do better with in-person relationships. The pandemic helped us recognize the deep and valuable experience of being with people in person, whether it's talking to a grocery store clerk, seeing people's faces without masks, hanging out with a group of peers, or hugging a best friend. We are built for face-to-face social connection. So be sure to highlight this to your kid.

People are natural sponges for reading faces and voices. It is estimated that there are 10,000 nonverbal cues in every minute of face-to-face social interaction. This rich tapestry of visual communication cannot possibly be fully captured on Zoom. And worse, we have nothing but a few emojis to help fill in the often vital gaps that are left when we are texting. How often do we yearn for a bit of facial expression or tone of voice when someone texts us back something as simple as "Ok"?

Major advancements in technology, from the printing press to the industrial revolution, have carried both amazing opportunities and deeply damaging side effects for the many humans caught in the change. Now is one of those unprecedented times when a new technology has radically changed how we live. The crucial difference for today's world is the pace of change. Research cannot move fast enough for us to truly comprehend what kind of impact social media will have on people. A huge scientific experiment is going on right now, with our kids (and us) as the subjects, and we honestly don't fully know how it will turn out.

But some things will always be true. Humans are built to struggle between immediate gratification (like a ding notifying you of a response to your post) and delayed gratification (like a friendship cultivated gradually through shared activities). Finding a healthy balance and knowing how to manage this innate struggle is a valuable skill to teach our kids—and ourselves.

What You Can Do

PRESCHOOL: *Do It for Them*

Avoid using screens in place of free play. Unstructured play is by far the most brain-building activity young children can engage in.

ELEMENTARY: *Limit and Teach*

Provide your kids with IRL physical materials: fabric and scissors instead of a dressmaking app; a brush and some paints rather than a drawing app; gel pens and a paper journal rather than the Notes app. Sit or work nearby, also without a screen, if possible, when your kids are just messing around, letting their minds wander.

TEEN: *Gradual Transfer of Power, With Curiosity*

Discuss the power of mind-wandering with them. Ask them if/how they can limit technology (even educational activities such as podcasts and audiobooks) and how to create some non-tech zones in their life, such as when driving, in the shower, during walks, and so on.

Essential #6

INDEPENDENCE
Developing Digital Freedom

Unfun fact: A study on teenagers' smartphone use while doing homework showed that kids experienced distraction and mind-wandering over 37 percent of the time.

We have yet to speak to a parent who didn't wish their child could independently manage their technology use. We all want to work ourselves out of the thankless job of "screen monitor." But in order to do so, we need to give our kids the preparation and practice to do it for themselves (and let them make mistakes along the way). When our kids are young, we set rules to help them learn how to live with some limits ("Don't cross the street by yourself."). When our kids get older, we want to transition them into setting their own boundaries ("You can walk to the store by yourself and should look both ways when crossing the street."). Building up our kids' ability to be smart consumers is the goal of digital independence.

One key to being able to be the boss of your technology is to learn the concept of "pre-commitment." Much of tech uses a limitless model—as soon as one piece of content is over, the next one begins automatically rolling. To combat this never-ending stream, teach kids to use pre-committing systems to plan ahead in order to limit the amount of time they will be on their devices.

What You Can Do

PRESCHOOL: *Do It for Them*
Don't expect your preschooler to independently regulate. Pre-commit for them. Don't bring devices into a restaurant; bring a coloring book. Don't have your phone available for them in the car; provide physical toys such as animals and dolls instead.

ELEMENTARY: *Limit and Teach*
Avoid power struggles by asking your child to join with you as an ally in fighting the devices. For example, you might say, "Hey, I want to give our brains a tech break on our trip to visit Grandpa, but we might be tempted. Where do you think we can hide the iPad so that we can't reach it? And what shall we do instead?"

TEEN: *Gradual Transfer of Power, With Curiosity*
Talk to your teen about the importance of pre-committing to how much time they will spend on their device or content stream, both in one sitting and in a day/weekend/week. Help them find systems, such as embedding their own time limits on certain apps, so they can help their Future Self with the sometimes-Herculean effort of disengaging from technology.

Essential #7
MOTIVATION
Being Bored Is Motivating

Sean Parker, founding president of Facebook, speaking about the creation of the platform, said their thought process "was all about: 'How do we consume as much of your time and conscious attention as possible?' And that means that we need to sort of give you a little dopamine hit every once in a while, because someone liked or commented on a photo or a post or whatever. And that's going to get you to contribute more content, and that's going to get you . . . more likes and comments. . . . It's a social validation feedback loop. . . . You're exploiting a *vulnerability in human psychology. . . . The inventors, creators—it's me, it's Mark [Zuckerberg], it's Kevin Systrom on Instagram, it's all of these people—understood this consciously. And we did it anyway."*

Tech is designed to be insanely motivating. But guess what? Boredom is motivating, too. The feeling of boredom can be experienced as quite painful, especially for kids. Yet without boredom, we have no drive. Part of the struggle with technology is that it hijacks the dopamine reward system in our brain, making intrinsic motivation particularly challenging to muster in the moment. Filling every bored second with stimulation drains our dopamine, making it harder to engage in those oh-so-important, low-dopamine activities such as practicing and learning.

What You Can Do

PRESCHOOL: *Do It for Them*

Avoid using screens as much as possible so as not to accidentally get kids too accustomed to high-dopamine activities. Help little kids tune in to the pleasurable sensations of low-dopamine activities, such as watching a tadpole swim in a pond, snuggling up near a window with a soft blanket to look at a book, or smelling cinnamon or peppermint.

ELEMENTARY: *Limit and Teach*

Create a bit of natural boredom with some technology scarcity. Set limits on easy high-dopamine technology so that kids will be drawn toward slower but still rewarding low-dopamine activities. If your child wants to practice the violin but feels drawn to their tablet instead, help them. Don't expect them to generate their own willpower over the experts at Candy Crush whose jobs depend on keeping them hooked.

TEEN: *Gradual Transfer of Power, With Curiosity*

At this age, they will have the ability to "sneak" tech, so you will need to get their input and buy-in. They actually don't want to be hostage to their devices any more than you do. So ask them for some creative ways they can develop their own artificial tech scarcity.

Essential #8

COMPASSION AND GRATITUDE
The Global Green-Eyed Monster

Heather worked with parents whose four-year-old son, Peter, loved watching Vlad and Niki (86 million subscribers and counting) unboxing videos on YouTube. The pace was slow and sweet, and the content seemed harmless. Then one day Anna, his mother, found Peter despondent in the Walmart toy aisle, sad that his (economically secure) family was too "poor" to afford the number of toys that (ultrarich) Vlad and Niki got to unbox every week.

Humans are evolutionarily wired for social comparison. And jealousy is an evolutionarily useful feeling: Knowing whether we have access to as much food as our caveman neighbors could be the difference between life or death. But in the global digital age, the new "neighbors" we use for social comparison are often the wealthiest, the most physically beautiful, and the most talented (or the most carefully curated, artfully airbrushed and filtered, or even flat-out fabricated). This natural social comparison of ourselves against people on the extremes saps our gratitude for who we are and what we have. Instead, we end up feeling either jealous or entitled, which then wreaks havoc on our sense of compassion for others.

What You Can Do

PRESCHOOL: *Do It for Them*

Avoid exposing young children to programming and advertising that preys on their natural wants and desires. If kids engage in any programming at all, look for it to be more balanced as to how real children live, such as *Sesame Street*. And avoid content that includes advertising to young kids.

ELEMENTARY: *Limit and Teach*

Limit programming that can create a focus on material goods. Avoid, for example, video games that involve your kids "buying" items for their digital animal. Avoid exposure to (digital) children living lives out of step with your values. Watching virtual kids eating sugary cereals, receiving lots of new toys,

and taking Disney trips may seem harmless, but it sets a tone that happiness and pleasure come from material possessions.

TEEN: *Gradual Transfer of Power, With Curiosity*
Ask your teen for examples that they themselves have noticed about how social media, TV shows, and movies create a sense that an expensive material life is both normal and desirable. Encourage them to consider the financial incentives that influencers have to share their "lives" with them. Make a game out of finding product placements in media. Share examples of how your own digital world also can sometimes trick you into thinking you "need" something that really is just a "want."

Essential #9
RESILIENCE
Learning to Recalibrate
The human spirit must prevail over technology.
—Albert Einstein

If resilience is the compilation of all the other Essentials, then the ability to self-regulate one's own behavior is a special superpower. No one is perfect at keeping their technology use exactly in check. We overindulge, pull back, and then recalibrate, all the while trying to stay balanced on the high wire of moderation so we can be the boss of our brain and behavior. Making sure we build in room for mistakes and learning how to adjust and try again will make our kids resilient consumers of technology as well as resilient people. And if you find that technology has begun to take over your family life, don't despair! Instead, talk to your kids. Course correct and adjust, try some different rules, and teach your kids to do the same for themselves. We all need to have a flexible relationship with technology and adapt as the technology advances. Find compassion for kids when they struggle with this ever-present frustrating task, and don't let them catch a whiff of your judgment or criticism. After all, the goal is to equip them to self-regulate, not to force them into temporary compliance.

What You Can Do

PRESCHOOL: *Do It for Them*
Avoid being digitally distracted while you're with your children. They are highly aware of when your attention is diverted! When you need to answer an email or return a phone call during your child-centered time, or when you realize you have gone down a Twitter rabbit hole, apologize, and show them how you right your tech ship.

ELEMENTARY: *Limit and Teach*
Use collaborative problem-solving to better understand where they are coming from, and then have them work with you to recalibrate. For example, you might say, "So what I'm hearing from you is that playing *Dragon Masters* online is one of the best ways to hang out with your friends, and you will be left out if you don't play, too. I get it; friends are important! And you heard Dr. Ramirez remind us that every kid needs an hour of unplugged play a day. What should we do? How can we make both work?"

TEEN: *Gradual Transfer of Power, With Curiosity*
When teens' tech use becomes too much, don't blame and shame, but do have an honest conversation about it: "Julia, I've noticed that you are looking at Instagram even while we're watching the movie. And I confess I was checking my own emails earlier. But I love this movie, and I love being with you. Could we both put our phones in the next room while we watch the rest? Would you be cool with that?"

Essential #10
LIVING THE PLAYBOOK

Anyone wish they could have a few "do as I say, not as I do" free parenting passes? As modern humans surrounded by abundance, we *all* struggle with limiting ourselves. So—surprise!—we suggest you go back through our digital age essentials, but now turn the lens on yourself with an honest self-assessment. Decide where your own tech struggle points are and how you can address them. Use the ideas on yourself. Aim for progress, not perfection. And ask your kid for help! Kids often know more about technology managment than their parents do. Invite them into your struggle and try their advice. One of the many joys of parenting is learning something about ourselves from our children, rather than always teaching.

DEEPER DIVE FOR THE DIGITAL AGE

Stolen Focus: Why You Can't Pay Attention—and How to Think Deeply Again by Johann Hari

> Hari is a journalist who wanted to learn why he was struggling to focus. His deeply researched answer is that our focus and attention have been stolen for corporate profit, and offers refreshingly practical solutions.

Attention Span: A Groundbreaking Way to Restore Balance, Happiness, and Productivity by Gloria Mark, PhD

> Dr. Mark's decades-long meticulous research into human attention is providing us evidence that our attention spans are shrinking. Her highly readable book outlines the issues and offers solutions.

iGen: Why Today's Super-Connected Kids Are Growing Up Less Rebellious, More Tolerant, Less Happy—and Completely Unprepared for Adulthood—and What That Means for the Rest of Us by Jean Twenge, PhD

> Dr. Twenge has been at the forefront of observing and highlighting the changes in the generation of kids who grew up in the age of smartphones. She is a leading voice in the effects of the digital age on children's psychological development.

Common Sense Media (commonsensemedia.org)

> This website can be a parent's best friend in navigating technology and evaluating media. There are resources for every age, stage, and digital parenting concern.

Wait Until 8th (waituntil8th.org)

> This website has a specific focus on providing parents with the information and tools to slow down granting adolescents access to smartphones.

For Kids

The Couch Potato by Jory John, illustrated by Pete Oswald

> This fun picture books extols the virtues of balancing play time with screen time.

For Adolescents

Posted by John David Anderson

> This chapter book is appropriate for ages 9 and up and offers a story about words being used as weapons that is highly relevant in the digital age.

8th Grade, directed by Bo Burnham

> *8th Grade* is about a media-savvy but socially awkward middle school girl. While references to sex and drugs may create some cringeworthy moments when watching with your teen, we think it's worth it. The film makes an excellent conversation starter about the challenges and pressures of the digitally connected lives of adolescents.

NOTES

WHAT'S GOING ON IN YOUR KID'S BRAIN

The human brain hasn't changed much in the past 30,000 years. Simon Neubauer, J. J. Hublin, and P. Gunz, "The Evolution of Modern Human Brain Shape," *Science Advances* 4, no. 1 (2018), doi.org/10.1126/sciadv.aao5961.

The amygdala is our threat detection center. J. E. LeDoux and D. S. Pine, "Using Neuroscience to Help Understand Fear and Anxiety: A Two-System Framework," *American Journal of Psychiatry* 173, no. 11 (2016): 1083–93, doi.org/10.1176/appi.ajp.2016.16030353; J. E. LeDoux, "The Amygdala Is Not the Brain's Fear Center," blog post on the *Psychology Today* website, August 10, 2015; and P. Nair, "QnAs with Joseph LeDoux," Proceedings of the National Academy of Sciences 111, no. 8 (2014): 2860–61, doi.org/10.1073/pnas.1323534111.

Neuroscientist Joseph LeDoux, one of the early researchers of anxiety, was able to map out, within the brain itself, how our unconscious threat detector, the amygdala, synaptically interacted with our conscious thoughts. J. E. LeDoux, *Anxious: Using the Brain to Understand and Treat Fear and Anxiety* (New York: Penguin Books, 2016).

Ta-da! We now could see how these survival circuits create the human experience of anxiety. A. Petersen, *On Edge: A Journey through Anxiety* (New York: Crown, 2017).

Dr. Jay Giedd and his colleagues at the National Institute of Mental Health revolutionized the way we look at child brain development. D. R. Weinberger, B. Elvevåg, and J. Giedd, "The Adolescent Brain: A Work in Progress" (Washington, DC: National Campaign to Prevent Teen Pregnancy, 2005).

Their research showed that the PFC is the last part of the brain to develop and remains a neuroplastic "work in progress" through young adulthood. J. N. Giedd, M. Stockman, C. Weddle, M. Liverpool, A. Alexander-Bloch, G. L. Wallace, N. R. Lee, F. Lalonde, and R. K. Lenroot, "Anatomic Magnetic Resonance Imaging of the Developing Child and Adolescent Brain and Effects of Genetic Variation," *Neuropsychology Review* 20, no. 4 (2010): 349–361, doi.org/10.1007/s11065-010-9151-9.

Giedd's study looked at MRIs of young people's brains every two years from the ages of 3 through 25. N. Gogtay, J. N. Giedd, L. Lusk, K. M. Hayashi, D. Greenstein, A. C. Vaituzis, T. F. Nugent, et al., "Dynamic Mapping of Human Cortical Development during Childhood through Early Adulthood," *Proceedings of the National Academy of Sciences* 101, no. 21 (2004): 8174–79, doi.org/10.1073/pnas.0402680101.

In babies and young children, brain neurons grow like bushes. J. Sakai, "Core Concept: How Synaptic Pruning Shapes Neural Wiring during Development and, Possibly, in Disease," *Proceedings of the National Academy of Sciences* 101, no. 28 (2020): 16096–16099, doi.org/10.1073/pnas.2010281117.

. . . all the way down to the molecular and chemical level. A. F. T. Arnsten, "Stress Signaling Pathways That Impair Prefrontal Cortex Structure and Function," *Nature Reviews Neuroscience* 10, no. 6 (2009): 410–22, doi.org/10.1038/nrn2648.

Conversely, high levels of uncontrollable stress (such as when we are living through a global pandemic) activate the amygdala response, which impairs the PFC. A. Arnsten, "The Effects of Stress on Brain Function," YouTube video, April 17, 2017.

As noted by Dr. Giedd and his colleagues, neuroplasticity is paradoxical. "Interview: Jay Giedd," posted online as part of the *Frontline* series "Inside the Teenage Brain," January 31, 2002, WGBH (PBS) website.

The brain's plasticity—its ability to grow, strengthen, and prune neural connections in response to the environment—can have negative effects as well as positive ones, leaving kids' brains more vulnerable to the effects of chronic high stress. L. Eiland and R. D. Romeo, "Stress and the Developing Adolescent Brain," *Neuroscience* 249 (2013): 162–71, doi.org/10.1016/j.neuro science.2012.10.048; S. M. Houston, M. M. Herting, and E. R. Sowell, in *The Neurobiology of Childhood*, ed. S. L. Andersen and D. S. Pine (Berlin, Heidelberg: Springer, 2013), 3–17; Elsevier, "Stress May Cause the Brain to Become Disconnected." ScienceDaily. sciencedaily.com/releases/2009/03/090316075845.htm, March 16, 2009.

Research shows that stress can cause neurons to die and neural networks to shrink or retract. B. S. McEwen, "Physiology and Neurobiology of Stress and Adaptation: Central Role of the Brain," *Physiological Reviews* 87, no. 3 (2007): 873–904, doi.org/10.1152/physrev.00041.2006; B. S. McEwen and P. J. Gianaros, "Stress- and Allostasis-Induced Brain Plasticity," *Annual Review of Medicine* 62, no. 1 (2011): 431–45, doi.org/10.1146/annurev-med-052209-100430; B. S. McEwen and J. H. Morrison, "The Brain on Stress: Vulnerability and Plasticity of the Prefrontal Cortex over the Life Course," *Neuron* 79, no. 1 (2013): 16–29, doi.org/10.1016/j .neuron.2013.06.028.

As our favorite neuropsychologist, Dr. William Stixrud, often says, "The more anxious and stressed you are, the more anxious you become." W. Stixrud and N. Johnson, *The Self-Driven Child: The Science and Sense of Giving Your Kids More Control over Their Lives* (New York: Penguin, 2019).

We are wired to constantly work to reduce and resolve uncertainty. A. Peters, B. S. McEwen, and K. Friston, "Uncertainty and Stress: Why It Causes Diseases and How It Is Mastered by the Brain," *Progress in Neurobiology* 156 (2017): 164–88, doi.org/10.1016/j.pneurobio.2017 .05.004.

Recent research has shown that the feeling of "anticipatory anxiety" comes from a part of the brain near the amygdala called the bed nucleus of the stria terminalis (BNST), sometimes also known as the "extended amygdala." M. Davis, D. L. Walker, L. Miles, and C. Grillon, "Phasic vs Sustained Fear in Rats and Humans: Role of the Extended Amygdala in Fear vs Anxiety," *Neuropsychopharmacology* 35, no. 1 (2010): 105–35, doi.org/10.1038/npp.2009.109; and A. S. Fox, J. A. Oler, D.P.M. Tromp, J. L. Fudge, and N. H. Kalin, "Extending the Amygdala in Theories of Threat Processing," *Trends in Neurosciences* 38, no. 5 (2015): 319–29, doi.org/10 .1016/j.tins.2015.03.002.

The BNST is involved in sustained fear reactions, and in the long-lasting icky unease that is typical of anxiety and switched on by apprehension. A. Petersen, *On Edge: A Journey through Anxiety* (New York: Crown, 2017).

Dr. Martin Seligman described the concept of "learned helplessness": the idea that when people experience a stressful situation repeatedly and feel like they cannot see a way out, they may eventually give up trying to change or solve the situation, even when paths to the solution present themselves. S. F. Maier, M.E.P. Seligman, and C. Peterson, *Learned Helplessness: A Theory for the Age of Personal Control* (United Kingdom: Oxford University Press, 1993).

Age of Anxiety. W. H. Auden, *The Age of Anxiety: A Baroque Eclogue. The Collected Poetry of W. H. Auden*, edited by Edward Mendelson (Vintage, 1991), 190–204.

Essential #1
GETTING YOUR THREE RS: REST, RECREATION, AND ROUTINE

Sleep deprivation has been shown to quadruple the risk of teenage depression and significantly increase the risk for teen suicidality. L. M. Lyall, C. A. Wyse, N. Graham, A. Ferguson, D. M. Lyall, B. Cullen, C. A. Celis Morales, et al., "Association of Disrupted Circadian Rhythmicity with Mood Disorders, Subjective Wellbeing, and Cognitive Function: A Cross-Sectional Study of 91 105 Participants from the UK Biobank," *The Lancet Psychiatry* 5, no. 6 (2018): 507–14, doi.org/10.1016/S2215-0366(18)30139-1; University of Reading, "Poor

Sleep Significantly Linked with Teenage Depression: Depression Group Slept 30 Minutes Less per Night than Other Groups in Study," *ScienceDaily* (online), June 17, 2020; F. Orchard, A. M. Gregory, M. Gradisar, and S. Reynolds, "Self-Reported Sleep Patterns and Quality amongst Adolescents: Cross-Sectional and Prospective Associations with Anxiety and Depression," *Journal of Child Psychology and Psychiatry* 61, no. 10 (2020): 1126–1137, doi.org /10.1111/jcpp.13288; and C. T. Fitzgerald, E. Messias, and D. J. Buysse, "Teen Sleep and Suicidality: Results from the Youth Risk Behavior Surveys of 2007 and 2009," *Journal of Clinical Sleep Medicine* 7, no. 4 (2011): 351–56, doi.org/10.5664/JCSM.1188.

A recent study from the University of California at Berkeley concluded that deep sleep seems to be a natural inhibitor of anxiety. A. Rossi, A. G. Harvey, and M. P. Walker, "Overanxious and Underslept," *Nature Human Behaviour* 4, no. 1 (2020): 100–110, doi.org/10.1038/s41562-019 -0754-8.

We can think of this sleep-time CSF flush as a nightly "power-wash" of the brain, preventing the buildup of adrenaline and toxic waste by-products. S. Makin, "Deep Sleep Gives Your Brain a Deep Clean," *Scientific American* (online), November 1, 2019. scientificamerican.com /article/deep-sleep-gives-your-brain-a-deep-clean1/.

. . . sleep plays a critical role in learning and memory. M. P. Walker and R. Stickgold, "Sleep-Dependent Learning and Memory Consolidation," *Neuron* 44, no. 1 (2004): 121–33, doi.org /10.1016/j.neuron.2004.08.031; "Sleep, Learning, and Memory," video from the Healthy Sleep website from the Division of Sleep Medicine at Harvard Medical School and WGBH Educational Foundation, accessed February 24, 2021, healthysleep.med.harvard.edu/video /sleep07_stickgold_learning; and E. Ben Simon, A. Rossi, A. G. Harvey, and M. P. Walker, "Overanxious and Underslept," *Nature Human Behaviour* 4, no. 1 (2020): 100–110, doi.org /10.1038/s41562-019-0754-8.

As early as 2010, researchers showed that when students unplugged and significantly reduced their screen use, they reported a dramatic improvement in their quality of life. International Center for Media & the Public Agenda (ICMPA) at the University of Maryland, *The World Unplugged*, a global media project, 2010, accessed May 9, 2021, theworldunplugged.wordpress.com/.

. . . unplugging completely after the workday resulted in feeling recharged. Y. Park, C. Fritz, and S. M. Jex, "Relationships between Work-Home Segmentation and Psychological Detachment from Work: The Role of Communication Technology Use at Home," *Journal of Occupational Health Psychology* 16, no. 4 (2011): 457–67, doi.org/10.1037/a0023594.

When less oxygen circulates in the bloodstream, the feeling of fatigue increases and results in lower energy and motivation levels. Mayo Clinic Staff, "Exercise: 7 Benefits of Regular Physical Activity," Mayo Clinic website, October 8, 2021, mayoclinic.org/healthy-lifestyle/fitness /in-depth/exercise/art-20048389; and T. Golen and H. Ricciotti, "Does Exercise Really Boost Energy Levels?" Harvard Health Publishing website, July 1, 2021, health.harvard .edu/exercise-and-fitness/does-exercise-really-boost-energy-levels.

Experts in human evolution have shown that fun and recreation—exercise, movement, laughter, time spent outside, time to be social, unstructured playtime—are essential for the growth and development of children's brains and even the survival of our species. S. Brown and C. Vaughan, *Play: How It Shapes the Brain, Opens the Imagination, and Invigorates the Soul* (reprint, Avery, 2010); and Peter Gray, "Evolutionary Functions of Play: Practice, Resilience, Innovation, and Cooperation," in *The Cambridge Handbook of Play: Developmental and Disciplinary Perspectives*, ed. P. K. Smith and J. Roopnarine (Cambridge, UK: Cambridge University Press, 2019), 84–102.

Studies have shown that older kids who are highly playful report less stress and better coping skills than their less-playful peers. C. Magnuson and L. Barnett, "The Playful Advantage: How Playfulness Enhances Coping with Stress," *Leisure Sciences* 35 (2013): 129–144, doi.org /10.1080/01490400.2013.761905.

Studies show that simply spending ninety minutes outside, in a natural setting, stimulates beneficial changes in the PFC. G. N. Bratman, J. P. Hamilton, K. S. Hahn, G. C. Daily, and J. J. Gross, "Nature Experience Reduces Rumination and Subgenual Prefrontal Cortex Activation," *Proceedings of the National Academy of Sciences* 112, no. 28 (2015): 8567–72, doi.org/10.1073 /pnas.1510459112.

Time spent in green spaces and outdoors can improve cognition . . . F. E. Kuo and A. Faber Taylor, "A Potential Natural Treatment for Attention-Deficit/Hyperactivity Disorder: Evidence from a National Study," *American Journal of Public Health* 94, no. 9 (2004): 1580–86.

Daily contact with nature lowers stress . . . S. Gritzka, T. E. MacIntyre, D. Dörfel, J. L. Baker-Blanc, and G. Calogiuri, "The Effects of Workplace Nature-Based Interventions on the Mental Health and Well-Being of Employees: A Systematic Review," *Frontiers in Psychiatry* 11 (2020): 323, doi.org/10.3389/fpsyt.2020.00323.

Daily contact with nature lowers stress, improves mood, and reduces anxiety. R. Louv, *Last Child in the Woods: Saving Our Children from Nature-Deficit Disorder*, updated and expanded edition (Chapel Hill, NC: Algonquin Books, 2008).

The experience of unstructured play is crucial for nerve cell connections being made in kids' growing PFCs. S. M. Pellis, B. T. Himmler, S. M. Himmler, and V. C. Pellis, "Rough-and-Tumble Play and the Development of the Social Brain: What Do We Know, How Do We Know It, and What Do We Need to Know?," chapter 12 in *The Neurobiology of Brain and Behavioral Development*, ed. R. Gibb and B. Kolb (London: Academic Press, 2018), 315–37, doi.org /10.1016/B978-0-12-804036-2.00012-1.

. . . meaning free play without rules or directions from parents, teachers, coaches, or other adults. E. Entin, "All Work and No Play: Why Your Kids Are More Anxious, Depressed," *The Atlantic*, October 12, 2011. theatlantic.com/health/archive/2011/10/all-work-and -no-play-why-your-kids-are-more-anxious-depressed/246422/.

. . . brain-derived neurotrophic growth factor (BDNF). S. Bathina, U. N. Das, "Brain-derived Neurotrophic Factor and Its Clinical Implications," *Archives of Medical Science*. December 10, 2015; 11(6):1164–78. doi.org/10.5114/aoms.2015.56342

. . . "Miracle-Gro" for the brain. J. J. Ratey and Eric Hagerman (collaborator), *Spark: The Revolutionary New Science of Exercise and the Brain* (New York: Little, Brown and Co., 2008).

BDNF boosts memory and IQ . . . M. Miranda, J. F. Morici, M. B. Zanoni, and P. Bekinschtein, "Brain-Derived Neurotrophic Factor: A Key Molecule for Memory in the Healthy and the Pathological Brain," *Frontiers in Cellular Neuroscience* 13 (2019): 363, doi.org/10.3389 /fncel.2019.00363.

There is evidence that BDNF stimulates neurogenesis in older adults, including people with Alzheimer's. J. J. Ratey and J. E. Loehr, "The Positive Impact of Physical Activity on Cognition during Adulthood: A Review of Underlying Mechanisms, Evidence, and Recommendations," *Reviews in the Neurosciences* 22, no. 2 (2011): 171–85, doi.org/10.1515 /RNS.2011.017.

. . . even a shorter life span. S. M. Rothman and M. P. Mattson. "Activity-Dependent, Stress-Responsive BDNF Signaling and the Quest for Optimal Brain Health and Resilience throughout the Lifespan." *Neuroscience* 239 (2013): 228–40. https://doi.org/10.1016/j.neuro science.2012.10.014; *It can make us feel overwhelmed and trigger a sensation of "brain fog."* D. Gilbert, *Stumbling on Happiness* (New York: Vintage, 2007); and D. W. Grupe and J. B. Nitschke, "Uncertainty and Anticipation in Anxiety," *Nature Reviews Neuroscience* 14, no. 7 (2013): 488–501, doi.org/10.1038/nrn3524.

. . . getting to at least 70 percent of your maximum heart rate for thirty minutes, four or five times a week. J. J. Ratey and E. Hagerman (collaborator), *Spark: The Revolutionary New Science of Exercise and the Brain* (New York: Little, Brown and Co., 2008).

Several studies have found that having active daytime routines promotes healthier sleep cycles. A. Bond, "Daily routines may influence sleep quality, quantity," Reuters (online), (January 3, 2014); and Lyall et al., "Association of Disrupted Circadian Rhythmicity with Mood Disorders, Subjective Wellbeing, and Cognitive Function." doi.org/10.1016 /S2215-0366(18)30139-1.

. . . family routines help reduce oppositional and negative behaviors in children. H. I. Lanza and D.A.G. Drabick, "Family Routine Moderates the Relation between Child Impulsivity and Oppositional Defiant Disorder Symptoms," *Journal of Abnormal Child Psychology* 39 (2011): 83–94, doi.org/10.1007/s10802-010-9447-5.

. . . the body is still set to On Alert, not yet used to the surroundings. M. Tamaki, J. Won Bang, T. Watanabe, Y. Sasaki, "Night Watch in One Brain Hemisphere during Sleep Associated with the First-Night Effect in Humans," *Current Biology* 26, no. 9 (2016): 1190–1194, doi.org/10.1016/j.cub.2016.02.063.

. . . soothes the brain and tricks it into feeling that the task is being handled. E. J. Masicampo and R. F. Baumeister, "Consider It Done! Plan Making Can Eliminate the Cognitive Effects of Unfulfilled Goals," *Journal of Personality and Social Psychology* 101, no. 4 (2011): 667–83, doi.org/10.1037/a0024192.

A recent study looked at the sleep habits of more than two thousand first-year medical residents. Y. Fang, D. B. Forger, E. Frank, S. Sen, and C. Goldstein, "Day-to-Day Variability in Sleep Parameters and Depression Risk: A Prospective Cohort Study of Training Physicians," *npj Digital Medicine* 4, no. 1 (2021): 1–9, doi.org/10.1038/s41746-021-00400-z.

Keeping a regular sleep schedule is as important as . . . P. Moore, "Good Sleep Means More than Getting Enough Hours. A Consistent Schedule Matters, Too," *Washington Post* (online), April 30, 2021.

. . . lowering the temperature to around 65°F in the room before bedtime and during sleep . . . E. C. Harding, N. P. Franks, and W. Wisden, "Sleep and Thermoregulation," *Current Opinion in Physiology* 15 (2020): 7–13, doi.org/10.1016/j.cophys.2019.11.008.

. . . five to ten minutes of morning sun . . . M. B. Figueiro, B. Steverson, J. Heerwagen, K. Kampschroer, C. M. Hunter, K. Gonzales, B. Plitnick, B., and M. S. Rea, "The Impact of Daytime Light Exposures on Sleep and Mood in Office Workers," *Sleep Health* 3, no. 3 (2017): 204–15, doi.org/10.1016/j.sleh.2017.03.005.

. . . humor is also important for cognitive and emotional development. M. N. Neely, E. Walter, J. M. Black, and A. L. Reiss, "Neural Correlates of Humor Detection and Appreciation in Children," *Journal of Neuroscience* 32, no. 5 (2012): 1784–90, doi.org/10.1523/JNEURO SCI.4172-11.2012.

. . . outdoors into fresh air and use the walking time to connect with your child. Experimental Biology 2017, "How Walking Benefits the Brain: Researchers Show That Foot's Impact Helps Control, Increase the Amount of Blood Sent to the Brain," *ScienceDaily* (online), April 24, 2017.

Research supports the idea that tracking a behavior helps to change the behavior. M. Duncan, B. Murawski, C. E. Short, A. L. Rebar, S. Schoeppe, S. Alley, C. Vandelanotte, and M. Kirwan, "Activity Trackers Implement Different Behavior Change Techniques for Activity, Sleep, and Sedentary Behaviors," *Interactive Journal of Medical Research* 6, no. 2 (2017), doi.org/10.2196/ijmr.6685.

. . . the brain gets flooded with dopamine. M. Palaus, E. M. Marron, R. Viejo-Sobera, and D. Redolar-Ripoll, "Neural Basis of Video Gaming: A Systematic Review," *Frontiers in Human Neuroscience* 11 (2017), doi.org/10.3389/fnhum.2017.00248; M. J. Koepp, R. N. Gunn, A. D. Lawrence, V. J. Cunningham, A. Dagher, T. Jones, D. J. Brooks, C. J. Bench, and P. M. Grasby, "Evidence for Striatal Dopamine Release during a Video Game," *Nature* 393, no. 6682 (1998): 266–68, doi.org/10.1038/30498; and C. Montag and J. D. Elhai, "Discussing Digital Technology Overuse in Children and Adolescents during the COVID-19 Pandemic and Beyond: On the Importance of Considering Affective Neuroscience Theory," *Addictive Behaviors Reports* 12 (2020): 100313; doi.org/10.1016/j.abrep.2020.100313.

. . . irritability and boredom during most off-screen activities. C. Montag and J. D. Elhai, "Discussing Digital Technology Overuse in Children and Adolescents during the COVID-19 Pandemic and Beyond," *Addictive Behaviours Reports* 12 (2020): 100313; doi.org/10.1016/j.abrep.2020.100313; and M. Richtel, "Children's Screen Time Has Soared in the Pandemic, Alarming Parents and Researchers," *New York Times* (online), January 16, 2021.

Research shows that kids of all ages better understand time when it's visual. G. Shabiralyani, "Impact of Visual Aids in Enhancing the Learning Process Case Research: District Dera Ghazi Khan," *Journal of Education and Practice* 6, no. 19 (2015).

More and more studies are showing that the food we eat affects brain development and composition, brain function, and mood. F. Gómez-Pinilla, "Brain Foods: The Effects of Nutrients on Brain Function," *Nature Reviews Neuroscience* 9, no. 7 (2008): 568–78, doi.org/10.1038/nrn2421.

Fats, or lipids, account for nearly 60 percent of our brain composition, and come in the form of fatty acids. M. Haag, "Essential Fatty Acids and the Brain," *Canadian Journal of Psychiatry* 48, no. 3 (2003): 195–203.

. . . like a superconductor. S. C. Dyall, "Long-Chain Omega-3 Fatty Acids and the Brain: A Review of the Independent and Shared Effects of EPA, DPA and DHA," *Frontiers in Aging Neuroscience*, April 21, 2015, doi.org/10.3389/fnagi.2015.00052 and R. Avallone, G. Vitale, and M. Bertolotti, "Omega-3 Fatty Acids and Neurodegenerative Diseases: New Evidence in Clinical Trials," *International Journal of Molecular Science* 20, no. 17 (2019): 4256, doi.org/10.3390/ijms20174256.

". . . optimizing brain health." N. Parletta, D. Zarnowiecki, J. Cho, A. Wilson, S. Bogomolova, A. Villani, C. Itsiopoulos, et al., "Mediterranean-Style Dietary Intervention Supplemented with Fish Oil Improves Diet Quality and Mental Health in People with Depression: A Randomized Controlled Trial (HELFIMED)," *Nutritional Neuroscience* 22, no. 7 (2019): 474–87, doi.org/10.1080/1028415X.2017.1411320 and F. N. Jacka, A. O'Neil, R. Opie, C. Itsiopoulos, S. Cotton, M. Mohebbi, D. Castle, et al., "A Randomized Controlled Trial of Dietary Improvement for Adults with Major Depression (the 'SMILES' trial)," *BMC Medicine* 15, no. 23 (2017), doi.org/10.1186/s12916-017-0791-y.

"Some research indicates that we can reduce anxiety and improve mood when we make dietary changes to enhance the good bacteria in our gut." L. Harrison, "Manipulating the Microbiome to Improve Mood," *Medscape*, June 7, 2019, medscape.com/viewarticle/913817; "Personal Microbiomes Shown to Contain Unique 'Fingerprints,'" press release, Harvard T. H. Chan School of Public Health, May 11, 2015, hsph.harvard.edu/news/press-releases/personal -microbiomes-contain-unique-fingerprints/; and E. A. Franzosa, K. Huang, J. F. Meadow, D. Gevers, K. P. Lemon, B. J. M. Bohannan, and C. Huttenhower, "Identifying Personal Microbiomes Using Metagenomics Codes," *Proceedings of the National Academy of Sciences* 112, no. 22 (2015): E2930–38, doi.org/10.1073/pnas.1423854112.

There is a lot of emerging evidence that the gut biome can affect the brain. J. A. Foster, L. Rinaman, and J. F. Cryan, "Stress & the Gut-Brain Axis: Regulation by the Microbiome," *Neurobiology of Stress* 7 (2017): 124–36, doi.org/10.1016/j.ynstr.2017.03.001.

. . . *Columbia University psychiatrist Dr. Drew Ramsey* . . . D. Ramsey, *Eat to Beat Depression and Anxiety: Nourish Your Way to Better Mental Health in Six Weeks* (New York: HarperCollins, 2021).

Essential #2
LEARNING TO FOCUS: ATTENTION AND SELF-CONTROL

Some research shows that attention and self-control are limited resources that become depleted, like a muscle. R. F. Baumeister, E. Bratslavsky, M. Muraven, and D. M. Tice, "Ego Depletion: Is the Active Self a Limited Resource?" *Journal of Personality and Social Psychology* 74, no. 5 (1998): 1252–65.

Other research shows attention and self-control can be strengthened and grown. K. McGonigal, *The Willpower Instinct: How Self-Control Works, Why It Matters, and What You Can Do to Get More of It* (New York: Avery/Penguin Group USA, 2012).

. . . *research shows there are ways to increase the strength and number of the synaptic pathways in a developing brain.* . . R. F. Baumeister, K. D. Vohs, and D. M. Tice, "The Strength Model of Self-Control," *Current Directions in Psychological Science* 16, no. 6 (2007): 351–55, doi.org/10 .1111/j.1467-8721.2007.00534.x and R. Douglas Fields. "White matter in learning, cognition and psychiatric disorders." *Trends in Neurosciences* 31, no. 7 (2008): 361–70. doi.org/10.1016/j .tins.2008.04.001.

Functional MRI (fMRI) studies have looked at the adult brain and the adolescent brain while they were performing a simple self-control task. R. Marsh, H. Zhu, R. T. Schultz, G. Quackenbush, J. Royal, P. Skudlarski, and B. S. Peterson, "A Developmental fMRI Study of Self-Regulatory Control," *Human Brain Mapping* 27, no. 11 (2006): 848–63, doi.org/10.1002/hbm.20225.

Studies show children can sometimes exhibit even better self-control than adults, at least for brief periods. R. Marsh, H. Zhu, R. T. Schultz, G. Quackenbush, J. Royal, P. Skudlarski, and B. S. Peterson, "A Developmental fMRI Study of Self-Regulatory Control," *Human Brain Mapping* 27, no. 11 (2006): 848–63, doi.org/10.1002/hbm.20225.

The development of self-control advantageously wires a child's brain, helping to reduce the risk of mental disorders in adulthood. L. M. Paschke, D. Dörfel, R. Steimke, I. Trempler, A. Magrabi, V. U. Ludwig, T. Schubert, C. Stelzel, and H. Walter, "Individual Differences in Self-Reported Self-Control Predict Successful Emotion Regulation," *Social Cognitive and Affective Neuroscience* 11, no. 8 (2016): 1193–204, doi.org/10.1093/scan/nsw036; T. Moffitt, R. Poulton, and A. Caspi, "Lifelong Impact of Early Self-Control," *American Scientist* 101, no. 5 (2013): 352, doi.org/10.1511/2013.104.352; and T. E. Moffitt, L. Arseneault, D. Belsky, N. Dickson, R. J. Hancox, H. Harrington, R. Houts, et al. "A Gradient of Childhood Self-Control Predicts Health, Wealth, and Public Safety," *Proceedings of the National Academy of Sciences* 108, no. 7 (2011): 2693–98, doi.org/10.1073/pnas.1010076108.

. . . *Dr. Dan Siegel* . . . *founded the Mindsight Institute.* D. J. Siegel, *Mindsight: The New Science of Personal Transformation* (New York: Bantam Books, 2011).

This is because numerous studies show that focusing on "wins" in self-control actually decreases the chances of you maintaining that control later, while getting curious about and predicting your own failures is highly correlated with increased willpower. Kelly McGonigal, *The Willpower Instinct: How Self-Control Works, Why It Matters, and What You Can Do to Get More of It.* (New York: Avery/Penguin Group USA, 2012).

Essential #3
FEELING UNCOMFORTABLE: TOLERATING DIFFICULT FEELINGS

There is clear evidence that suppressing emotions can lead to some serious problems down the line, including an increase in the risk of depression, anxiety, substance abuse, and eating disorders.

K. S. Young, C. F. Sandman, M. G. Craske, *Positive and Negative Emotion Regulation in Adolescence: Links to Anxiety and Depression. Brain Sciences* 9, no. 4 (2019): 76, doi.org/10.3390/brainsci9040076.

B. Garssen, "Repression: Finding Our Way in the Maze of Concepts," *Journal of Behavioral Medicine* 30, no. 6 (2007): 471–81, doi.org/10.1007/s10865-007-9122-7; and M. Cullen, "How to Regulate Your Emotions without Suppressing Them," *Greater Good Magazine,* January 30, 2020, greatergood.berkeley.edu/article/item/how_to_regulate_your_emotions _without_suppressing_them.

Research has also linked emotional suppression to physical health issues . . . B. P. Chapman, K. Fiscella, I. Kawachi, P. Duberstein, and P. Muennig, "Emotion Suppression and Mortality Risk over a 12-Year Follow-Up," *Journal of Psychosomatic Research* 75, no. 4 (2013): 381–85, doi.org/10.1016 /j.jpsychores.2013.07.014; N. A. Roberts, R. W. Levenson, and J. J. Gross, "Cardiovascular Costs of Emotion Suppression Cross Ethnic Lines," *International Journal of Psychophysiology* 70, no. 1 (2008): 82–87, doi.org/10.1016/j.ijpsycho.2008.06.003; K. L. Weihs, T. M. Enright, S. J. Simmens, and D. Reiss, "Negative Affectivity, Restriction of Emotions, and Site of Metastases Predict Mortality in Recurrent Breast Cancer," *Journal of Psychosomatic Research* 49, no. 1 (2000): 59–68, doi.org/10.1016/S0022-3999(00)00143-4; and H. Koechlin, R. Coakley, N. Schechter, C. Werner, and J. Kossowsky, "The Role of Emotion Regulation in Chronic Pain: A Systematic Literature Review," *Journal of Psychosomatic Research* 107 (2018): 38–45, doi.org/10.1016/j.jpsychores.2018.02.002.

Emotional suppression can also affect our sense of empathy and our ability to connect with others. H. R. Karnilowicz, S. F. Waters, and W. B. Mendes, "Not in Front of the Kids: Effects of Parental Suppression on Socialization Behaviors during Cooperative Parent–Child Interactions," *Emotion* 19, no. 7 (2018): 1183–91, doi.org/10.1037/emo0000527; Washington State University, "Emotional Suppression Has Negative Outcomes on Children," *ScienceDaily* (online), November 26, 2018; and J. W. Burns, P. J. Quartana, W. Gilliam, J. Matsuura, C. Nappi, and B. Wolfe, "Suppression of Anger and Subsequent Pain Intensity and Behavior among Chronic Low Back Pain Patients: The Role of Symptom-Specific Physiological Reactivity," *Journal of Behavioral Medicine* 35, no. 1 (2012): 103–14, doi.org/10.1007/s10865 -011-9347-3.

Window of tolerance. . . D. Siegel, "Self-Regulation," chapter 7 in *The Developing Mind: How Relationships and the Brain Interact to Shape Who We Are* (New York: Guilford Press, 1999).

. . . participants' ability to hold their breath underwater (that is, people who were able to tolerate feeling uncomfortable) for longer periods of time correlated with their ability to function well under difficult circumstances.

G. Y. Thompson-Lake, R. De La Garza II, P. Hajek, "Breath holding endurance: stability over time and relationship with self-assessed persistence," *Heliyon,* 3, no. 9 (2017): e00398, doi.org/10.1016/j.heliyon.2017.e00398.

"Brett Ford and her colleagues at University of California at Berkeley devised a series of clever experiments to assess a nonjudgmental approach toward negative feeling states." B. Q. Ford, P. Lam, O. P. John, and I. B. Mauss, "The Psychological Health Benefits of Accepting Negative Emotions and Thoughts: Laboratory, Diary, and Longitudinal Evidence," *Journal of Personality and Social Psychology* 115, no. 6 (2018): 1075–92, doi.org/10.1037/pspp0000157.

... optimism ... can be a barrier to equanimity and acceptance. K. McGonigal, *The Willpower Instinct: How Self-Control Works, Why It Matters, and What You Can Do to Get More of It* (New York: Avery/Penguin Group USA, 2012), 92–98.

Science tells us that kids function best and recover more quickly when they can recognize, name, and most importantly, accept their feelings. D. J. Siegel and T. P. Bryson, *The Whole-Brain Child: 12 Revolutionary Strategies to Nurture Your Child's Developing Mind* (New York: Bantam Books, 2012).

... feeling (and exhibition) of shame by someone who'd made a mistake ... allowing that person to maintain their membership. D. Sznycer, D. Xygalatas, S. Alami, X.-F. An, K. I. Ananyeva, S. Fukushima, H. Hitokoto, et al., "Invariances in the Architecture of Pride across Small-Scale Societies," *Proceedings of the National Academy of Sciences* 115, no. 33 (2018): 8322, doi.org/10.1073/pnas.1808418115.

previously unfaithful marital partner ... D. Sznycer, D. Xygalatas, S. Alami, X.-F. An, K. I. Ananyeva, S. Fukushima, H. Hitokoto, et al., "Invariances in the Architecture of Pride across Small-Scale Societies," *Proceedings of the National Academy of Sciences* 115, no. 33 (2018): 8322, doi.org/10.1073/pnas.1808418115.

... avoiding feelings of shame, just like avoiding feelings of fear, can actually be more destructive ... J. Sabini and M. Silver, "In Defense of Shame: Shame in the Context of Guilt and Embarrassment," *Journal for the Theory of Social Behaviour* 27 (1997): 1–15, doi.org/10.1111/1468-5914.00023.

... mindfulness practice can literally grow physical connections in the brain ... Y. Y. Tang, B. K. Holzel, and M. I. Posner, "The Neuroscience of Mindfulness Meditation," *Nature Reviews Neuroscience* 16, no. 4 (2015): 213–25.

... short periods of consistent meditation can physically change brain structure and increase synaptic connections. K.C.R. Fox, S. Nijeboer, M. L. Dixon, J. L. Floman, M. Ellamil, S. P. Rumak, P. Sedlmeier, and K. Christoff, "Is Meditation Associated with Altered Brain Structure? A Systematic Review and Meta-Analysis of Morphometric Neuroimaging in Meditation Practitioners," *Neuroscience and Biobehavioral Reviews* 43 (2014): 48–73; and R. Tang, K. J. Friston, and Y.-Y. Tang, "Brief Mindfulness Meditation Induces Gray Matter Changes in a Brain Hub," *Neural Plasticity* 2020, no. 8830005 (2020): 1–8, doi.org/10.1155/2020/8830005.

NPR journalist Michaeleen Doucleff and her 3-year-old child, Rosy, lived with and investigated child-rearing practices in three of the oldest world cultures, including the Inuit of Northern Canada. M. Doucleff and E. Trujillo, *Hunt, Gather, Parent: What Ancient Cultures Can Teach Us about the Lost Art of Raising Happy, Helpful Little Humans* (New York: Avid Reader Press, 2021).

Essential #4
AVOIDING AVOIDANCE: ACCEPTING ANXIETY

If there ever was a time in history to become a resident expert on how to teach our kids to better manage anxiety, that time is right now. T. Chansky, *Freeing Your Child from Anxiety, Practical Strategies to Overcome Fears, Worries, and Phobias and Be Prepared for Life—from Toddlers to Teens,* revised and updated edition (New York: Harmony Books, 2014).

Statistically, we are significantly safer than our ancestors were in the prehistoric world for which our brain's threat detector is designed. R. Veenhoven, "Life is Getting Better: Societal Evolution and Fit with Human Nature," *Social Indicators Research* 97, no. 1 (2010): 105–122, doi.org/10.1007/s11205-009-9556-0.

Pre-pandemic, the National Institutes of Health found that nearly one in three children ages 13 to 18 will develop an anxiety disorder and depression will increase by 24 percent. National Institute of Mental Health (NIMH), "Any Anxiety Disorder," on the NIMH website, accessed April 8, 2021, nimh.nih.gov/health/statistics/any-anxiety-disorder.shtml.

Stanford psychologist Dr. Kelly McGonigal . . . has also helped transform how we look at stress. C. B. Parker, "Embracing Stress Is More Important than Reducing Stress, Stanford Psychologist Says," *Stanford News* (online), May 7, 2015, news.stanford.edu/2015/05/07 /stress-embrace-mcgonigal-050715/; K. McGonigal, *The Upside of Stress: Why Stress Is Good for You, and How to Get Good at It* (New York: Avery, 2016); K. McGonigal, *"How to Make Stress Your Friend,"* TED Talk, Edinburgh, Scotland, June 2013, ted.com/talks/kelly _mcgonigal_how_to_make_stress_your_friend/transcript.

Specifically, Dr. McGonigal challenges us to consider that it is our "toxic relationship with stress"— not stress itself—that is problematic. McGonigal, *"How to Make Stress Your Friend."*

Research studies support that shifting our mindset about stress changes our stress response, and that a "stress-is-enhancing-not-harmful" mindset may have lasting positive effects. A. Keller, K. Litzelman, L. E. Wisk, T. Maddox, E. R. Cheng, P. D. Creswell, and W. P. Witt, "Does the Perception That Stress Affects Health Matter? The Association with Health and Mortality," *Health Psychology* 31, no. 5 (2012): 677–84, doi.org/10.1037/a0026743; A. J. Crum, M. Akinola, A. Martin, and S. Fath, "The Role of Stress Mindset in Shaping Cognitive, Emotional, and Physiological Responses to Challenging and Threatening Stress," *Anxiety, Stress, and Coping* 30, no. 4 (2017): 379–95, doi.org/10.1080/10615806.2016.1275585.

Experiencing stress may also actually have positive correlations with lifespan. M. G. Marmot, G. D. Smith, S. Stansfeld, C. Patel, F. North, J. Head, I. White, E. Brunner, and A. Feeney, "Health Inequalities among British Civil Servants: The Whitehall II Study," *The Lancet* 337, no. 8754 (1991): 1387–93, doi.org/10.1016/0140-6736(91)93068-k; Keller et al., "Does the Perception That Stress Affects Health Matter?" *Health Psychology* 31, no. 5 (2011): 677–84, doi.org/10.1037/a0026743; P. Jaret, "The Surprising Benefits of Stress," *Greater Good Magazine*, October 20, 2015, greatergood.berkeley.edu/article/item/the_surprising _benefits_of_stress; E. D. Kirby, S. E. Muroy, W. G. Sun, D. Covarrubias, M. J. Leong, L. A. Barchas, and D. Kaufer, "Acute Stress Enhances Adult Rat Hippocampal Neurogenesis and Activation of Newborn Neurons via Secreted Astrocytic FGF2," eLife 2 (2013): e00362, doi.org/10.7554/eLife.00362.

We often remind our clients that there is an upside-down U-shaped relationship between stress and performance. R. M. Yerkes and J. D. Dodson, "The Relation of Strength of Stimulus to Rapidity of Habit-Formation," *Journal of Comparative Neurology and Psychology* 18, no. 5 (1908): 459–82; B. Salehi, M. I. Cordero, and C. Sandi, "Learning under Stress: The Inverted-U-Shape Function Revisited," *Learning & Memory* 17, no. 10 (2010): 522–30, doi.org/10.1101 /lm.1914110.

. . . parent's response to a child, and even a parent's own anxiety, can reduce or amplify the cortisol response of their child. A. M. Parenteau, N. V. Alen, L. K. Deer, A. T. Nissen, A. T. Luck, and C. E. Hostinar, "Parenting Matters: Parents Can Reduce or Amplify Children's Anxiety and Cortisol Responses to Acute Stress," *Development and Psychopathology* 32, no. 5 (2020): 1799– 809, doi.org/10.1017/S0954579420001285; F.-S. Koch, J. Ludvigsson, and A. Sepa, "Parents' Psychological Stress over Time May Affect Children's Cortisol at Age 8," *Journal of Pediatric Psychology* 35, no. 9 (2010): 950–59, doi.org/10.1093/jpepsy/jsp132; and V. K. Johnson and S. E. Gans, "Parent Cortisol and Family Relatedness Predict Anxious Behavior in Emerging Adults," *Journal of Family Psychology* 30, no. 7 (2016): 802–11, doi.org/10.1037/fam0000236.

Children who are especially sensitive to fear stimuli send frequent cries for help to their parent, and MRI studies have shown a correlation between increased amygdala size in children with anxiety disorders. S. Qin, C. B. Young, X. Duan, T. Chen, K. Supekar, and V. Menon, "Amygdala Subregional Structure and Intrinsic Functional Connectivity Predicts Individual Differences in Anxiety during Early Childhood," *Biological Psychiatry* 75, no. 11 (2014): 892–900, doi.org/10.1016/j.biopsych.2013.10.006.

New research suggests that especially sensitive and fearful children truly have less natural oxytocin available to them. E. R. Lebowitz, W. K. Silverman, A. M. Martino, O. Zagoory-Sharon, R. Feldman, and J. F. Leckman, "Oxytocin Response to Youth–Mother Interactions in Clinically Anxious Youth Is Associated with Separation Anxiety and Dyadic Behavior," *Depression and Anxiety* 34, no. 2 (2017): 127–36, doi.org/10.1002/da.22585; D. S. Carson, S. W. Berquist, T. H. Trujillo, J. P. Garner, S. L. Hannah, S. A. Hyde, R. D. Sumiyoshi, et al., "Cerebrospinal Fluid and Plasma Oxytocin Concentrations Are Positively Correlated and Negatively Predict Anxiety in Children," *Molecular Psychiatry* 20, no. 9 (2015): 1085–90, doi.org/10.1038/mp.2014.132.

. . . the kid may be affecting their parent right back . . . M. A. Lippold, P. Molenaar, S. Lee, K. D. Chandler, and D. M. Almeida, "Daily Parent-Adolescent Cortisol Associations: Unpacking the Direction of Effects," *Psychoneuroendocrinology* 116 (2020): 104652, doi.org /10.1016/j.psyneuen.2020.104652.

. . . In an early rescue has been challenged by new research. E. R. Lebowitz, *Addressing Parental Accommodation When Treating Anxiety in Children* (New York: Oxford University Press, 2019).

Dr. Lebowitz has developed a highly effective treatment for reducing childhood anxiety called Supportive Parenting for Anxious Childhood Emotions (SPACE). E. Lebowitz, *Breaking Free of Child Anxiety and OCD: A Scientifically Proven Program for Parents* (New York: Oxford University Press, 2021).

Essential #5
STAYING FLEXIBLE: PSYCHOLOGICAL ADAPTABILITY

Meditation teacher, psychologist, and podcast host Dr. Tara Brach brought the term radical acceptance *to the forefront in her powerful popular book by that title.* T. Brach, *Radical Acceptance: Embracing Your Life with the Heart of a Buddha* (New York: Bantam Books, 2004).

Research supports the idea that practicing acceptance not only improves general emotional well-being but is a powerful component in the treatment of multiple psychiatric conditions, including anxiety and depression. T. Brach, *Radical Acceptance: Embracing Your Life with the Heart of a Buddha* (New York: Bantam Books, 2004).

Dr. Brach takes her definition of radical acceptance a step further: "Recognizing what we are feeling in the present moment and regarding that experience with compassion." T. Brach, *Radical Acceptance: Embracing Your Life with the Heart of a Buddha* (New York: Bantam Books, 2004).

In a New York Times *article about using radical acceptance to cope with the COVID-19 pandemic, Dr. Brach said, "Life regularly and inevitably involves emotional stress, anger, fears around health, shame around failed relationships, but anything short of fully accepting our human experience will keep us caught in those emotions."* J. Taitz, "Radical Acceptance Can Keep Emotional Pain from Turning into Suffering," *New York Times* (online), April 22, 2021.

In weaving together the traditions of psychotherapy and Buddhism in her 2019 bestselling book Radical Compassion, *she offers the marvelously simple pneumonic RAIN.* T. Brach, *Radical Compassion: Learning to Love Yourself and Your World with the Practice of RAIN* (New York: Penguin Life, 2019).

The process isn't about ignoring difficult emotions and thoughts. It's about holding those emotions and thoughts loosely, facing them courageously and compassionately, and then moving past them. S. David, "The Gift and Power of Emotional Courage," TED Talk, New Orleans, Louisiana, November 2017, ted.com/talks/susan_david_the_gift_and_power_of_emotional_courage ?language=en.

. . . rigid thinking is correlated with poorer outcomes in terms of relationships, success, and contentment. S. David, *Emotional Agility: Get Unstuck, Embrace Change, and Thrive in Work and Life* (New York: Avery, 2016).

These mental shortcuts are often helpful and allow us to do many things at once, but research shows us over and over that they also make us deeply vulnerable to thinking errors. D. Kahneman, *Thinking, Fast and Slow* (New York: Farrar, Straus and Giroux, 2011).

Dr. Jennifer Daks and her colleagues published one of the first studies confirming that parental psychological flexibility—and inflexibility—appeared to directly impact families during the pandemic. J. S. Daks, J. S. Peltz, and R. D. Rogge, "Psychological Flexibility and Inflexibility as Sources of Resiliency and Risk during a Pandemic: Modeling the Cascade of COVID-19 Stress on Family Systems with a Contextual Behavioral Science Lens," *Journal of Contextual Behavioral Science* 18 (2020): 16–27, doi.org/10.1016/j.jcbs.2020.08.003.

The early stages of the pandemic were associated with increased levels of distress, depressive, and anxiety symptoms globally, with the mental health fallout particularly affecting children and adolescents.

M. É. Czeisler, "Mental Health, Substance Use, and Suicidal Ideation during the COVID-19 Pandemic—United States, June 24–30, 2020," *Morbidity and Mortality Weekly Report* 69 (2020), doi.org/10.15585/mmwr.mm6932a1.; M. Feider, *The State of Teen Mental Health during COVID-19 in America: A 4-H and Harris Poll Youth Mental Health Survey, Harris Poll,* June 23, 2020, 4-h.org/wp-content/uploads/2020/06/4-H-Mental-Health -Report-6.1.20-FINAL.pdf; R. T. Leeb, "Mental Health–Related Emergency Department Visits among Children Aged 18 Years during the COVID-19 Pandemic—United States, January 1–October 17, 2020," *Morbidity and Mortality Weekly Report* 69 (2020), doi.org/10 .15585/mmwr.mm6945a3; and F. Manjoo, "The Hidden 'Fourth Wave' of the Pandemic," *New York Times* (online), December 9, 2020.

Much of the current mental health crisis in the country occurred well before the pandemic. From 2009 to 2021, the proportion of American high-school students who said they felt "persistent feelings of sadness or hopelessness" rose from 26 percent to 44 percent, according to a CDC study. CDC-DASH. "Youth risk behavior survey: data summary & trends report 2009-2019." cdc.gov /healthyyouth/data/yrbs/pdf/YRBSDataSummaryTrendsReport2019-508.pdf; CDC Press Release, March 31, 2022. "New CDC data illuminate youth mental health threats during the COVID-19 pandemic." cdc.gov/media/releases/2022/p0331-youth-mental-health-covid -19.html; D. Thompson, "Why American Teens Are So Sad," *The Atlantic,* April 11, 2022.

Now signs are emerging that since the pandemic began, some kids may actually be developing new, more flexible thinking and better adaptability to changing circumstances. E. Soneson, S. Puntis, N. Chapman, K. L. Mansfield, K. L., M. Fazel, "Happier during lockdown: a descriptive analysis of self-reported well-being in 17,000 UK school students during COVID-19 lockdown." *European Child & Adolescent Psychiatry,* 1–16. Advance online publication. doi.org/10.1007/s00787-021-01934-z.

While some kids suffered deeply, a substantial number were largely unaffected, with some even possibly doing better during the pandemic. T. Ford, A. John, D. Gunnell, "Mental health of children and young people during pandemic." *BMJ* 2021;372:n614, bmj.com/content/372 /bmj.n614.

Long-term follow-up has shown remarkable signs of resiliency, with many kids displaying the ability to bounce back and adapt. E. Soneson, S. Puntis, N. Chapman, K. L. Mansfield, M. Fazel, "Happier during lockdown: a descriptive analysis of self-reported well-being in 17,000 UK school students during Covid-19 lockdown." *European Child & Adolescent Psychiatry,* 1–16. Advance online publication. doi.org/10.1007/s00787-021-01934-z.

The most effective treatment for OCD is to practice feeling uncertainty over longer and longer periods of time. C. M. Pinciotti, B. C. Riemann, and J. S. Abramowitz, "Intolerance of Uncertainty and Obsessive-Compulsive Disorder Dimensions," *Journal of Anxiety Disorders* 81, no. 102417 (2021), doi.org/10.1016/j.janxdis.2021.102417.

Neuroscientist Dan Siegel describes mental and emotional agility as a river, with chaos on one side and rigidity on the other. D. J. Siegel and T. P. Bryson, "Get in the Flow: Navigating the Waters between Chaos and Rigidity," in *The Whole-Brain Child: 12 Revolutionary Strategies to Nurture Your Child's Developing Mind* (New York: Bantam Books, 2012).

Essential #6
LETTING GO: BUILDING INDEPENDENCE

Harvard's Grant Study, spanning more than seventy-five years found strong support for chores as a path to develop work ethic. G. E. Vaillant, C. C. McArthur, and A. Bock, "Grant Study of Adult Development, 1938–2000," *Harvard Dataverse*, 2019, V4, doi.org/10.7910/DVN /48WRX9.

Another study from the University of Minnesota found the single best predictor for future relationship success with family, friends, and romantic partners is doing chores at ages 3 and 4 years old of age. University of Minnesota, "Involving Children in Household Chores: Is It Worth the Effort?" *ResearchWorks*, University of Minnesota College of Education and Human Development, 2002, ww1.prweb.com/prfiles/2014/02/22/11608927/children -with-chores-at-home-University-of-Minnesota.pdf.

Dr. Richard Rende's research at Brown University has also shown chores, increasing at specific ages, are strongly correlated with a decreased risk of alcohol and drug abuse, increased school engagement, and increased family connectedness through a sense of shared responsibility. R. Rende, "The Developmental Significance of Chores: Then and Now," *Brown University Child and Adolescent Behavior Letter* 31, no. 1 (2015): 1–7, doi.org/10.1002/cbl.30009.

Dr. Roger Hart, an environmental psychologist, observed eighty-six children between the ages of 3 and 12 daily for two and a half years in a small town in Vermont in the 1970s. "World with No Fear," episode of *Invisibilia*, an NPR program, January 15, 2015, npr.org/2015/01/16 /377517810/world-with-no-fear.

A recent study led by Stanford University professor Jelena Obradović examined parents' behaviors when their kindergarten-aged kids were playing, cleaning up toys, learning a new game, and discussing a problem. J. Obradović, M. J. Sulik, and A. Shaffer, "Learning to Let Go: Parental Over-engagement Predicts Poorer Self-Regulation in Kindergartners," *Journal of Family Psychology* 35, no. 8 (2021): 1160–70, doi.org/10.1037/fam0000838.

As many as 30 percent of first-year college students don't return for their sophomore year of college, even though many of them are fully prepared academically for college content and rigor. "U.S. College Dropout Rate and Dropout Statistics," August 12, 2014, updated June 29, 2018, *College Atlas* (online), collegeatlas.org/college-dropout.html.

The First Year College Experience survey found that 60 percent of first-year college students said they wished they had more help getting emotionally ready for college. JED Foundation, Partnership for Drug-Free Kids, and Jordan Porco Foundation, *The First-Year College Experience, a Harris Poll*, October 8, 2015, settogo.org/wp-content/uploads/2017/01 /First-Year-College-Experience-Data-Report-for-Media-Release-FINAL.pdf.

Half of the students said they felt stressed "most or all of the time," and more than a third felt they did not feel as if they were "in control of managing the stress of day-to-day college life." JED Foundation et al., *The First-Year College Experience*.

She cites a 2013 study showing a whopping 95 percent of college counseling center directors said the number of students with significant psychological problems is a growing concern on their campus. J. Lythcott-Haims, *How to Raise an Adult: Break Free of the Overparenting Trap and Prepare Your Kid for Success* (New York: Henry Holt and Co., 2015); B. J. Mistler, D. R. Reetz, B. Krylowicz, and V. Barr, *The Association for University and College Counseling Center Directors Annual Survey: Reporting Period: September 1, 2011 through August 12, 2012* (AUCCCD, 2013), files.cmcglobal.com/Monograph_2012_AUCCCD_Public.pdf.

Seventy percent of directors believed that the number of students with severe psychological problems on their campus had increased in the past year. At the top was anxiety in 41% of college students, followed closely by depression at 36.4 percent. American College Health Association–National College Health Assessment II (ACHA-NCHA II), Spring 2013 Reference Group Executive Summary (ACHA, Spring 2013), acha.org/documents/ncha/ACHA-NCHA-II_Reference Group_ExecutiveSummary_Spring2013.pdf.

Our colleagues Dr. William Stixrud and Ned Johnson explain why the transition to college is treacherous for some kids in their book The Self-Driven Child. W. Stixrud and N. Johnson, *The Self-Driven Child: The Science and Sense of Giving Your Kids More Control over Their Lives* (New York: Penguin Publishing Group, 2019).

"As we see it, there are two critical issues at hand. First, college life is a highly dysregulated environment with inconsistent sleep patterns and diets, little structure, and an abundance of binge-drinking, pot-smoking, and abuse of stimulants like Adderall. Second, students haven't been given control of their own lives until way too late. You wouldn't tell a kid to merge onto the freeway the first time he gets behind the wheel of a car, and yet that's essentially what we do in expecting students to go from parental control to near-total freedom." W. Stixrud and N. Johnson, "When a College Student Comes Home to Stay," *New York Times* (online), November 19, 2018.

Essential #7
TRUSTING THE SPARK: MOTIVATION

But dopamine does not just passively arrive with pleasure—it also makes us go after it. C. Buckley, "UConn Researcher: Dopamine Not about Pleasure (Anymore)," *UConn Today*, November 30, 2012, today.uconn.edu/2012/11/uconn-researcher-dopamine-not-about-pleasure-anymore.

"Low levels of dopamine make people and other animals less likely to work for things, so [dopamine] has more to do with motivation and cost/benefit analyses than pleasure itself," explains dopamine expert Dr. John Salamone. J. D. Salamone. M. Correa, J.-H. Yang, R. Rotolo, and R. Presby, "Dopamine, Effort-Based Choice, and Behavioral Economics: Basic and Translational Research," *Frontiers in Behavioral Neuroscience* 12 (2018), doi.org/10.3389/fnbeh.2018.00052.

Vanderbilt researchers found differences in dopamine levels among individuals throughout the motivation spectrum. M. T. Treadway, J. W. Buckholtz, R. L. Cowan, N. D. Woodward, R. Li, M. S. Ansari, R. M. Baldwin, A. N. Schwartzman, R. M. Kessler, and D. H. Zald, "Dopaminergic Mechanisms of Individual Differences in Human Effort-Based Decision-Making," *Journal of Neuroscience* 32, no. 18 (2012): 6170-76, doi.org/10.1523/JNEUROSCI.6459-11.2012.

Many motivation professionals rely on Edward Deci and Richard Ryan's landmark self-determination theory, which they laid out in 1985, but others have confirmed decade after decade, to explain the complex relationship between our motivation, personality, and functioning. R. M. Ryan and E. L. Deci, *Self-Determination Theory* (New York: Guilford Publications, 2018).

Hundreds of studies have demonstrated that when children are rewarded for doing a task they find inherently enjoyable, they tend to lose interest in doing the task for enjoyment's sake. S.-H. Tang and V. C. Hall, "The Overjustification Effect: A Meta-Analysis," *Applied Cognitive Psychology* 9, no. 5 (1995): 365–404, doi.org/10.1002/acp.2350090502.

Edward Deci first showed this happening in an experiment with college students working on a puzzle. E. L. Deci, "Effects of Externally Mediated Rewards on Intrinsic Motivation," *Journal of Personality and Social Psychology*, 18, no. 1 (1971): 105–15, doi.org/10.1037/h0030644.

Carol Dweck's groundbreaking research on mindsets has revolutionized how we think about potential across many domains including intelligence and talent. C. S. Dweck, *Mindset: The New Psychology of Success* (New York: Random House Digital, Inc., 2008).

Another landmark study with young children by Mark Lepper, David Greene, and Richard Nisbett in 1973 involved a drawing task with children who already loved to draw. M. R. Lepper, D. Greene, and R. E. Nisbett, "Undermining Children's Intrinsic Interest with Extrinsic Reward: A Test of the 'Overjustification' Hypothesis," *Journal of Personality and Social Psychology* 28, no. 1 (1973): 129–37, doi.org/10.1037/h0035519.

Essential #8
BEING HUMAN: COMPASSION AND GRATITUDE

The skills of compassion and gratitude are hugely important for overall well-being, and are linked to increased happiness, better health, and greater life satisfaction in all people. S. Allen, "The Science of Gratitude," white paper prepared for the John Templeton Foundation (Greater Good Science Center at UC Berkeley, May 2018), ggsc.berkeley.edu/images/uploads/GGSC-JTF_White _Paper-Gratitude-FINAL.pdf; and E. Seppala, "Compassionate Mind, Healthy Body," *Greater Good Magazine*, July 24, 2013, greatergood.berkeley.edu/article/item/compassionate _mind_healthy_body.

We are evolutionarily wired for compassion, and it is one of the traits that can keep us well liked, well fed, and more likely to spread our DNA. J. L. Goetz, D. Keltner, E. Simon-Thomas. "Compassion: An Evolutionary Analysis and Empirical Review," *Psychological Bulletin* 136, no. 3 (2010): 351–74, doi.org/10.1037/a0018807; P. Gilbert, "Compassion: From Its Evolution to a Psychotherapy," *Frontiers in Psychology* 11 (2020): 586161, doi.org/10.3389 /fpsyg.2020.586161.

Practicing gratitude, turning the mind toward others, can lead us to feel more compassion for others. R. A. Emmons, *Thanks! How Practicing Gratitude Can Make You Happier* (New York: Houghton Mifflin, 2007).

And compassion is a value that, when lived, brings deep fulfillment and social connection, increases oxytocin (that feel-good chemical, helps us make social connections, and binds us even more closely to others who may love and care for us. D. Keltner, "The Compassion Instinct," *Greater Good Magazine*, March 1, 2004, greatergood.berkeley.edu/article/item/the_compassionate _instinct; and D. Keltner, "The Compassionate Species," *Greater Good Magazine*, July 31, 2012, greatergood.berkeley.edu/article/item/the_compassionate_species.

Nobody says it better than the Greater Good Science Center: "Compassion is not the same as empathy or altruism, thought the concepts are related. While empathy refers more generally to the ability to take the perspective of and feel the emotions of another person, compassion is when those feelings and thoughts include the desire to help." greatergood.berkeley.edu/topic/compassion/definition.

Dr. Dacher Keltner, founding director of the Greater Good Science Center at the University of California at Berkeley, is an expert on the science of compassion. Dacher Keltner | Profile. (n.d.). *Greater Good Magazine*. Retrieved April 10, 2021, from greatergood.berkeley.edu/profile /dacher_keltner.

His research has helped show how the human "compassionate instinct" has ensured our survival as a species. D. Keltner, "The Evolutionary Roots of Compassion," video, part of the *Science of a Meaningful Life* video series on the website of *Greater Good Magazine*, July 2012, greatergood .berkeley.edu/video/item/dacher_keltner_the_evolutionary_roots_of_compassion.

Physical pain activates a part of our brain called the anterior cingulate. D. Keltner, *Born to Be Good: The Science of a Meaningful Life* (New York: W. W. Norton & Company, 2009).

In Dr. Keltner's words, "We have the same pain response to other people's pain as we do our own experience of pain. We are wired to empathize." Keltner, "The Compassionate Species." (See above.)

The vagus nerve—our nervous system's longest wandering nerve, which stretches from the brain to the abdomen—also shows activity when we feel compassion. J. E. Stellar, A. Cohen, C. Oveis, and D. Keltner, "Affective and Physiological Responses to the Suffering of Others: Compassion and Vagal Activity," *Journal of Personality and Social Psychology* 108, no. 4 (2015): 572–85, doi.org/10.1037/pspi0000010.

Research by Keltner and others suggests that we are evolutionarily wired to care about other people and that compassion may have ensured our survival because of its massive benefits to our species as a whole. D. Keltner, J. Marsh, and J. A. Smith, eds., *The Compassionate Instinct: The Science of Human Goodness* (New York: W. W. Norton, 2010); Keltner, "The Compassion Instinct"; and Keltner, "The Compassionate Species."

The science indicates that compassion makes us more resilient to the effects of stress, strengthens our immune response, and may improve longevity. E. Diener and M.E.P. Seligman, "Beyond Money: Toward an Economy of Well-Being," Psychological Science in the Public Interest 5, no. 1 (2004): 1–31, doi.org/10.1111/j.0963-7214.2004.00501001.x; S. Konrath, A. Fuhrel-Forbis, A. Lou, and S. Brown, "Motives for Volunteering Are Associated with Mortality Risk in Older Adults," *Health Psychology* 31, no. 1 (2012): 87–96, doi.org/10.1037/a0025226; and M.E.P. Seligman, *Flourish: A Visionary New Understanding of Happiness and Well-Being* (New York: Atria Books, 2012).

Cultivating compassion has been shown to increase daily positive emotions, reduce depressive symptoms, decrease amygdala response, improve emotion regulation, and increase life satisfaction. A. Lutz, L. L. Greischar, D. M. Perlman, and R. J. Davidson, "BOLD signal in Insula Is Differentially Related to Cardiac Function during Compassion Meditation in Experts vs. Novices," *NeuroImage* 47, no. 3 (2009): 1038–46, doi.org/10.1016/j.neuroimage.2009.04.081.; C. A. Hutcherson, E. M. Seppala, and J. J. Gross, "Loving-Kindness Meditation Increases Social Connectedness," *Emotion* 8, no. 5 (2008): 720–24, doi.org/10.1037/a0013237.

Social scientists James Fowler of the University of California at San Diego and Nicholas Christakis of Harvard have shown that kindness behavior spreads from person to person to person. University of California–San Diego, "Acts of Kindness Spread Surprisingly Easily: Just a Few People Can Make a Difference," *ScienceDaily* (online), March 10, 2010.

When people benefit from kindness, they "pay it forward" by helping others, creating a cascade of kindness and trickle-down effect in a social network. University of California–San Diego, "Acts of Kindness Spread Surprisingly Easily: Just a Few People Can Make a Difference."

There's empirical support for the idea of a "set point" to happiness, meaning that we each tend to have a default level of happiness that is determined by a combination of temperament, mood, and emotions, and not by life circumstances. G. Hülür and D. Gerstorf, "Set Point," entry in *The SAGE Encyclopedia of Lifespan Human Development*, ed. M. Bornstein (SAGE Publications, Inc., 2018), 1958–60, dx.doi.org/10.4135/9781506307633.n728.

For example, in the spectrum of completely life changing experiences, studies have shown that people who have had life changing lottery wins, after an initial bump in euphoria, reported no more baseline happiness that those who have had life-changing spinal cord injuries. P. Brickman, D. Coates, and R. Janoff-Bulman, "Lottery Winners and Accident Victims: Is Happiness Relative?" *Journal of Personality and Social Psychology* 36, no. 8 (1978): 917–27, doi.org/10.1037//0022-3514.36.8.917.

Gratitude has been shown to be an effective method for increasing well-being and contentment, both day-to-day and by nudging our set point of happiness upward. Harvard Health Publishing, "Giving Thanks Can Make You Happier," *HealthBeat* (e-newsletter), August 14, 2021, health.harvard.edu/healthbeat/giving-thanks-can-make-you-happier.

Research has linked gratitude to happiness in children by as early as age 5. S. P. Nguyen and C. L. Gordon, "The Relationship between Gratitude and Happiness in Young Children," *Journal of Happiness Studies* 21 (2020): 2773–87, doi.org/10.1007/s10902-019-00188-6.

A study of middle school children, from ages 11 through 13, showed that children who expressed gratitude were more optimistic, had better social support, and were overall happier. J. J. Froh, W. J. Sefick, and R. A. Emmons, "Counting Blessings in Early Adolescents: An Experimental Study of Gratitude and Subjective Well-Being," *Journal of School Psychology* 46, no. 2 (2008): 213–33, doi.org/10.1016/j.jsp.2007.03.005.

And an adolescent study (ages 14 to 19) showed that grateful teens were more satisfied with their lives, more likely to want to improve their communities, and overall more engaged with and successful in their schoolwork. A.J.S. Youssef, J. J. Froh, M. E. Muller, and T. Lomas, "Measuring Gratitude in Youth: Assessing the Psychometric Properties of Adult Gratitude Scales in Children and Adolescents," *Psychological Assessment* 23, no. 2 (2011): 311–24, doi.org/10.1037/e711892011-001.

Studies of adults and gratitude have found similar effects. A. M. Wood, J. J. Froh, and A. W. Geraghty, "Gratitude and Well-Being: A Review and Theoretical Integration," *Clinical Psychology Review* 30, no. 7 (2010): 890–905, doi.org/10.1016/j.cpr.2010.03.005; C. V. Witvliet, F. J. Richie, L. M. R. Luna, and D. R. V. Tongeren, "Gratitude Predicts Hope and Happiness: A Two-Study Assessment of Traits and States," *Journal of Positive Psychology* 14, no. 3 (2016): 271–82, doi.org/10.1080/17439760.2018.1424924.

Gratitude has even been linked to better physical health in adults. E. R. Simon-Thomas, "A 'Thnx' a Day Keeps the Doctor Away," *Greater Good Magazine*, December 19, 2012, greatergood .berkeley.edu/article/item/a_thnx_a_day_keeps_the_doctor_away; Summer Allen, "The Science of Gratitude." John Templeton Foundation, May 1, 2018. ggsc.berkeley.edu/images /uploads/GGSC-JTF_White_Paper-Gratitude-FINAL.pdf.

Several studies have found that people who feel more gratitude also experience better sleep, less fatigue, and lower levels of cellular inflammation. L. I. Hazlett, M. Moieni, M. R. Irwin, K. E. Byrne Haltom, I. Jevtic, M. L. Meyer, E. C. Breen, S. W. Cole, and N. I. Eisenberger, "Exploring Neural Mechanisms of the Health Benefits of Gratitude in Women: A Randomized Controlled Trial," *Brain, Behavior, and Immunity* 95 (2021): 444–53, doi.org/10.1016/j.bbi .2021.04.019.

In one study of heart failure patients, participants who kept a gratitude journal for eight weeks had reduced signs of inflammation afterward, giving evidence of the direct effect of gratitude on health. L. S. Redwine, B. L. Henry, M. A. Pung, K. Wilson, K. Chinh, B. Knight, S. Jain, et al., "Pilot Randomized Study of a Gratitude Journaling Intervention on Heart Rate Variability and Inflammatory Biomarkers in Patients with Stage B Heart Failure," *Psychosomatic Medicine* 78, no. 6 (2016): 667–76, doi.org/10.1097/PSY.0000000000000316.

A national poll conducted in 2021 asked parents of kids age 4 to 10 if their kids are "grateful for what they have." C. S. Mott Children's Hospital, University of Michigan Health, "Parent Efforts to Teach Children about Gratitude," *Mott Poll Report* 39, no. 5 (November 22, 2021), mottpoll.org/reports/parent-efforts-teach-children-about-gratitude.

One study found that writing daily gratitude lists for just two weeks increased positive moods, happiness, and life satisfaction and reduced negative moods and depression symptoms. R. A. Emmons and M. E. McCullough, "Counting Blessings versus Burdens: An Experimental Investigation of Gratitude and Subjective Well-Being in Daily Life," *Journal of Personality and Social Psychology* 84, no. 2 (2003): 377–89, doi.org/10.1037/0022-3514.84.2.377.

Research suggests that there are actions we can take, even short term, that can increase our own and our child's feelings of gratitude. A. M. Hussong, H. A. Langley, W. A. Rothenberg, J. L. Coffman, A. G. Halberstadt, P. R. Costanzo, and I. Mokrova, "Raising Grateful Children One Day at a Time," *Applied Developmental Science* 23, no. 4 (2019): 371–84, doi.org/10.1080 /10888691.2018.1441713; A. Morin. "How to Teach Children Gratitude," Verywell Mind website, November 11, 2020, verywellmind.com/how-to-teach-children-gratitude-4782154; "How to Help Kids Develop Gratitude," post on the Harvard Graduate School of Education Making Caring Common Project website, 2022, mcc.gse.harvard.edu/resources-for-families /develop-gratitude; and "10 Tips for Raising Grateful Kids," Child Mind Institute website, September 9, 2021, childmind.org/article/10-tips-raising-grateful-kids/.

Essential #9
BOUNCING BACK: RESILIENCE

Behavioral epigenetics is a fascinating field of study pioneered by Drs. Michael Meaney and Moshe Szyf. M. J. Meaney and M. Szyf, "Environmental Programming of Stress Responses through DNA Methylation: Life at the Interface between Dynamic Environment and a Fixed Genome," *Dialogues in Clinical Neuroscience* 7, no. 2 (2005): 103–23.

Subsequent research has found support for the idea that not just trauma but resilience may be genetically heritable. S. J. Russo, J. W. Murrough, M. H. Han, D. S. Charney, and E. J. Nestler, "Neurobiology of Resilience," *Nature Neuroscience* 15, no. 11 (2012): 1475–84, doi.org/10.1038/nn.3234.

Until recently, very little was known about the mechanisms underlying resiliency, but exciting emerging research has found specific genetic variants that contribute to human capacity for psychological resilience under trauma and stress. R. G. Hunter, J. D. Gray, and B. S. McEwen, "The Neuroscience of Resilience," *Journal of the Society for Social Work and Research* 9, no. 2 (2018): 305–39; K. Niitsu, M. J. Rice, J. F. Houfek, S. F. Stoltenberg, K. A. Kupzyk, and C. R. Barron, "A Systematic Review of Genetic Influence on Psychological Resilience," *Biological Research for Nursing* 21, no. 1 (2019): 61–71, doi.org/10.1177/1099800418800396.

Researchers looking at a group of several thousand military veterans found that one year into the pandemic, 43 percent of them had experienced COVID-19-associated posttraumatic growth (a type of positive psychological change resulting from a traumatic situation), including appreciation of life, better relating to others, and greater personal strength. R. H. Pietrzak, J. Tsai, and S. M. Southwick, "Association of Symptoms of Posttraumatic Stress Disorder with Posttraumatic Psychological Growth among US Veterans during the COVID-19 Pandemic," *JAMA Network Open* 4, no. 4 (2021): e214972, doi.org/10.1001/jamanetworkopen.2021.4972.

The most significant of these factors has consistently been connectedness: Having a stable and committed relationship with at least one adult, no matter the environmental stressors, strengthens a child's resilience. "Key Concepts: Resilience," post on the Center on the Developing Child at Harvard University website, retrieved May 3, 2021, developingchild.harvard.edu/science/key-concepts/resilience/; A. S. Masten and A. J. Barnes, "Resilience in Children: Developmental Perspectives," *Children* (Basel, Switzerland) 5, no. 7 (2018): 98, doi.org/10.3390/children5070098.

Northwestern University researcher Dashun Wang calls failure "the essential prerequisite for success." D. Noonan, "Failure Found to Be an 'Essential Prerequisite' for Success," *Scientific American*, October 30, 2019, scientificamerican.com/article/failure-found-to-be-an-essential -prerequisite-for-success/.

His team's analysis of data sets from three diverse fields—scientific research, entrepreneurship, and terrorism (!)—found the same pattern: People who eventually succeeded and people who eventually failed did not differ in sheer persistence (they had nearly identical numbers of attempts). Y. Yin, Y. Wang, J. A. Evans, and D. Wang, "Quantifying the Dynamics of Failure across Science, Startups and Security," *Nature* 575 (2019): 190–94, doi.org/10.1038/s41586-019-1725-y.

Essential #10
ALL TOGETHER NOW: LIVING THE PLAYBOOK

Dr. Suniya Luthar, who has led decades of groundbreaking research on the mental health of children and adolescents, surveyed a diverse group of more than 46,000 students in sixth through twelfth grade beginning in 2019. She found that the strongest predictors of depression and anxiety in the kids were, first, their perception that their parents were dissatisfied with them and, second, their parents' mood. J. Warner, "How to Help Your Adolescent Think about the Last Year," *New York Times* (online), April 11, 2021 (updated April 14, 2021).

RAISING A KID IN THE DIGITAL AGE

The technology journalist Johann Hari, after interviewing numerous "attention engineers" . . . J. Hari, *Stolen Focus: Why You Can't Pay Attention—and How to Think Deeply Again* (New York: Crown, 2022).

It came from a headline-grabbing Microsoft report that appeared in dozens of news stories in multiple countries. Maybin, "Busting the Attention Span Myth," BBC World Service, March 10, 2017, bbc.com/news/health-38896790.

Yet the nuance—that the statistic was cited in the Microsoft research paper but was NOT actually a finding of the Microsoft study—was completely lost. S. Maybin, "Busting the Attention Span Myth," BBC World Service, March 10, 2017, bbc.com/news/health-38896790.

It turns out it's pretty difficult to study attention spans in general because our ability to sustain attention depends on a bunch of constantly changing variables, such as our mood, our health, the time of day, and of course the specific task that we are doing at that moment. J. M. Lodge and W. J. Harrison, "The Role of Attention in Learning in the Digital Age," *Yale Journal of Biology and Medicine* 92, no. 1 (2019): 21–28.

A 2021 large-scale survey of British adults found that half of respondents felt their attention span had gotten shorter. Data tables are available at the website of Savanta ComRes; see also "Are Attention Spans Really Collapsing? Data Shows UK Public Are Worried—but Also See Benefits from Technology," *King's College London News Centre*, February 16, 2022, kcl.ac.uk /news/are-attention-spans-really-collapsing-data-shows-uk-public-are- worried-but-also -see-benefits-from-technology.

The Journal of the American Medical Association *reports a large-scale study that followed more than 2,500 high school students.* C. K. Ra, J. Cho, M. D. Stone, J. De La Cerda, N. I. Goldenson, E. Moroney, I. Tung, S. S. Lee, and A. M. Leventhal, "Association of Digital Media Use with Subsequent Symptoms of Attention-Deficit/Hyperactivity Disorder among Adolescents," *JAMA* 320, no. 3 (2018): 255–63, doi.org/10.1001/jama.2018.8931.

Numerous studies have found that the mere presence of a smart phone impairs attention and cognitive capacity. A. F. Ward, K. Duke, A. Gneezy, and M. W. Bos, "Brain Drain: The Mere Presence of One's Own Smartphone Reduces Available Cognitive Capacity," *Journal of the Association for Consumer Research* 2, no. 2 (2017): 140, doi.org/10.1086/691462.

Thus, multitasking is, technically speaking, neurologically impossible. "Why Multitasking Doesn't Work," Cleveland Clinic Health Essentials website, March 10, 2021, health.clevelandclinic. org/science-clear-multitasking-doesnt-work/; J. S. Rubinstein, D. E. Meyer, and J. E. Evans, "Executive Control of Cognitive Processes in Task Switching," *Journal of Experimental Psychology: Human Perception and Performance* 27, no. 4 (2001): 763–97, doi.org/10.1037/0096 -1523.27.4.763.

Miller explains that when we think we are multitasking, we are actually switching from one task to another very rapidly and incurring what is called the "switch cost effect"—the expense of cellular energy required to switch between multiple tasks. E. Miller, "Multitasking: Why Your Brain Can't Do It and What You Should Do about It," presentation for the Hack Your Mind series hosted by Radius at the Massachusetts Institute for Technology, April 11, 2017, available at radius.mit.edu/programs/multitasking-why-your-brain-cant-do-it-and-what -you-should-do-about-it.

And then, thanks to these dopamine hits, our brain gives us the false feedback that we are totally rocking it, when in reality we are spread thin and doing a mediocre job. D. Sanbonmatsu, D. Strayer, N. Medeiros-Ward, and J. Watson, "Who Multi-Tasks and Why? Multi-Tasking Ability, Perceived Multi-Tasking Ability, Impulsivity, and Sensation Seeking," *PLoS One* 8, no. 1 (2013): e54402, doi.org/10.1371/journal.pone.0054402.

Additionally, Stanford researchers are finding evidence that heavy multitaskers have reduced memory, reduced overall concentration, and less creativity over time. M. R. Uncapher and A. D. Wagner, "Minds and Brains of Media Multitaskers: Current Findings and Future Directions," *Proceedings of the National Academy of Sciences* 115, no. 40 (2018): 9889–96, doi.org/10.1073/pnas.1611612115.

Dr. Jonathan Smallwood, a leader in the study of mind wandering . . . J. Smallwood and J. Schooler, "The Science of Mind Wandering: Empirically Navigating the Stream of Consciousness," *Annual Review of Psychology* 66 (2014): 487–515, doi.org/10.1146/annurev-psych-010814-015331.

As former Google design ethicist Tristan Harris stated in testimony to the US Senate in 2019, "You can try having self-control, but there are a thousand engineers on the other side of the screen working against you." T. Harris, comments made at the US Senate Committee on Commerce, Science, and Transportation's hearing "Optimizing for Engagement: Understanding the Use of Persuasive Technology on Internet Platforms," Washington, DC, June 25, 2019, commerce.senate.gov/services/files/96E3A739-DC8D-45F1-87D7-EC70A368371D.

It's not your fault. J. Hari, *Stolen Focus: Why You Can't Pay Attention—and How to Think Deeply Again* (New York: Crown, 2022).

Numerous studies have found that the mere presence of a smartphone impairs attention and cognitive capacity. A smartphone within sight, even if it's turned off and upside down, appears to reduce the ability to focus and perform tasks. A. F. Ward, K. Duke, A. Gneezy, and M. W. Bos, "Brain Drain: The Mere Presence of One's Own Smartphone Reduces Available Cognitive Capacity." *Journal of the Association for Consumer Research* (2018). doi.org/10.1086/691462.

Unfun fact: a recent study found today's teenagers now focus on any one task for an average of 65 seconds (for adults, it's 3 minutes, also not awesome). J. Hari, *Stolen Focus: Why You Can't Pay Attention—and How to Think Deeply Again* (New York: Crown, 2022).

Research clearly shows correlations between social media use and depression in some teens. J. M. Twenge, "Have Smartphones Destroyed a Generation?" *The Atlantic*, September 2017.

Teens who used social media more than five hours a day were found to be twice as likely to be depressed as nonusers. J. M. Twenge, "Increases in Depression, Self-Harm, and Suicide among U.S. Adolescents after 2012 and Links to Technology Use: Possible Mechanisms," *Psychiatric Research & Clinical Practice* 2, no. 1 (2020): 19–25, doi.org/10.1176/appi.prcp .20190015.

. . . girls appear to be disproportionately affected. J. M. Twenge, T. E. Joiner, M. L. Rogers, and G. N. Martin, "Increases in Depressive Symptoms, Suicide-Related Outcomes, and Suicide Rates among U.S. Adolescents after 2010 and Links to Increased New Media Screen Time," *Clinical Psychological Science* 6, no. 1 (2018): 3–17, doi.org/10.1177/2167702617723376.

. . . Facebook's own research found that heavy Instagram use . . . G. Wells, J. Horowitz, D. Seetharaman, "Facebook Knows Instagram Is Toxic for Teen Girls, Company Documents Show," *Wall Street Journal* (online), September 14, 2021; and R. Cohen, T. Newton-John, and A. Slater, "The Relationship between Facebook and Instagram Appearance-Focused Activities and Body Image Concerns in Young Women," *Body Image* 23 (2017): 183–87, doi.org/10.1016/j.bodyim.2017.10.002.

Newer, larger studies show that social media use . . . A. Orben and A. K. Przybylski, "The Association between Adolescent Well-Being and Digital Technology Use," *Nature Human Behavior* 3, no. 2 (2019): 173–82, doi.org/10.1038/s41562-018-0506-1; and A. K. Przybylski and N. Weinstein, "A Large-Scale Test of the Goldilocks Hypothesis," *Psychological Science* 28, no. 2 (2017): 204–15, doi.org/10.1177/0956797616678438.

. . . kids with depression, anxiety, and ADHD. C. Odgers, "Smartphones Are Bad for Some Teens, Not All," *Nature* 554, no. 7693 (2018): 432–34, doi.org10.1038/d41586-018-02109-8; C. L. Odgers and M. R. Jensen, "Annual Research Review: Adolescent Mental Health in the Digital Age: Facts, Fears, and Future Directions," *Journal of Child Psychology and Psychiatry* 61, no. 3 (2020): 336–48, doi.org/10.1111/jcpp.13190; Child Mind Institute, "Smartphones and Social Media," in 2017 Children's Mental Health Report (Child Mind Institute, 2017), childmind.org/awareness-campaigns/childrens-mental-health-report/2017-childrens-mental-health-report/; and C. Miller, "Does Social Media Use Cause Depression?," post on the Child Mind Institute website, April 14, 2022, childmind.org/article/is-social-media-use-causing-depression/.

. . . preexisting conditions may actually cause increased social media use . . . T. Heffer, M. Good, O. Daly, E. MacDonell, and T. Willoughby, "The Longitudinal Association between Social-Media Use and Depressive Symptoms among Adolescents and Young Adults: An Empirical Reply to Twenge et al. (2018)," *Clinical Psychological Science* 7, no. 3 (2019): 462–70, doi.org/10.1177/2167702618812727; L. Raudsepp and K. Kais, "Longitudinal Associations between Problematic Social Media Use and Depressive Symptoms in Adolescent Girls," *Preventive Medicine Reports* 15 (2019): 100925, doi.org/10.1016/j.pmedr.2019.100925; A. Vannucci, K. M. Flannery, and C. M. Ohannessian, "Social Media Use and Anxiety in Emerging Adults," *Journal of Affective Disorders* 207 (2017): 163–66, doi.org/10.1016/j.jad.2016.08.040; C. K. Ra, J. Cho, M. D. Stone, J. De La Cerda, N. I. Goldenson, E. Moroney, I. Tung, S. S. Lee, and A. M. Leventhal, "Association of Digital Media Use with Subsequent Symptoms of Attention-Deficit/Hyperactivity Disorder among Adolescents," *JAMA* 320, no. 3 (2018): 255–63, doi.org/10.1001/jama.2018.8931; and S. W. Nikkelen, P. M. Valkenburg, M. Huizinga, and B. J. Bushman, "Media Use and ADHD Related Behaviors in Children and Adolescents: A Meta-Analysis," *Developmental Psychology* 50, no. 9 (2014): 2228–41.

There appear to be specific ages when teenagers are most vulnerable to the negative effects of social media . . . A. Orben, A. K. Przybylski, S. J. Blakemore, and R. A. Kievit, "Windows of Developmental Sensitivity to Social Media," *Nature Communications* 13, no. 1649 (2022), doi.org/10.1038/s41467-022-29296-3.

It's not all bad news. J. Hancock, S. X. Liu, M. Luo, and H. Mieczkowski, "Psychological Well-Being and Social Media Use: A Meta-Analysis of Associations between Social Media Use and Depression, Anxiety, Loneliness, Eudaimonic, Hedonic and Social Well-Being," paper, posted in the SSRN online library March 9, 2022, dx.doi.org/10.2139/ssrn.4053961.

It appears the risks of social media are specific to each individual child . . . M. Espinosa and V. Chang, "Webinar Focuses on 'Tech and Teen Wellbeing' during the Pandemic," *Stanford Daily* (online), July 8, 2020, stanforddaily.com/2020/07/08/webinar-focuses-on-tech-and-teen-wellbeing-during-the-pandemic/.

Sean Parker, founding president of Facebook, speaking about the creation of the platform, said their thought process "was all about: 'How do we consume as much of your time and conscious attention as possible?'" E. Pandey, "Sean Parker: Facebook Was Designed to Exploit Human Vulnerability," *Axios*, November 9, 2017, axios.com/2017/12/15/sean-parker-facebook-was-designed-to-exploit-human-vulnerability-1513306782.

INDEX

GRATITUDE LIST

This section of the book has been the easiest to write and the hardest to edit. We have had so much support along the way and wish we could thank dozens more people by name. We hope you know how much we have appreciated your contributions.

First, to our wonderful editor Maisie Tivnan: It has been a privilege and a pleasure to work with you. We are incredibly grateful for the close collaboration, your tremendous expertise, and for your confidence that three is better than one!

To the team at Workman Publishing, who understood our vision for this book and were all in on making it the best it could be: our fearless Illo Captain Analucia Zepeda, designer Rae Ann Spitzenberger, typesetters Annie O'Donnell and Barbara Peragine, production manager Erica Jimenez, production editor Beth Levy, copyeditor Nancy Ringer, wordsmith David Schiller, and our marketing and PR dream team of Cindy Lee, Ilana Gold, Moira Kerrigan, and Rebecca Carlisle.

To our amazing agent, Anna Worrall, we thank you from the bottom of our hearts for believing in us and helping others to believe as well. Your knowledge and good humor grounded and guided us throughout this process more than you know.

To Sarah Letteney, whose engaging illustrations fill this book and help make it the kind of resource we always envisioned. To Seyoung Hong, whose beautiful draft illustrations enabled us to experiment at this book's earliest stages. To Qinglan Wang, for your early guidance and vote of confidence. And to Emily Murdoch Baker, who helped us craft our proposal and who led us to Anna.

To our friends and colleagues who were early readers and cheerleaders: Dana Carstarphen, Kate Clavijo, Elizabeth Hale, Tina Jin, Dawn Koons, Kathy Lynch, Brad Sachs, Alix Spiegel, Melissa Sporn, Bill Stixrud, and Bruce Wilhelm—thank you for your time, talent, and enthusiasm.

To our many colleagues, clients, and patients—thank you for the privilege of working with you.

And to our families: We three have shared many struggles and successes over the almost three years of this project and we couldn't have done so without incredible support in our personal lives. We'd like to thank our spouses and children who, in innumerable ways large and small, have pitched in and shown tremendous love and patience.

Catherine

First and foremost, I would like to thank my amazing patients, who surprise and inspire me every day and make me realize I have one of the most rewarding jobs in the world. To so many colleagues and dear friends, thank you for your constant support and belief in me.

To Dr. Susan Trachman and Dr. Molly Sebastian, thanks for serving as my expert medical sounding boards and for laughing at most of my jokes. To Dr. Tiffany Elias, my practice director, your tireless work allowed me to focus on this book. And to Deb Murphy, you were the first to educate me about the publishing world.

To my daughter Kate, your first cover design sprouted into the tree illustration that grounds each of the Essentials chapters.

To my son Tom, thank you for your rock-solid patience and compassion in helping me improve my limited computer skills.

To my husband, Kevin, thanks for your countless hours and personal sacrifice of the three Rs as you formatted and edited the entire manuscript to ensure it was perfect before we brought it to our publisher. My gratitude surpasses words.

Heather

To my wonderful village of friends and family who have listened to me talk about this book for far longer than I have been writing it, and who are always there in the highs, lows, and everything in between—I am rich beyond measure with your love and support.

To my children, Sophie, Will, and Henry, who teach me, inspire me, and fill me with so much gratitude, joy, and love—being your mom(ster) is my greatest gift.

And to my husband, Joe, my partner in all things, who dreams bigger, sees farther, and believes in me endlessly—thank you for building and sharing a beautiful life with me.

3-2-1, I love my family!

Jennifer

To all my colleagues past and present at Weaver and Associates, I love the energy and quality of our clinical hive mind, and I learn so much from you fellow therapy nerds.

Thank you, Kelin, for your care all these years, and Peer Soups, for your wisdom and guidance.

To my wonderful friends who make me feel worthy and loved and who sometimes think I'm funny, especially my QC's, BC, VABC, and of course my Assets.

To JenJ, my most grounded connection in this world. And to my beautiful, compassionate Hermanita, what would I do without you?

To my children, Linus, Milo, and Franny, thank you for your love and patience with me and your subtle guidance in helping me become the person I really want to be. Words cannot express my love for you guys.

To Christopher, my husband and most ardent supporter, I can't imagine my life without you and your love.